COMPANIONS

FIFTY YEARS OF DOCTOR WHO ASSISTANTS

An unofficial non-fiction reference book based on
the BBC television programme Doctor Who

Andy Frankham-Allen

CANDY JAR BOOKS · CARDIFF
A Chaloner & Russell Company
2013

The right of Andy Frankham-Allen to be identified as the
Author of the Work has been asserted by him in accordance
with the Copyright, Designs and Patents Act 1988.

Copyright © Andy Frankham-Allen 2013
Additional material: Richard Kelly
Editor: Shaun Russell
Assistant Editors: Hayley Cox & Justin Chaloner

Doctor Who is © British Broadcasting Corporation, 1963, 2013.

Published by
Candy Jar Books
113-116 Bute Street,
Cardiff Bay, CF10 5EQ
www.candyjarbooks.co.uk

A catalogue record of this book is available
from the British Library

ISBN: 978-0-9571548-8-9

Printed and bound in the UK by
CPI Antony Rowe
Chippenham, Wiltshire, UK

Foreword

When I was very young I fell in love with *Doctor Who* – it was a series that 'spoke' to me unlike anything else I had ever seen. And of course, my main way of entering its weird, scary, thrilling, subversive worlds was through the eyes of the Doctor's friends, his assistants, his companions.

So what is the companion there for? Somewhat accurately, but cynically, pointing out a flaw in the show's format back in 1971, the writers described the companion as someone who was there to pass the Doctor his test tubes and tell him he was brilliant. However this is a rather unfair generalisation and had the people responsible for that swipe subsequently shaken up what they perceived as the status quo and done something to change that conception, one might be more forgiving of their little piece of whimsey.

Because the companion is far far more important than that. Yes, of course they are a sounding board, someone to pat him on the back, or get into trouble and need rescuing, or point out the bleedin' obvious when he gets all spacey and alien and misses the little details. But above all else, the companion is there to be his best friend. And, as a result, the viewer, especially the under tens, become the Doctor's best friend by default. Because they identify with the companion. More than anything else, if I was in any way the 'typical' viewer back in the 1960s and 1970s, I wanted to *be* the companion. We aspire to be the companion, we want to find our own magical police box and be whisked off into space and time, fighting Daleks, stopping Cybermen, facing down the Weeping Angels. Because that's exactly what we'd do to help the Doctor.

1

That's why this show so captured the imaginations of generations, yes generations, of children. The need, and the love the viewer has for the companion, is as valid and true in 2013 as it was on that foggy night in November 1963.

My first 'best friends' were Ben and Polly. My first tears shed when a companion said goodbye was for Jo Grant. My first 'blimey she's sexy' was Leela. My first 'I don't like this companion' was K9 (sorry, but I cannot abide cute robots and much as I respect the little mutt now, back in 1977 I wanted to punt him into outer space). Yes, the middle-aged *Doctor Who* fan I am now can look back and say 'that one worked well' and 'that one wasn't really that well developed as a character' and 'what were they thinking?' – but the pre-teen inside me who fell in love with this madcap, insane and brilliant show, still looks at each and every companion, from Susan to Clara, via Jamie, Sarah Jane, Tegan and Mel and all the others, with affection, admiration and of course a huge amount of jealousy. Because they got to do what I never did. They found their madman with a box.

Which brings us neatly to this book, and Andy Frankham-Allen's guide to each and every one of those companions (and a few other friends that don't quite count as companions but were of equal importance to the Doctor at any given moment). Of course there have been books about companions before – but few of them going into this amount of detail, display this amount of in-depth knowledge and above all, this amount of love. As a celebration of everything that makes the Doctor's (and therefore our) best friends unique and special, this book is essential.

Whether you were there through the days of Ian & Barbara, Victoria and Zoe, Liz and the men of UNIT, the two Romanas, Adric and Nyssa, Peri, Ace and Grace – or whether you only discovered your Doctor through the eyes of Rose, Martha, Donna or Amy & Rory, this is the book for you.

So step aboard your own Police Box and take a trip through the Doctor's outer-space Rolodex and get reacquainted with old chums, or discover some fantastic new ones. It's good to know who these guys are – because if you do find that Police Box of your own, you might just need to know what they did to ensure you don't get exterminated in the first five minutes!

Gary Russell
Cardiff, 2013

Fifty Years in...

Doctor Who began, unsurprisingly, with mystery. A Police Box sitting in a junkyard, letting out a mysterious hum. It took over half an episode before we discovered the truth behind the Police Box, because before that we had to learn a few important things. Our guides on that journey of discovery were two school teachers: Mr Ian Chesterton, who taught science, and Miss Barbara Wright, who taught history. These two characters were destined to be the voice of the audience for the next year and a half, the (initially) unwilling co-travellers on a fantastic journey through space and time with a mysterious old man called the Doctor...

...And so began the greatest show in the galaxy. Alas, due to the lack of timey-wimeyness in my life I wasn't there at the very beginning. I'm far too young! Plus, the odd truth of the matter is I only really happened upon Doctor Who just as it was about to embark on a lengthy hiatus. The party seemed to be wrapping up when I accidentally turned the television to BBC One in 1987 and found myself watching episode two of Time and the Rani. Certainly as a child I remember watching Doctor Who; I have very precise memories of watching Logopolis at my Nana Allen's in 1981, and even vague memories of seeing Leela and K9 in the late '70s. Doctor Who was never really far from me – via the occasional novelisation or magazine – but it wasn't until the 1980s drew to a close that I really found myself caught up in the universe of Doctor Who – just as it was (unofficially) cancelled.

I'm a voracious collector, and when I get *into* something I don't hold back. Before the final episode of Survival was transmitted in

1989 I had every novelisation available, and even all the videos (yep, no DVDs back then), not that there were many at that point. I was discovering the past through print, learning about Ian Chesterton via *An Exciting Adventure with the Daleks*, discovering all about the Brigadier and Liz during *The Auton Invasion*, and falling in love with Sarah and Harry as they dealt with *The Loch Ness Monster* (these titles will not be familiar to those of you young 'uns who've discovered the 'classic' series through DVDs, but don't worry, keep reading and it'll all make sense). Back then I really had no idea of the journey I had embarked on.

When asked by my publisher to write a book celebrating fifty years of *Doctor Who,* my first thought was to do a guide to the companions. It made perfect sense to me; other than the Doctor and the TARDIS, the only thing that's consistently been a part of the ongoing saga of *Doctor Who* are the people who travel with him. There have been other books about the Doctor's companions over the decades, but since the show returned in 2005 there has not really been one book that has taken a proper look at every single companion to travel by the Doctor's side – and there have been many!

And that's the point. It's about time we had the information in one place, to see how all these characters influence the Doctor's adventures, to show that despite the sixteen-year gap (not including the one-off *Television Movie* in 1996) *Doctor Who* has been one long narrative, from the opening of the gates at Totter's Lane in *An Unearthly Child* right through to the dramatic revelations at Trenzalore in *The Name of the Doctor*. It's all one story, one adventure seen through the eyes of many individuals. The story of the *Last of the Time Lords* as witnessed by humans, aliens and – once or twice – by robots. Make no mistake, these people have changed the Doctor; they've taught him much more than he's ever taught them. He may have shown them the wonders of the universe, but they have shown him what it is to care for those he meets, to understand the importance of every life he touches.

You'll be forgiven for thinking that, if you've seen every episode of the television series (and believe me, that's quite a feat in itself), you've seen every companion. You would, of course, be quite mistaken. During the sixteen-year gap (the Wilderness Years, as it's commonly known) *Doctor Who* continued primarily in prose, and as with the parent show, companions came and went. It started with Ace, continuing from the final television story, but soon all-new companions were introduced. Their place in the annals of *Doctor Who* history is not to be overlooked. They are as important, in some ways more so, as any companion seen on television. The continued growth and development began with Ace in *Remembrance of the Daleks*, and prepared the way for the companions that were soon to join the Ninth, Tenth and Eleventh Doctors. And they are all included in this tome (although it's possible that one or two may be missing – if so, I raise my hand and totally blame the Last Great Time War for erasing them), prose companions like Professor Bernice Summerfield all the way through to Trix MacMillan, to the companions introduced in the Big Finish audios like Evelyn Smythe through to Molly O'Sullivan, plus a few more obscure companions who appeared in the various incarnations of the *Doctor Who* comic strips.

In writing this book decisions needed to be made. It's an age-old argument among *Doctor Who* fans – what makes a companion? Who counts? Is Astrid a companion? What about Grace? Sara Kingdom...? For the purpose of this book we've decided to follow the *intent* of the production team. For instance; Grace Holloway from the *Television Movie* is not regarded as a companion because the *intent* was that she'd become the Doctor's companion had a series been picked up on the success of the *Television Movie*. No such series materialised, however, and so Grace becomes another in a long list of people the Doctor has met who were *almost* companions – much like Astrid Peth in *Voyage of the Damned*, or Adam Mitchell – the literal *almost* companion. But someone like Katarina, although having much less screen time than Sara

Kingdom, is regarded as a companion because she was created to be so – yes, even Kamelion, who only appeared in two adventures (introduced in one, and written out in the other), since he was *intended* to be a companion.

It's inevitable, however, that some will disagree with our selection process, and that's OK. Every fan has their own standard upon which they choose their *canon* companions, and you're more than welcome to disagree. Much like the TARDIS, *Doctor Who* fandom is infinite in its view and no one view is better than the other.

We follow the series Doctor by Doctor, each with two chapters. The first is the ongoing narrative of the television series, thus all information can be considered official, while the second chapter will look at the Expanded Universe (a term lifted, with some resistance, from *Star Wars* fans) of the novels, comics and audios, exploring the companions never seen on television, while looking into some of the more interesting information revealed about the television companions in adventures never screened. Often the material contained in the Expanded Universe is contradictory, even more so than on television, but it is not the job of this book to fit everything together into one whole (Lance Parkin's excellent *Ahistory* does that), but rather to collect together the more interesting points.

So, read on, and meet the Doctor's granddaughter, Susan, and begin your fifty year journey of *Doctor Who* as seen through the eyes of the companions, your guides on a fantastic adventure through space and time…

The First Doctor
William Hartnell

*'It all started out as a mild curiosity in the junkyard
and now it's turned out to be quite a spirit of adventure.'*
The Doctor – *The Sensorites*

*Susan – Carole Ann Ford (An Unearthly Child to The Dalek Invasion
of Earth and The Five Doctors)*

If there is one main character in *Doctor Who* we know less about
than the Doctor, it is Susan. For a start we don't even know her
real name. Susan Foreman is almost certainly a fiction; the
surname we know she took from the name painted on the doors
of the junkyard in which we first see the TARDIS – IM Foreman.
Even in the second episode Ian & Barbara question this. In all
likelihood her forename is incorrect too, given what we later learn
about her home-world. For not only is she an alien, but she heralds
from the same world as the Doctor; indeed, she is his
granddaughter. At least, that is what they both claim, and there
has been no proof to the contrary. We only see her on screen for
a year, and in that time we learn so little about her that when she
remains on Earth in the twenty-second century, we feel as if we
barely know her.

    In the very first story we learn only a little: she is from 'another
time, another world', a place where the children would be insulted
if they were compared to human adults like Ian & Barbara. Her
home is far in advance of twentieth century Earth, and this is
confirmed by her technical and scientific knowledge: she is very
dismissive of Ian's experiment with the litmus paper, and is baffled
by the notion that there are only three dimensions.

But for all her knowledge, for all her supposed alienness, she is still very much a child. Indeed, in some ways, she is more child-like than her 'peers' at Coal Hill School. This ought not be much of a surprise, really, when one considers that Gallifreyans are a long-lived people, and fifteen must be extremely young (the Doctor explains in *The Sound of Drums* that, 'Children on Gallifrey are taken from their families at the age of eight to enter the Academy' [perhaps Susan somehow escaped that fate?] and much later states in *The Stolen Earth* that ninety is young). Her reactions tend to be of someone much younger than fifteen years of age, seemingly living in a heightened emotional state (perhaps there is a reason the children of Gallifrey are rarely seen). Yet, that isn't to say she is not brave.

Witness her mission to find a cure for the radiation sickness that has struck her and her travelling companions in the second story. She is clearly horrified to discover that she is the only one able to go, but more than anything else, it is the sight of her grandfather deteriorating that urges her to swallow her fear and press on. This fear of the unknown; of being on her own, is her constant companion during her mission through the radiation-soaked jungle of Skaro, yet still she goes. And later, when she is travelling in Marco Polo's caravan across China, she displays an impressive level of bravery. After all the dangers faced on that journey, the travellers manage to gain entry to the TARDIS once again, and thus can finally escape. Susan, however, insists on saying goodbye to her friend, Ping-Cho. This puts first herself in danger, and then her friends, as she is used against them. It shows the foolish level of bravery Susan excels at; brash and impulsive, often without any thought as to how it may affect others.

Another minor thing we learn about Susan in *The Sensorites* is that she is telepathic, although this doesn't appear to be a well-developed ability. The Doctor is surprised to learn that Susan has this gift, which begs the question: why? It is later established that all Time Lords are telepathic to some extent (to the point where the Doctor states in *Logopolis* that in some ways they all 'have the same mind'). The Doctor suggests she will be better trained when they return home; could this be because she is developing early, a consequence of her travels in the TARDIS?

It is also interesting to note that in the very first story Susan states she 'made up the name TARDIS from the initials Time And Relative Dimension In Space'. In the context of the series as a whole, this implies a lot about Susan, since we later learn that all Gallifreyan timeships are called TARDISes. Although when you consider that in the early days of the show the Doctor most often referred to the TARDIS as 'the ship', is it possible that the name Susan coined caught on after they left Gallifrey? As with most things related to Susan, we are only given a tantalising hint, but few firm facts.

Susan, it would appear, is out of her depth a lot of the time. Taken out of the comfort of her home... Or did she choose to go with her grandfather? One can assume she did; after all, when talking to Ping-Cho in *Marco Polo,* she expresses her frustration at being stuck on Earth, when she should be out among the stars. Like almost everything else about Susan, we never know. Much has been revealed about her in other media (see page 25), but on TV all we ever get are intriguing hints of a character that could have been so much more.

The Doctor himself forces Susan to leave in *The Dalek Invasion of Earth* after seeing her grow closer to freedom fighter David Campbell. It is a subtle romance, although it is never quite believable, and it almost comes as a surprise to the viewer when Susan considers remaining on Earth. But she is fearful of leaving her grandfather, thinking he needs her, when in truth it is perfectly obvious that she is dependent on him. That she should end up settling on Earth makes a certain sense, however, considering how much she enjoyed her time in 1963, and considering the five months living in the twentieth century as the happiest of her life.

We only ever see Susan once more, almost twenty years later when she is taken to Gallifrey and reunited with her grandfather. And, although she is clearly older, it does not appear she has changed at all. As ever with Susan we are given nothing new with which to work; she is simply the Doctor's granddaughter, although as soon as she spots the Dark Tower she realises that she is on Gallifrey thus confirming that she is definitely *from* there.

Susan's fate remains unknown. In *The Empty Child* the Doctor tells Rose, 'My entire planet died. My whole family.' Later, after Doctor Constantine mentions he used to be 'a father and a grandfather. Now I'm neither, but I'm still a doctor,' the Doctor points out, 'Yeah, I know the feeling'.

Compared to Susan, the rest of the Doctor's companions were pretty straightforward – at least during the initial twenty-six year run of the series, although some were more fleshed out than others. Some with well defined back-stories, some with less so...

Ian Chesterton & Barbara Wright – William Russell & Jacqueline Hill (*An Unearthly Child* to *The Chase*)

Along with Susan, we are introduced to two of the most defined companions; Ian Chesterton & Barbara Wright. Unusually for *Doctor Who*, indeed it has only happened twice (arguably three times if we include Rose and Mickey), Ian & Barbara become synonymous with each other. It almost becomes impossible to separate them. They start together, they finish together, and even when mentioned in the 2010 episode of *The Sarah Jane Adventures* episode, *Death of the Doctor*, they are still together. They are as much defined by their relationship to each other as they are as individuals. Both were teachers at Coal Hill School, Ian teaching Science and Barbara teaching History, and both had their curiosity piqued by the mystery that was Susan. It is worth noting that these two are, in some respect, more important than either the Doctor or Susan during the first year of *Doctor Who*. While Susan was the child who would always get in trouble, it was Barbara who often proved to be the voice of reason, always ready to challenge the more alien aspects of the Doctor's reasoning. Ian is the man of action, displaying a broad range of skills one might not expect from a comprehensive school teacher. Barbara is also the very first person in *Doctor Who* to meet a Dalek. Make no mistake; these two ordinary teachers are the key players in a series of extraordinary adventures.

It is through their eyes that we see the initial adventures. They take us into the Doctor's strange world; forcing their way into the TARDIS, all the way to Skaro and the historical first encounter with the Daleks. Neither expected what was to follow, but both had to assuage their curiosity and followed Susan home, to a junkyard in London. Worried for Susan's safety they both force their way into the old Police Box, and immediately find themselves challenging their own perceptions of everything they have ever known. Both are equally incredulous and unbelieving, but while Ian tries to reason things with science, Barbara attempts a more common sense approach, certain that it is just an elaborate illusion created by Susan's grandfather.

Although an unwilling adventurer, Barbara's compassion often overrides her own fear, as seen in the very first journey in *An Unearthly Child* when Za, a caveman on pre-historic Earth, is attacked by a tiger. Even though Za was willing to sacrifice them a short while earlier, Barbara cannot leave the wounded man unattended. This is a trait that continues; even after being sold as a slave in ancient Rome (*The Romans*), Barbara still helps her fellow prisoner rather than worrying about her own safety. Such is her compassion that Ian remarks that she probably has stray cats in her flat in London.

Barbara is not only compassionate, but also full of passion, which comes out in anger and frustration. Note that when the travellers are all trapped in the TARDIS (*The Edge of Destruction*) and the Doctor accuses Ian & Barbara of sabotaging the ship, it is Barbara who confronts him with a verbal slap that would've had the most callous of men reeling in shock, 'How dare you! Do you realise, you stupid old man, that you'd have died in the Cave of Skulls if Ian hadn't made fire for you? And what about what we went through with the Daleks? Not just for us, but for you and Susan, too, and all because you tricked us into going down to the city. Accuse us? You ought to get down on your hands and knees and thank us. But gratitude's the last thing you'll ever have, or any sort of common sense, either.'

Such is the power behind her words that the Doctor does ultimately apologise to her. Her passion for history is also a driving force during their travels, most notably when she is mistaken for the reincarnation of the Aztec High Priest Yetaxa (*The Aztecs*). She is convinced that she can prevent the human sacrifices, and brings the Aztecs out of their superstitious ways so their society can flourish. She fails, of course, but she learns a valuable lesson. Although they are travellers in time, they cannot affect history on a big scale. This lesson stands Barbara in good stead when they later visit such periods as the French Revolution (*The Reign of Terror*) and the fall of Rome (*The Romans*). Not to say that Barbara doesn't get involved; an unwilling adventurer she may be, but she was never going to be a quiet one too.

On the other hand, Ian adapts to adventuring relatively quickly. His National Service prepares him for the challenges ahead, and he displays a remarkable set of useful skills, including horse riding, sword fighting, and how to disable an opponent with pressure points. On Earth he is a man of reason, but he soon learns that reason alone is simply not enough when travelling to dangerous times and places. Such is his level of bravery and courage that he is even knighted by King Richard the Lionheart as Sir Ian of Jaffa in *The Crusades*.

An interesting, and not often explored, trait of Ian's is his familiarity with popular youth culture, in particular the music, and his ease with children. National Service may have prepared him for adventuring, but his understanding of young people prepared him for the varied people he was to meet on his travels.

Ian & Barbara were always close, at least close enough initially that it was in Ian that Barbara confided her doubts about Susan in the very first episode. This obvious closeness develops through their travels, as Ian becomes something of a protector for Barbara. The most obvious hint at the level of intimacy between the two comes when they are alone at the villa on the outskirts of Rome (*The Romans*). The familiarity they display with each other, both physically and verbally, hints at much more. It is never expressly stated, but to consider some kind of romantic interest between them isn't much of a stretch.

Always throughout their travels is the thought of returning home, although they become less vocal about it over time, when presented with the first opportunity, Barbara takes hold of it without question. Ian is a little more cautious, but he soon comes around. The Doctor, clearly upset by their departure, responds obstinately, almost point blank refusing to help them. But once again they win him over – because of them this grumpy old alien softens, becoming almost kindly in his dealings with others. Through Ian & Barbara the Doctor learns compassion.

It is unfortunate that we never hear of Ian & Barbara again – they were such a huge part in establishing *Doctor Who* as a success, and defining the future relationships the Doctor has with his travelling companions and, ultimately, his friends and extended family. Ian almost returns in the 1983 adventure *Mawdryn Undead*, but due to William Russell being unavailable, it never came to pass. However, in 2010, we did finally get a clue about what happened to them. Sarah Jane Smith had taken to looking up the Doctor's old companions, and she learned that there were two professors in Cambridge, Ian & Barbara Chesterton, who, according to rumour, had not aged since the 1960s. It is an intriguing rumour, but regardless, it is great to know that Ian & Barbara remain, as they began, together.

With the departure of Susan, there was a void in the Doctor's life. He had grown very close to his granddaughter, so it was unsurprising, although convenient (at least so it seems, but in *The Doctor's Wife* the TARDIS explained that she always took the Doctor to where he needed to be, and this may well be a case in point), that the next destination brought the Doctor, Ian & Barbara to the planet Dido, and the young orphan, Vicki.

Vicki – Maureen O'Brien (The Rescue to The Myth Makers)

Almost immediately Vicki forms a close bond with the Doctor, both having lost the most important people in their lives. When the Doctor asks her to join them on their adventures, Vicki jumps at the chance. It is very interesting to note that Vicki is the first person the Doctor asks to go with him. The next being Victoria (also an orphan, see page 48).

Vicki's mother and father died following the crash of the *UK-201* on Dido. Her only companion on the desolate world is a man called Bennett who, it transpires, is quite insane and has murdered all the survivors of the crash.

Vicki comes from an Earth where the children are taught advanced academic subjects at a young age; she herself claims to have studied medicine, physics, chemistry and various other subjects when she was only ten. A fact that she shares when Barbara explains that she taught using the three Rs – at which point Vicki exclaims that she didn't realise Barbara taught at a nursery. This shows that either Vicki liked to tease Barbara, or was simply being naive at her own rudeness.

This yearning for adventure grows during the month they all spend at the villa on the outskirts of Rome. This isn't the life Vicki had been expecting, and she convinces the Doctor to take her to Rome. As their travels continue we see much of this spirit of adventure; an outlook that brings Vicki and the Doctor closer together, developing a very gentle relationship. In fact it is this closeness that allows her to convince the Doctor to do things he might otherwise resist. A good example in *The Chase* is when Ian & Barbara realise they could use the Daleks' time ship to return home; the Doctor refuses to show them how it works. But Vicki gets through his anger and convinces him to let them go – even though she doesn't want to see them leave. After all, along with the Doctor, Ian & Barbara became something of a foster family for her.

Vicki's sharp and deductive brain comes into good use on Xeros in *The Space Museum* when she enables the subjugated Xerons to override the Moroks' computer, and later on in *Galaxy Four* when she works out that the Chumblies only respond to movement directly in front of them. She also fixes the meaning of the name TARDIS when she tells Steven that the D stands for 'Dimensions', possibly recognising the equational and grammatical inaccuracy in the acronym when it was told to her as 'Dimension'.

Vicki has a habit of giving the aliens they meet strange names, for example the beast on Dido she calls Sandy because it lives in the sand and the little robot servants of the Rills she calls Chumblies due to the way they move. This inclination of hers could well be an indication of the loneliness she feels as she seeks to find a place to call home once again. Her loneliness is evident in the way she quickly draws close to the Doctor, and later with Steven with whom she develops an almost sibling-like relationship.

It is when the TARDIS brings them to Asia Minor just before the Fall of Troy (*The Myth Makers*) that Vicki's desire for a family again becomes most obvious. She finds her way into Troy on her own and is immediately taken in by King Priam who is equally impressed by her. She even accepts the new name of Cressida from Priam. During the course of the siege, she finds herself responding to the affections of Priam's son, Troilus, and realises she will be quite happy settling there with him, even though he is only seventeen and she sixteen (when Troilus tells Vicki his age she says, 'That's barely older than me,' the first time her age is inferred). We never get to see exactly how the Doctor reacts to Vicki's news, as this happens off-screen, but he does not appear to oppose. He appears to be more concerned with Steven's wound suffered during the battle between the Greeks and the Trojans. The last we ever see of Vicki is shortly after the TARDIS departs and she finds Troilus watching the destruction of his people – he thinks she has betrayed them, but she convinces him otherwise. And from there they pass into history, through tales by Chaucer ('*Troilus and Criseyde'*) and Shakespeare ('*Troilus and Cressida*'), from which we can, at least, infer something of Vicki's later life...

As with Susan and Vicki, a replacement was waiting in the wings once Ian & Barbara returned to their own time. This new companion joined the Doctor's travels by what would become the most popular method of all; stowing away in the TARDIS.

Steven Taylor – Peter Purves (The Chase to The Savages)

When the Doctor, with Ian & Barbara and Vicki, first meet him he introduces himself as Steven Taylor, Flight Red Fifty. He has already spent two years as a prisoner of the robotic Mechanoids on the planet Mechanus, in an undisclosed period of Earth's future. Steven is an astronaut, his ship having crashed on that planet; his only companion his stuffed panda, Hi-Fi. Despite two years of captivity he is a man of good humour, grateful of some human company at last. He happily assists the Doctor and company in escaping the Mechanoids' city, but at the last minute returns for Hi-Fi. He manages to escape the burning city himself, and stumbles through the jungle, disorientated, and into what he describes as a door.

'I went through it,' he says. 'I must have flaked out. I remember registering that, well, it didn't look like a ship – it was very small. I must have been delirious.'

After his initial incredulity, and mocking of Vicki's explanations, he soon adapts to time travel. Granted, his scepticism is supported when he discovers a wristwatch in a small woods in Northumbria in 1066 (*The Time Meddler*) but events reveal the truth. Steven is a man prone to natural sarcasm and bouts of frustrated anger, but to counter these less positive attributes, he is also a man of great courage and resourcefulness.

He becomes very close to Vicki, and develops a strong

sibling-like bond with her, displaying the typical bickering one would expect to find in an older brother/younger sister relationship, most notable when they are both imprisoned in Troy and Vicki becomes the object of Troilus' affections. Both are determined in their mind sets, and often conflict over the simplest of things, but ultimately they stand by each other. His relationship with Dodo is, in contrast, merely that of two friends. Steven's natural cynicism is often contrasted by Dodo's enthusiasm for everything they encounter, and she tends to bring out the child in him, as shown during the games of the Celestial Toymaker and Steven's joy at being in the 'Wild West' of American legend (*The Gunfighters*).

By the time they arrive on the 'Ark', a space craft taking the survivors of Earth to the world of Rufusis, Steven's good humour has already been sorely tried by his experiences in Paris and the Massacre of St Bartholomew's Eve. He spends most of the time without the Doctor's company, getting embroiled in the political and religious strife that is plaguing Paris, despite the Doctor warning him not to, and becomes angered greatly by the Doctor's refusal to involve himself in events – an act that, in Steven's eyes, means the death of a young woman he has befriended, Anne Chaplet. This anger is compounded by all the other deaths he had witnessed recently, including that of Katarina and Sara Kingdom, both of whom died during the Doctor's effort to prevent the Daleks from gaining control of the Time Destructor. Such is his anger that as soon as the TARDIS arrives on Wimbledon Common in the 1960s he storms out of the ship, intent on leaving the Doctor for good. It is only the presence of police officers that change his mind, and he returns forthwith to warn the Doctor to move the TARDIS. He is immediately concerned about Dodo, who has just happened upon the TARDIS, wondering what her parents will think of her disappearing, but that concern soon fades when he realises that Dodo is a likely descendant of Anne Chaplet, suggesting that the young French girl has survived the massacre after all. Even with this positive news, Steven still contains some anger in his belly, which erupts when he is put on trial by the humans on the Ark and he expresses his distaste for humanity and the fear that always seems to drive them.

Nonetheless, despite his growing dislike for his own race, Steven is still the compassionate man he has always been and is willing to sacrifice his freedom for both the Doctor and Dodo when faced with the dilemma of how to escape the Toymaker's celestial domain.

He learns much during his journeys, and when he is asked to help the Elders and the Savages find a way to live together in peace, he resists, not wanting to walk out on the Doctor and Dodo. But the Doctor insists he take up the offer, a position he is now ready for. Steven agrees, but only if both sides wish him to, which they do. He takes his leave of the Doctor and Dodo, and we never hear of him again.

Katarina, the handmaiden of Cassandra of Troy, was one of the shortest-lived companions of the Doctor, and the first to die.

Katarina – Adrienne Hill (The Myth Makers to The Daleks' Masterplan)

Cassandra, fearful of the false prophetess, Cressida, sends Katarina to spy on Vicki. During the battle between the Greeks and the Trojans, Steven is wounded by a spear in the shoulder, and Katarina is tasked with caring for him. She helps him back to the TARDIS and is still aboard the ship when the Doctor quickly leaves the troubled land.

She has no understanding of the strange world she has entered, and believes the Doctor to be Zeus, the TARDIS his temple. She is, in her mind, on a journey to the Palace of Perfection – the afterlife. Out of her depth, she remains by Steven's side, practically worshipping at the Doctor's feet. Such is her devotion, that when the criminal Kirksen holds her hostage to force the Doctor to return the *Spar*, stolen from the planet Kembel where the Daleks are waiting, she understands enough to know that it cannot be. She sacrifices her life, by blowing the airlock in which she and Kirksen stand, and the two of them are swept out into the depths of space.

Dorothea 'Dodo' Chaplet was one of only two companions to find herself inside the TARDIS after mistaking it for a real Police Box. Having witnessed an accident on Wimbledon Common, she rushed to it to get help...

Dorothea 'Dodo' Chaplet – Jackie Lane (The Massacre to *The War Machines)*

Dodo adapts very quickly to TARDIS life, although with the usual level of incredulity, to the idea that it is a time machine. Due to the police officers rushing towards the TARDIS, the Doctor has no choice but to leave Wimbledon Common, and when Steven voices his concerns about leaving with Dodo she points out that she doesn't care. She has no parents and no reason to stay in London. One suspects that it is not just the arrival of the police that causes the Doctor to take Dodo away with them, but rather the fact that he thinks she looks a little bit like his absent granddaughter, Susan.

During the initial journey Dodo finds the time to root through the TARDIS' wardrobe, something she continues to avail herself of throughout her short time as companion. When arriving in a jungle, Dodo refuses to accept it might be an alien world, instead believing it to be Whipsnade Zoo, and shows a keen awareness and liking for nature. Indeed she is almost smug about her knowledge, presenting a very 'know it all' attitude. Of course, she is soon proven wrong when they discover the jungle is just a small part of a space craft taking refugees from the dying Earth. She dubs the ship 'the Ark', and accidentally infects all its inhabitants with her cold – something that has not existed on Earth for centuries. She feels terrible for causing so much trouble and does everything she can to assist the Doctor in finding a cure, especially when Steven, who has no antibodies to combat the cold, also succumbs to it.

While pitted against the dolls created by the Toymaker (*The Celestial Toymaker*), Dodo takes the view that they are as much victims as she and Steven – even arguing her point about free will, although she never convinces Steven of her stance. This is probably another example of her contrary nature and her single-mindedness. As she points out when they land on the world of the Savages and Elders, she never did like guided tours and preferred to wander off the assigned route. Or, as Steven once said, 'If it wasn't allowed, Dodo would be first in line.' This is evidenced a lot during their visit to Tombstone (*The Gunfighters*). Dodo is a big fan of the Wild West and has always wanted to meet Wyatt Earp, thus she throws herself into the period, giving herself over to every cliché of the 'western', even to the point where she seems to enjoy being forced to play the piano at gunpoint. Steven is more perturbed, but Dodo encourages him to sing, and shows an ability to not only play but also read music. She is also taken in by Doc Holliday's charm, barely batting an eye at his propensity for killing almost everybody they meet, even though she is, ultimately, his captive.

She is upset by Steven's sudden departure, and wonders if she will ever see him again. The Doctor explains how unlikely it is, and is proven to be correct when they next land back in London, 1966 (*The War Machines*). Glad to be back in familiar surroundings, Dodo quickly bonds with Polly, the secretary of Professor Brett, who takes her to the Inferno nightclub where they both meet Able Seaman Ben Jackson. WOTAN, an intelligent machine, brainwashes Dodo in an attempt to remove the Doctor, but the Doctor sees through the conditioning and is able to break it. He sends Dodo to a house in the country to recover, and she is never seen again.

After showing such enthusiasm for her travels, and growing attached to the Doctor, it is very odd that she doesn't return to at least say goodbye to him. Instead she passes on a message to him through Ben & Polly, saying that she has decided to remain in London. What is the reason for such a drastic shift in her character? We never find out on television, but several other reasons have been offered up in the *Doctor Who* Expanded Universe (see page 36).

As with Ian & Barbara the next companions came as a 'couple' – they joined together, they left together and, according to Sarah in 2010 they are still together.

Ben Jackson & Polly – Michael Craze & Anneke Wills (The War Machines to The Faceless Ones)

Polly is the secretary of Professor Brett, a young 'dolly bird' with an active social life, enjoying the night life of the Inferno club. When Polly meets Ben Jackson she takes it on herself to cheer him up, with mixed results. Despite this, Ben defends Polly against the attentions of an unwanted admirer, a trait that continues throughout their time together.

Polly has a tendency to tease those she likes, Ben in particular. He soon gets used to this and takes to calling her 'Pol'. After assisting the Doctor in defeating WOTAN and the War Machines, it is Polly who is curious as to why the Doctor enters a Police Box. Ben is less bothered, more concerned about returning to his own ship, but Ben remembers the key that had fallen out of the Doctor's pocket earlier. At her urging, Ben joins her and they both enter the Police Box mere seconds before it dematerialises.

Both are somewhat sceptical of the Doctor's claims about the TARDIS, but Polly adapts to things a lot quicker than Ben who is, upon arriving on a beach in Cornwall, sure that the Doctor is a hypnotist or something. Throughout their harrowing adventures in the seventeenth century (*The Smugglers*), Polly finds herself enjoying the notion of time travel, while Ben is more concerned about getting home and back to his ship. Even when the Doctor insists they have to stay and sort out the problem with the pirates and the smugglers, it takes both him and Polly to convince Ben that it is the right thing to do. Polly's humour is also something Ben takes a while to get used to, coming across as positively miserable next to her cheekiness. But he does take some pleasure in her horror at seeing a rat, despite them both being imprisoned at the time and facing a likely death sentence, a fact that does not seem to bother Polly too much. The humour soon infects Ben, too, when he begins to turn on his own cocky charm, even to the point of quipping, 'Polly, put the kettle on?' when he has to leave her for a short while.

By the time the TARDIS brings them to the South Pole some twenty years after their own native 1966, both seem to have adapted nicely to travelling with the Doctor. Faced with the emotionless Cybermen, in *The Tenth Planet*, it is Polly who first challenges them, while Ben tries to hold his 'duchess' back, fearing for her safety. Ben also stands up to the Cybermen, making inventive use of a projector to blind one, and then using its own weapon against it. It is an act Ben is not proud of – but he knows it is necessary. His courage is never far away, and when the Cybermen intend on taking Polly prisoner, Ben soon stands forward insisting he go in her place.

Ben & Polly are the first companions to meet the Cybermen, but also at the end of *The Tenth Planet* they are on hand to witness the most remarkable thing about the Doctor. His body wearing thin, the Doctor staggers back to the TARDIS, and it is there that a concerned Ben & Polly witness him collapse mere moments after setting the time machine in motion. They pull him over to check on him, and watch as his face begins to blur and change...

The First Doctor
Expanded Universe

Once again, we start with Susan, a character we know so little from TV, the Doctor's very own granddaughter. It isn't surprising that the stories contained in the Expanded Universe explore her origins and character in some extreme (and often conflicting) ways.

There are four distinct 'origin' stories for Susan. In one account (written by 1980s *Doctor Who* script editor, Eric Saward, and published in the *Radio Times 20th Anniversary Special*) she is the Lady Larna, whom the Doctor rescues when he escapes from Gallifrey. Larna is a descendent of Rassilon (the 'greatest single figure' in Time Lord history), and the last of Gallifrey's royal family. It draws from Anthony Coburn's original draft of the very first episode, in which he describes Susan as being of royal blood; an idea that never made it beyond that first draft.

A second origin is presented in the tongue-in-cheek radio broadcast *Whatever Happened to... Susan Foreman?* In this it is suggested that Susan's parents dispatch her to Earth with her grandfather because she is failing such subjects as French on Gallifrey, French being a common language in most galaxies, but she is fine with subjects such as thermodynamics. This account is full of contradictions and is not meant to be taken seriously.

A third, and much more complex idea is put forward in the 1997 novel *Lungbarrow* and it does not completely contradict established facts. In this Susan is the last child born on Ancient Gallifrey, and granddaughter of the mysterious Other – a mythical being who is said to form a triumvirate with Rassilon and Omega, and thus is one of the founders of Time Lord society. This Other, in this account, is reincarnated centuries later as the Doctor, who, when escaping Gallifreyan life, finds himself in his planet's past where both Susan and he recognise each other. She then joins him on his travels. Epic, yes, but it does fit in with some of the hints from stories late in the classic era's run, such as *Remembrance of the Daleks* and *Silver Nemesis* in which it is implied that the Doctor was present at the birth of the Time Lords.

What gives this account some credence is that it was written by a TV script writer, Marc Platt, using the so-called 'Cartmel Masterplan' – a name given to the long-term plans of script editor, Andrew Cartmel – the basis upon which much of the final two years of *Doctor Who*'s original twenty-six-year run on TV was informed. This origin story has been acknowledged by many of the novels that follow, and still remains the most popular theory (although, it is important to point out that it has never been confirmed by anything seen or said in *Doctor Who* since 2005 – indeed, the Doctor has said that he 'was a dad once', which at least confirms that he had children and, presumably, grandchildren, of which Susan is most certainly one).

Her origins are further expanded upon in the novella *Frayed*, which is set before the first TV story. In this we learn that the name Susan was given to her by an Earth colonist called Jill, after her mother. And in a short story published in *Doctor Who Magazine #214*, it is revealed that Susan's real name is Arkytior, which is High Gallifreyan for 'rose' (an interesting link between the first companions of the original series' run and that of the 2005 revival; even more so when you consider the short story was published in 1994).

A final piece is mentioned in the short story *Ash*, wherein the Doctor tells Steven that Susan's parent entrusted her care to him.

Little more is added to Susan during the period she travelled with Ian & Barbara, despite the many Expanded Universe journeys written. However, one area people seem keen to explore is her life after she left the Doctor. As one might expect, the accounts are contradictory.

Only one thing has been consistent in these accounts; Susan

and David marry and have children. In the novelisation of *The Five Doctors*, author Terrance Dicks mentions that she has three children. This idea was revisited by John Peel when he wrote *Legacy of the Daleks* which sees a reunion between Susan and her grandfather, now in his eighth incarnation. In this book we learn that she and David had helped rebuild England after the Dalek invasion, and adopted three war orphans, who they named Ian, Barbara and David Junior. The reason for the adoption is that Susan is not able to conceive with David. She also ages slower than humans, and often has to wear make-up to disguise her younger appearance. During the course of the story, she is taken captive by the Doctor's nemesis, the Master, and brought to the planet Tersurus. She leaves that planet in his TARDIS, believing she has killed the Master.

This interesting, grittier side of Susan has never been further explored, since she never returns to the novels. However the audio production company Big Finish offer their own version of events post-*The Five Doctors*. Again she reunites with the Doctor in his eighth incarnation, and again she is a mother. Only this time she and David have their own biological child, a son called Alex. Their son has only one heart, and Susan asks the Doctor to take Alex to Gallifrey to be better educated. She helps the Doctor repel a second Dalek invasion of Earth, which costs Alex his life in *To the Death*. She is left alone to deal with her son's death.

A curious detail is related by Susan when she tells the story *Here There Be Monsters*. In this story she claims that at the time of her travels with Ian & Barbara her actual age was more than theirs combined, even though she was still a baby by Gallifreyan standards (and the Doctor was only a child!). It is an interesting idea, but does not fit with anything ever revealed in fifty years on television.

In one further account, the entire universe is rewritten by a planar shift; an event so catastrophic that it destroys Gallifrey and rewrites the Doctor's entire timeline. In the final story, *Matrix Revelation* written by Dale Smith in 2006, it is revealed that Susan was copied into the Matrix, the repository of all Time Lord knowledge, when Earth's history was rewritten. It is there that she is eventually reunited with her grandfather, now in an alternative fifth incarnation.

One final piece of apocrypha should be mentioned, although technically it is fan theory, it does open up a whole universe of possibilities. In *The End of Time*, a mysterious Time Lady appears to guide Wilfred Mott into helping the Doctor. It is quite clear, at the end of the story, that both she and the Doctor recognise each other. It is never made clear who she is, but it has been inferred by some that she may be Susan; when Wilf asks the Doctor who the woman is, instead of answering he looks past Wilf, towards Donna, Wilf's *granddaughter*... As ever with Susan, it is an intriguing possibility.

As one might expect, the rest of the First Doctor's companions are dealt with in a much more straightforward manner in the Expanded Universe, mostly with writers content on filling the back-stories of those characters who on television, tended to have a past that was, barring a few hints, largely a blank slate. Another thing writers of the apocryphal material liked to play with was 'what happened after so-and-so left the Doctor?' with varying degrees of success.

Like on TV, Ian & Barbara's Expanded Universe appearances are mostly coherent. We learn more about Ian's past than Barbara's, discover a couple of new bits of information from their journeys with the Doctor, and we learn that they do indeed get married – long before it is confirmed in *The Sarah Jane Adventures* on television. They even have a son...

We discover that Ian was born in Reading, and grew up during the London Blitz, with a brother and a sister. He loved Jules Verne and HG Wells as a child; he was inspired by them to become a teacher of science, and he served in the British Army as a private for two years – confirming what we know about his

National Service from the television series. We also learn in *The Eleventh Tiger* that his great-great-grandfather, Major William Chesterton, looks a lot like an older Ian, when Ian was mistaken for him. Of Barbara's early life we learn very little – other than that she once dated a boy who carried a knife, that she has an aunt named Cecilia, that when she was a student teacher she had a flat in Cricklewood and that Ian and Barbara first met in a little tea shop on Tottenham Court Road.

Extra information about these two is a little thin on the ground, despite the amount of Expanded Universe adventures they had. We discover in *The Sorcerer's Apprentice* that Barbara has a fear of heights, something she is not aware of until she soars high into the sky on a broomstick. At one point (in the short story *Set in Stone*) they spend four months living in 1950s Shoreditch, believing that is the closest they will ever get to their own time. And, most curiously, there are two different accounts of the month between the opening scenes of *The Romans* that lead up to their moving into the villa on the outskirts of Rome – accounts that are hard to marry (in the short story *Romans Cutaway* and the novel *Byzantium!*).

But the oddest reveal of all is in *City at World's End* when Ian believes the Doctor and Susan to be human – even though he knows from the very first episode that this is not so!

There are also confused accounts of when Ian & Barbara first realise their love for each other. There are moments in the book *Venusian Lullaby* when Ian's true feelings are hinted at. The loss he feels when he believes Barbara has died in a spaceship explosion is crushing, to the point where he ponders suicide. And then in the later book *The Plotters* Barbara realises she is quite comfortable posing as Ian's wife. Further books set before *The Plotters* reveal that both Ian and Barbara have confessed their love for each other. In *Romans Cutaway* Ian admits that he loves Barbara, but is unable to tell her. Barbara finally tells Ian that she loves him in *The Eleventh Tiger* and Ian reciprocates. It is at this point that they both agree to get married when they return home.

However, the later audio book, *The Rocket Men,* has Ian realising he loves Barbara, even though this is set some time after the events of *The Eleventh Tiger.*

In the 1991 novel, *Timewyrm: Revelation,* we get the first mention of singer Johnny Chess (or Johnny Chester), who is idolised by future companion Ace at the age of fourteen. Johnny is the son of Ian & Barbara born in 1967, his full name being John Alydon Ganatus Chesterton, named after two Thals encountered in the television story *The Daleks* (the full name is not revealed until *Byzantium!* is released in 2001). Information on the events that lead to their marriage are not revealed until 1996 with the release of the novel, *Who Killed Kennedy?* According to that novel after returning to Earth Ian & Barbara excuse their two year absence by claiming they have been missionaries in Central Africa. Barbara takes up a position at a university lecturing, specialising on the Aztecs, while Ian gains a professorship within a year (which at least backs up the reference to Professor Chesterton in the novelisation of *The War Machines* set in 1966) and begins writing papers on astronomy. In the 2005 novel *The Time Travellers* we are treated to a scene set straight after *The Chase* in which Ian takes Barbara home to see her mother, Joan. More information is revealed when Ian & Barbara finally return to *Doctor Who* fiction in the 1998 novel *Face of the Enemy.* Set during the 1970s, Ian is in his late 30s and teaching at the RAF's college in Farnborough, while Barbara is teaching at a local comprehensive. They are called in to assist UNIT, thus helping the lifelong friend of the Doctor, Brigadier Alistair Lethbridge-Stewart (see page 330 to learn all about this key figure) and work alongside the Doctor's mortal enemy, the Master. During this novel we learn a bit more about their life post-Doctor – how they eloped on the first anniversary of their return home and how Ian has to sell everything he owns to get a new place, while Barbara stays with her parents. They also have plans to leave a journal for Susan, who they know will end up on Earth in 2167. During the course of the novel Ian believes Barbara has died in a car crash, and once again considers suicide as a way to end his pain.

In *Byzantium!* we are given a sneak peek into the life of Barbara in 1973, at which point she is thirty-two years old. It is said that she gave up teaching probably around the time of her son's birth (although she is still teaching in *Face of the Enemy* which is almost certainly set during the early '70s).

From Ian & Barbara's point of view, the first story to feature them post-*The Chase* is the comic strip *Hunters of the Burning Stone*, the fiftieth anniversary story published in *Doctor Who Magazine issues #456 to #461*. They are kidnapped by the Prometheans and placed in an illusionary world that looks like Coal Hill School. The Eleventh Doctor finds them there, but they have forgotten all their adventures with him. Eventually he is able to jog their memories, but Ian is not as willing to be convinced that the young man before them is the Doctor, although, as per *An Unearthly Child*, Barbara keeps a more open mind. Along with the Doctor they find themselves up against the Tribe of Gum, the cavemen primitives they encountered in the very first *Doctor Who* story in 1963, now a group of Hunters scouring the galaxy, having been given psychic metal by the Prometheans.

In terms of the ongoing narrative of the series, Ian & Barbara never surface again, until a *Brief Encounter* in which the Seventh Doctor bumps into an old Ian outside a conservatory in Greenwich. The Doctor says he is in the area visiting an old friend who is, unfortunately, out. Once home with his wife, Barbara, Ian is handed a present which has been delivered earlier that day; a Coal Hill School tie to replace the one destroyed on the surface of Vortis in the television story *The Web Planet*.

An older Ian also surfaces in the 2011 audio play *The Five Companions*. He is reunited with Steven Taylor, neither of whom have seen the Doctor since ending their travels, and both are much older now. When Ian first meets the Fifth Doctor he believes him to be a younger version of the Doctor he knew, but later learns about regeneration. He also explains that for thirty years he was a researcher, and after a bout of retirement he returned to teaching, which Barbara isn't happy about but then again she has started writing a new book.

Both of these encounters indicate that the 'rumour' Sarah Jane Smith heard about Ian & Barbara, that they had not aged since the 1960s, was just that. A rumour. Of course, like everything above, until it is confirmed in the television show it remains merely a possibility.

No Expanded Universe mention of Ian & Barbara would be complete without a mention of *Doctor Who in An Exciting Adventure with the Daleks*, the novelisation of the television story of the (almost) same name, published in 1964. It is the first Expanded Universe appearance of Ian & Barbara, and is the book that begins *Doctor Who*'s forty-nine-year publishing history. It presents a truly apocryphal introduction to *Doctor Who* by having Ian, apparently older than on television, relate a story that is basically the same as its TV counterpart but with a few important differences; he is after a job as an assistant research scientist at Donneby's (a big rocket component firm) who happens upon Barbara on Barnes Common, after she and Susan are involved in a car accident. Susan has mysteriously gone missing and Ian & Barbara meet the Doctor, who is as evasive as he was on television. They follow him to a Police Box on the common and, as per the show, they push their way in. It is interesting that neither Ian nor Barbara know each other, and he often refers to her as a 'girl in her early twenties', and Barbara is Susan's private tutor. It makes one wonder what might have happened if this narrative was continued in all Expanded Universe versions of *Doctor Who*.

The first truly alternative look at *Doctor Who* came along in 1965 with the first ever *Doctor Who* cinematic release, *Dr Who & the Daleks*. Essentially a re-telling of the first Dalek serial from 1963-1964, the film differs in many key ways. Both Susan (most often called 'Suzie') and Barbara are the granddaughters of Earth inventor, Dr Who, while Ian is Barbara's new boyfriend (the first occasion in which these two characters get romantically paired, and quite likely the origin of their perceived television romance, even though the film was released the day before Ian & Barbara departed the Doctor's company in *The Chase*). Susan is a little scientist, and the apple of Dr Who's eye, his protégé, while Barbara and Ian are very removed from their television counterparts; not a teaching credential between them. For the following film, *Daleks: Invasion Earth 2150AD*, released in 1966, things were changed a little and two new companions were introduced. First there is Louise, Dr Who's niece and Susan's cousin, and second there is police constable Tom Campbell (played by actor Bernard Cribbins, who would later go on to play Wilfred Mott in 2007-2010, the grandfather of future companion, Donna Noble), who stumbled into *Tardis* thinking it is a real Police Box.

Vicki has appeared in only a handful of Expanded Universe stories; less than ten short stories, only four novels and two audio books. It is not surprising, therefore, that we do not learn much that is new. The most we learn is in the 2001 novel, *Byzantium!* which reveals that she left Earth in 2493 and was only fourteen (an age contradicted by *The Myth Makers*). Her mother died when Vicki was eleven, and she wanted to call Vicki 'Tanni' (a name originally devised by the production team for Vicki) while her father preferred 'Vicki'. She thought it a stupid name, which ties nicely in with her willingness to change her name in *The Myth Makers*. Most importantly in that novel we are told that her surname is 'Pallister', a name used in most Expanded Universe appearances of Vicki. And in the 1996 novel *The Plotters* we learn that when she was five she was inoculated against many diseases by medical laser injection.

During her travels with the Doctor, Vicki finds herself confused, having grown used to Ian & Barbara's company, yet wishing they would find their way home. Her historical knowledge has as many gaps as it does on television; she confuses singer Dido with Sister Bliss, and has never heard of Plato, Archimedes or Socrates, although she is dimly aware of Charles

Dickens. She also thinks Shakespeare is good, but prefers the works of Lynda La Plante – ironic since she would end up meeting a young William Shakespeare a few years after leaving the Doctor.

She also finds herself the unwilling object of King James' affections in *The Plotters,* because she is posing as a boy called 'Victor', and in *The Empire of Glass* an alien Greld wishes to mate with her.

Two stories visit Vicki, or Cressida as she is known by then, a few years after *The Myth Makers*. First we have *Apocrypha Bipedium* which has the Eighth Doctor and his companion, Charley, arrive some time after the Fall of Troy. They are en route back to England, returning a young Shakespeare home. Vicki recognises the Doctor as a younger version of the man she knew, and so goes to great lengths to ensure that neither she nor her husband, Troilus, reveal any future knowledge of him. Eventually the Doctor explains things to Vicki and advises her and Troilus to move to Cornwall, as he is worried that she may end up becoming one of her own ancestors.

In the second of these stories, we come across an older Lady Cressida in 1164BC (confusingly twenty years before the traditional date of the Fall of Troy) in the 2007 audio book, *Frostfire*. She is living in Carthage, and tells a story of when she, Steven and the Doctor meet Jane Austen during the frost fair of 1814. During this adventure she witnesses the death of a phoenix, a cinder from which finds its way into Vicki's eye – and there it remains until Cressida and Troilus settle in Carthage many years later. One day, missing her old life and feeling so alone Cressida cries and the cinder escapes her eye. It is still alive and able to communicate with her. She keeps the cinder in an oil lamp and often talks to it, since it is the only thing that knows anything of her life with the Doctor.

Steven has managed a much better Expanded Universe life, with many appearances in short stories and audio books, but he has only been in three novels. However, surprisingly, not much new information has been given about his past, or his life post-Doctor.

We discover in the short story *Ash* that he was given learning pills as part of his education, and in *The Empire of Glass* we are told that he spent most of his adult career in cramped quarters, with the first new smell for him being the burning forest on Mechanus at the end of *The Chase*. Also in *The Empire of Glass* Steven is seen to be flirting with Christopher Marlowe, inferring perhaps that Steven may have been the first gay companion in *Doctor Who*. During his time in space Steven pilots a streamlined Terran ship made of modified Dalek technology, and at one point, while on shore leave on Roylus Prime, he witnesses a woman being savagely beaten yet does not lift a hand to help. This guilt tortures him for some time, and resurfaces in the novel *Salvation*, compounded by the recent deaths of Katarina and Sara.

In the novel *Bunker Soldiers*, Steven is still smarting from the conclusion of the television story *The Massacre* and initially sides against the Doctor, in favour of interceding and saving lives, but the Doctor convinces him why it would be wrong to do so. We also learn that he does not believe in heaven, despite claiming to be a Protestant in *The Massacre*, since in all his travels he has seen nothing to convince himself of such a place. Indeed, he has learned to expect a rational explanation for everything he sees, even if he cannot understand the explanation.

In one touching short story, Steven and the Doctor accidentally ruin the future of a young boy called Bobby Zierath, and with more than a little guilt for his own part in events, Steven gives Bobby his panda, Hi-Fi – which, of course, is never seen on TV after *The Time Meddler*.

It is not until the audio adventure, *The Five Companions*, that we meet Steven again. Many long years have passed since he has left the Doctor. At first he is reunited with Ian, followed by the Fifth Doctor, who like Ian, he believes to be a younger version of the Doctor he knew, until the Doctor explains about regeneration. Steven is very surprised to encounter an older Sara in this story, having witnessed her death many years previously while still with the Doctor. Sara never really explains to him the reason for her survival, only that even the Doctor never could quite understand it, either. Nonetheless he is happy to see Ian, Sara and the Doctor again and, like the others, is convinced that the Doctor will not return to look them up, despite his promises to the contrary.

Since Katarina literally went from Troy to Kembel and then sacrificed herself there is no time for other adventures. Regardless of this, the short story *Scribbles in Chalk* tells of a 'missing adventure'. There is not much that can be added to Katarina really – but this story does try to add a little something. We are told that Cassandra chose Katarina as her handmaiden because she had predicated Katarina's death. We also learn that, although she likes Steven, Katarina finds him arrogant.

Something interesting happens in the 2003 short story, *Katarina in the Underworld*. We follow Katarina as she journeys to the Elysian fields of the afterlife. She does not have the coins to pay her way across the River Styx, and so an old woman summons the Doctor to help her. Before Hades she explains how she sacrificed her life to save millions. Persephone vouches for Katarina and she is allowed into the Elysian fields. Even as she enters she ponders that this may have been just be a dream, but even so she is convinced that the Doctor inspired her to achieve her destiny.

Poor Dodo!

On television she had a pretty rum deal – joining the Doctor without preamble or an introductory story, and then cast aside by the Doctor for no real good reason, and thus denied a final adventure. She fares little better in the Expanded Universe prose.

Salvation, a novel published in 1999, attempts to give her a good introductory story, but only succeeds in messing up things even more. On television it is clearly stated that she ran into the TARDIS because she witnessed an accident on Wimbledon Common, but *Salvation* tells us otherwise. She is fleeing an increasingly insane alien metamorph called Joseph, who is one of six extra-dimensional beings who came into light as a result of the beliefs of those they encountered. This book also goes to great lengths to explain why Dodo's accent changes so drastically between scenes at the opening of *The Celestial Toymaker*.

'Dodo' starts out a horrible nickname in school, because of her inferior North London accent; she later takes the nickname on to spite her peers, and uses one accent as Dodo in everyday life, and the other as the 'proper schoolgirl' Dorothea. We also learn that her mother died in 1962, while her father was institutionalised shortly after, which led to Dodo living with her Aunt Margaret, a tyrannical woman if ever there was one. These background details are contradicted in *The Man in the Velvet Mask*, in which we are told that she grew up in one of the poorer parts of London, and her parents died when she was young. She then moved in with her aunt, who was a wealthy social climber. Dodo had trouble marrying her previously poor existence with this new life, and found herself reinventing herself depending on each situation, thus explaining that her accent was 'situational' at best.

Just to make her life a little bit worse, the Doctor implies in *Bunker Soldiers* that her remark to Dmitri in Kiev, 1240, may have been the inspiration for the Black Death over a hundred years later. After Dmitri orders his food is thrown to the pigs, Dodo tells him, 'You can't just throw something away because you don't like it,' which leads the half-mad Dmitri to order the plague-ridden bodies hurled over the walls of Kiev at the Mongol horde. A tactic that would be later remembered and passed on.

Still, the Expanded Universe authors are not finished with her. In the 1996 novel, *The Man in the Velvet Mask*, Dodo loses her virginity to Dalville, an actor in an alternative Paris in 1804, and is infected by a virus created by mad dwarf Minksi – a virus that infects all her future lovers and possible children. In that novel we also learn that she spent most of her French lessons learning how to kiss behind the gym.

The worst, however, is saved for when she leaves the Doctor.

COMPANIONS

The novel *Who Killed Kennedy?* details Dodo's life after the Doctor palms her off to recover in the country. It is revealed that she spends several months in the country, then returns to London to get a job. It does not work out too well for her as she starts experiencing blackouts and memory loss, a result of the conditioning from WOTAN. She goes to a series of psychiatric hospitals, and even undergoes fourteen months of electro-shock treatment. She is interrogated by the Master, once he learns she used to know the Doctor, who then wipes her memory of said event. She lives in a halfway house for homeless people and eventually gets in touch with journalist James Stevens, who is on a mission to expose UNIT and the cover-ups of alien invasions, after reading an article of his about mind control. They end up becoming lovers and she falls pregnant. While James investigates the Glasshouse, a special UNIT-funded hospital (secretly run by the Master – who was goading James to be a thorn in UNIT's side), she is shot in her home. She is buried in South London and one of the shorter-run Doctors (either the Second or Seventh) attends her funeral carrying a white rose.

Another gap that does not exist is the short time Ben & Polly travelled with the First Doctor, yet they do appear in a couple of stories, both in short form and in a novel. Understandably we learn very little (we learn more during their time with the Second Doctor – see page 54).

In the 2002 novel, *Ten Little Aliens*, we learn that Ben has an older brother who taught him how to swear when they were in school. He is a little conscious of his height, since Polly is a good inch taller than he. Polly tends to think of people as either cat or dog people, and considers Ben a dog person, whereas she is a cat person due to her independent nature. She seems to have had a rather privileged upbringing, being more used to Beaujolais Nouveau parties, and having attended a finishing school in South Kensington, London. When Polly becomes the object of Trooper Matthew Shade's affections, Ben finds himself becoming a little

38

jealous, even though he is getting close to Trooper Mel Narda. We also learn that the Doctor reminds Ben of his father, who had a knack for fixing things haphazardly.

As with all incarnations of the Doctor, the first has several companions that are exclusive to Expanded Universe, and the first were introduced in 1964 and still remain the most well-known; Dr Who's two grandchildren, John and Gillian. They travelled with Dr Who (during the '60s comics he was always referred to as such) for four years in total, until the first episode of *Invasion of the Quarks* in 1968, by which time they were travelling with the Second Doctor. There is no discernible moment when they leave and return, indeed it is strongly implied that they never did leave their grandfather and were, thus, with him for his regeneration in the comic-verse. More on their travels and eventual departure on page 61.

Over in the *Doctor Who Annual* Dr Who is joined by several companions, first in the 1966 annual story, *The Monster from Earth* (released in 1965). Playing hide and seek, brother and sister, Amy and Tony Barker, decide to hide in a Police Box and find themselves off on an adventure with the Sensorites (who barely resemble their TV counterparts), before the Doctor, after feeding them, take them back home. The following year a whole plethora of prose companions are introduced to readers, first in the novella-length release, *Doctor Who and the Invasion from Space* and later in the 1967 annual. Other than annoying Dr Who, the Mortimer (some sources say Mortimore) family does little except take up space and get into trouble. They are George and Helen, and their two children, Ida and Alan, who, at the beginning of the story, are fleeing the Great Fire of London and run into the TARDIS before it dematerialises. In the annual story, *The Devil-Birds of Corbo*, we are introduced to Harroll Strong, an Earth-maker looking for minerals on the planet Corbo, and his twin children, Jack and Dot. The Doctor rescues them from the Devil-Bird of the title, as well as three other astronauts, Shelly,

Chertzog and Hill. They return in the follow up story, *Playthings of Fo*, and at the end of that tale they set course for Earth. Other than John and Gillian, none of those Expanded Universe companions are heard of again.

The next Expanded Universe-only companion comes along in 2011, when we are introduced to Oliver Harper. A city trader from 1966, Oliver joins the Doctor and Steven in the audio book, *The Perpetual Bond,* and is killed two stories later in *The First Wave*. His mind continues to exist, and he remains with the Doctor (who is completely unaware of his presence) for the rest of his first incarnation until fading out when the Doctor regenerates.

The last Expanded Universe companion is, probably, the most interesting, in that she was created for television, but never intended to be an ongoing companion. Sara Kingdom appeared in the epic twelve-part story *The Daleks' Masterplan*, and was killed in the closing moments. Her position as companion has been hotly contested by fans for decades. A debate that was ratcheted up in 1989 when John Peel adapted the story into two books, fixing a very definite six month gap between episodes seven and eight. During that time, Sara continues to travel with the Doctor and Steven, as seen in several audio books and short stories. But in the audio book *Home Truths* we learn that Sara's mind is copied by a house, and later she is reincarnated as an older woman – and it is this Sara who appears in the audio play, *The Five Companions*.

The Second Doctor

Patrick Troughton

*'Our lives are different to anybody else's.
...Nobody in the universe can do what we're doing.'*
The Doctor – *The Tomb of the Cybermen*

With the change of Doctor a radical shift in the companion dynamic occurred. Up to this point the majority of the Doctor's companions were contemporary (and even when they were not, very little was made of the 'out of time' aspect of their characters), with a nice balance between male and female. But along came the Second Doctor, and off go Ben & Polly. Their replacements were three very distinctively different types of companions – and not one contemporary character among them – a fact that was tailored to the stories' benefit, and, indeed, the Doctor's.

Ben Jackson & Polly – Michael Craze & Anneke Wills continued... (*The War Machines* to *The Faceless Ones*)

During the rest of their travels with the Doctor, we learn very little about Ben & Polly, even though they continue with him for a further six adventures. It is a curious thing that from the start, despite having seen the Doctor's 'renewal', Ben refuses to accept that the Doctor is indeed who he claims to be. Once again Polly is the voice of reason, willing to accept what she has seen, even if she cannot really understand it. Throughout their adventure on the human colony on Vulcan (*The Power of the Daleks*) Ben continues to be irritable and highly strung, while Polly opts for calmness. It is only when a Dalek recognises the Doctor that Ben finally accepts this strange man in the frock coat is the same old man he had come to trust.

Throughout his travels, Ben is heard moaning and complaining a lot, often responding with aggression, but at his heart he is a good man; a hero of sorts, although sometimes he is not the sharpest of travelling companions. His lack of historical knowledge is proven when the TARDIS takes its occupants to the Battle of Culloden in 1746 (*The Highlanders*) but he displays an unexpected level of scientific knowledge on the Moonbase when helping Polly find a way to combat the Cybermen. He reveals himself to be a little ignorant of other cultures when he points out that Polly can speak 'foreign' and continues to be protective of Polly, calling her 'Duchess' on many occasions. When separated for some time, Ben's first thought on seeing the Doctor is always, 'Where's Polly?'

With the arrival of Jamie, Ben finds a kindred spirit – another young man who is not shy of taking action. They bond in an almost sibling-like way, although they almost come to blows when Ben suggests that Jamie 'cracks up' while on the Moonbase. His will is easily overcome by the Macra (*The Macra Terror*), who turn him against his travelling companions, but the brainwashing is eventually fixed by the Doctor, who has already prevented Polly from succumbing to the same brainwashing technique.

Polly maintains her usual level of optimism whilst travelling, although the horror of the events she has witnessed continues to affect her. She is sickened by the Daleks' slaughter of the human colonists on Vulcan, but despite her revulsion at witnessing the death of Gascoigne (*The Faceless Ones*) she still goes to check his body. Regardless of her outward 'dolly bird' appearance, and her well-to-do upbringing, she remains a strong and determined person, not ashamed to use her feminine wiles to gain the assistance of British soldier Finch, while on the Scottish highlands of 1746, as well as dominating the much weaker Kirsty McLaren, daughter of the Laird of the clan McLaren. She considers Ben a 'real man' and never loses hope that one day the Doctor will take her home (she thinks of Chelsea in *The Underwater Menace*, which suggests that is where she is from). She is partly responsible for Jamie joining the Doctor. It is her who suggests that he should come with them, rather than be left to fend for himself on the Scottish highlands.

Much like Dodo before them, during their last adventure set in London (*The Faceless Ones*) Ben & Polly are sidelined. In this case both disappear by the end of the second episode; Polly is replaced by an alien Chameleon in the first episode, calling itself Michelle Leuppi, while Ben is last seen in the second episode being frozen by the Chameleon, Spencer. The Doctor never gives up looking for them and eventually frees them at the end of episode six, in which they return for one final scene. Ben is the first to realise that the date, July 20th 1966, is the exact same day the pair joined the Doctor in *The War Machines*. Ben & Polly want to remain in London for a while, glad to be in a normal place again away from monsters. They both decide it is time to stop travelling, but only if the Doctor doesn't mind. The Doctor is saddened to see them go, but makes Polly promise to look after Ben, which she does.

We never see them again on television, but in 2010 we discover in *The Sarah Jane Adventures* that Polly made good on her promise, and she and Ben remained together running an orphanage in India.

James Robert McCrimmon was quite unique in *Doctor Who* history. Not only did he appear in more episodes than any other companion (not counting any return appearances), but he travelled with the Second Doctor for all but one of his adventures (the only companion who came close was Tegan Jovanka who travelled with the Fifth Doctor for all but two of his stories). It was, therefore, of little surprise to learn that even today the Doctor regarded Jamie with great affection, having mentioned him several times in later incarnations; he even used Jamie's full name as an alias when, in his tenth incarnation, the Doctor encountered

Queen Victoria on the moors of Scotland (*Tooth and Claw*).

Jamie McCrimmon – Frazer Hines (*The Highlanders* to *The War Games,* and *The Two Doctors*)

The Doctor first encounters Jamie in the Scottish highlands during the aftermath of the Battle of Culloden in 1746 (even though Jamie later explicitly states he comes from 1745 when being questioned by the Security Chief in *The War Games*). It is a violent first encounter, in which Jamie holds a dirk to Ben's throat, but the Doctor soon convinces the highlanders that he and his friends are not English spies. At the time Jamie is a piper for the McLaren clan. Surviving death at the gallows, Jamie helps the Doctor, Ben & Polly across the glen, suspecting they will become lost if they try to find their way on their own. Realising the danger, Polly convinces the Doctor to let Jamie go with them. Jamie is a little uncertain at first, wondering what he has 'come upon', but soon enters the TARDIS to be spirited away to Atlantis (*The Underwater Menace*).

The first thing to change about Jamie is his accent, which softens almost immediately. One might attribute this to travel, except it happens too quickly. The harder accent returns, however, when his features are temporarily changed in the Land of Fiction (*The Mind Robber)* but the soft familiar tones continue once his normal features are returned. It is interesting to note that once he is returned to his own time his original accent resurfaces, confirming his travels with the Doctor 'no longer happened for him'.

A product of the eighteenth century, Jamie's knowledge base is somewhat lacking, and he is constantly exposed to new things which he can barely understand. To cope he often equates such things with his own time period; calling a plane a 'flying beastie' for instance, or in the case of a hovercraft, a fairytale. He is initially fearful of flying in a helicopter in *The Enemy of the World*, despite having previously flown in an aeroplane sometime before in *The*

Faceless Ones, but by the time he is next in a helicopter, in *Fury from the Deep*, he is perfectly comfortable – just one instance in which Jamie displays his amazing adaptability to new situations. This lack of knowledge should never be mistaken as stupidity; he shows an amazing level of intelligence, resourcefulness and common sense throughout his travels, quickly learning to read and how to tell the time. Note, for example, how he finds a way onto the Chameleon Tours plane despite previously never having been in an airport.

It seems that at first Jamie doesn't quite know how to act around women; horrified by the notion of being pampered by a group of women on the leisure colony of *The Macra Terror*, and flustered by the attention of Samantha Briggs in *The Faceless Ones*, but he soon learns to adapt to her bolshie attitude and does his best to charm her. This experience leaves him in good standing, since in the next adventure (*The Evil of the Daleks*) he is quite happy to question the 'lassies' in a London cafe, and rather enjoys the experience, getting the required information with ease. When he is later transferred to 1866, he easily charms the Maxtible's maid, Molly. All these experiences prepare him for the arrival of Victoria.

Jamie's relationship with his travelling companions tends to be mostly affectionate, especially with the Doctor, Victoria and Zoe. He is competitive with Ben, often responding with bravado and aggression at some perceived insult.

Jamie is disappointed when Ben & Polly leave, since they had taken him under their wing and treated him much like a little brother (possibly it was them, in particular Polly, who encouraged him to learn to read). He promises to look out for the Doctor, a promise he takes very seriously over the course of the next two years. As he and the Doctor become close a strong relationship of trust and respect is built.

This relationship is almost brought to an abrupt end when the Doctor appears to ally himself with the Daleks (*The Evil of the Daleks*), putting Jamie through a series of dangerous tests as the Daleks attempt to define the 'human factor'. When Jamie discovers the Doctor's apparent betrayal, he is angry and calls him callous and uncaring. Uncharacteristically he appears to want to leave the TARDIS, but the Doctor manages to win him over. Jamie is later devastated when he believes the Doctor to be infected by the 'Dalek factor'. He is not entirely convinced by the Doctor's insistence that he is still actually himself. This presents a shift in their previous dynamic and Jamie continues to display a willingness to call the Doctor out when he believes the Doctor wrong. Nonetheless, despite that shift they still remain close, with Jamie considering himself responsible for the Doctor's safety.

Outwardly he treats new companion Victoria as a little sister, adopting the role of protective big brother. Jamie seems to hold a torch for her, as most clearly seen in *The Enemy of the World* after Victoria makes a disparaging remark about the future fashion of women's clothing, and Jamie suggests that she would look good in such garb herself with a solicitous smirk. This on its own could just be a case of Jamie's typical playfulness with those he is close to, but when coupled with his sadness when Victoria elects to remain on Earth in the 1970s it suggests something a little more. He tries to convince her to remain, and has a difficult time expressing his sadness to the Doctor, instead appearing gruff, until the Doctor points out that he too will miss her.

After leaving Victoria behind, the Doctor and Jamie find themselves in the twenty-first century (*The Wheel in Space*). It is in this story that Jamie first attributes the name 'John Smith' to the Doctor, having read it on a piece of medical equipment. While the Doctor is rendered unconscious Jamie is introduced to astrophysicist Zoe Herriot. It takes Jamie a while to warm to Zoe. He finds her too intelligent for her own good; with her 'big brain' she often laughs at his lesser intelligence, calling his kilt a 'skirt' and making snide comments. Zoe and Jamie soon settle into a friendly bickering relationship characterised by Jamie's usual protectiveness and Zoe's bossiness. His more simple thinking often wins out over Zoe's logic.

During his travels with the Doctor, Jamie grows a lot, both

emotionally and intellectually. By the time of *The War Games,* Jamie is quite willing to work with a redcoat to escape the prisoners' camp, the one-time sworn enemy of the highlanders. After some years travelling together, Jamie remains convinced that the Doctor hasn't betrayed the rebels, even though he appears to have allied himself with the War Chief, an old Time Lord acquaintance in *The War Games.* At the end of this adventure, the Doctor is left with no choice but to call his own people, and is ready to part company with Jamie and Zoe, fearing for their safety if the Time Lords catch up with them. Jamie doesn't care about the danger – he will not leave the Doctor's side.

Such is his loyalty to the Doctor that Jamie insists they attempt an escape from the Time Lords. He is angered by the Time Lord's insistence that he and Zoe must leave. It is only the Doctor's sad certainty that convinces Jamie that his adventures truly must end. A sad farewell follows, in which Jamie states that he will never forget the Doctor – not knowing that his memory is soon to be wiped by the Time Lords.

Jamie appears to return in *The Five Doctors* in 1983, although he, like Zoe, is only a phantom, an illusion created by the force of Rassilon's will. His appearance serves to help the Doctor solve a problem, since Jamie remembers the Brigadier, which is clearly impossible since his memory was wiped. How the Doctor could remember this wasn't going to be explored for some time, although the 1986 adventure *The Two Doctors* would provide clues. Although Jamie is returned to his own time, with only the memory of his first adventure with the Doctor remaining, he does return – *sixteen* years later! In *The Two Doctors,* Jamie and the Doctor appear to still be travelling together, both having aged considerably. The Doctor is seen to be working for the Time Lords, a fact fully known to Jamie. The familiar loyalty is evident, but now they have become very firm friends, much more so than they ever were when they were originally travelling together. There is no indication of how long they have been travelling together or indeed why (such explanations are bountiful in the

Expanded Universe material covered in page 56). It is, however, clear that the Sixth Doctor remembers his extra journeys with Jamie since he shows no surprise at his older appearance, or at the fact that his own second incarnation has grey hair. While stranded on Station Camera, believing the Doctor to be dead, Jamie reverts to a feral state, to the point where he attacks Peri – like an animal protecting its lair. He accepts the Sixth Doctor with ease. Even though the explanation makes little sense to Jamie he doesn't question it any further. He enjoys a good rapport with the Sixth Doctor, and becomes a little protective of Peri, much like he had once had been with Victoria and Zoe. He is last seen departing in the TARDIS with the Second Doctor, but not before giving Peri a quick peck on the cheek.

The teenage daughter of wealthy scientist, Edward Waterfield, Victoria was from 1866 and was very much a girl of her time. Well educated both academically and in the subject of manners and propriety.

Victoria Waterfield – Deborah Watling (*The Evil of the Daleks* to *Fury from the Deep*)

Victoria first meets Jamie while being held captive by the Daleks (*The Evil of the Daleks*), to ensure the continued assistance of her father and his associate Theodore Maxtible. She is understandably almost hysterical with fear, isolated with only the occasional appearance of a Dalek for company (it comes in barking orders at her, asking her to repeat her name constantly; an abject lesson in creating terror in a person). Even through her fear she continues to feed the birds that land on the sill of her cell window, despite repeated orders not to do so. It is as if she considers them the only contact she still has with a world she *does* understand. Her fear is not helped once Jamie and Kemel rescue her, since they are, for a time, barricaded in the cell. Later she and Kemel are transferred to Skaro in the distant future which Victoria has some difficulty accepting, but not as much as when Kemel is later killed. Death seems to follow her a lot and her father is also killed by the Daleks on Skaro, but not before he asks the Doctor to take care of Victoria for him.

Victoria accepts the Doctor's offer to join the TARDIS crew, with little other choice, since she is now an orphan, cut off and far from home. She is somewhat surprised by the TARDIS, and laughs at the idea that it is a time machine, having no knowledge of the experiments in time travel her own father conducted. Her laughter soon turns to concern when she realises just how old the Doctor is. This concern becomes even more evident when she tells him he probably needs rest being 'so old'. The Doctor, however, rebuffs this as he is quite sprightly really.

Victoria changes into clothes she considers far too short, until the Doctor points out that Jamie's kilt is not much different (although by *The Enemy of the World* she dons an even shorter skirt and calls it 'elegant', showing her acceptance of the new life she is living). This nineteenth century mindset continues with her for some time, but she still maintains an inquisitive mind, no doubt as encouraged by her father (as witnessed by her knowledge of science in *The Abominable Snowmen*) and evident in her dealings with the crew of the rocket that brings the archaeological team to Telos (*The Tomb of the Cybermen*). She talks down to them a lot, probably in the same manner she would have adopted speaking to servants back home – it is telling that she doesn't show the same attitude to the archaeologists themselves.

Although a product of her time, Victoria does show a surprising level of bravery, even when being held at gunpoint she holds her own and later stands up to Donald Bruce, the thuggish head of security for the World Zone Authority in *The Enemy of the World*. It appears she has been trained in firearms, or she is a very lucky shot, since she manages to hit a Cybermat with her first shot.

She often demonstrates a wide knowledge of academic subjects, including the sciences and geology, but she hasn't heard of the London Underground even though it existed in her native time. She is not afraid to lie if the situation requires it, for example when she professes knowledge of cooking, when it is clear she has never cooked in her life, spouting ingredients which she has most likely heard being mentioned before.

Victoria draws a great comfort from the Doctor's presence, looking upon him in almost a fatherly way. She learns how to cope with her own loss following his advice. With Jamie she develops a sibling-like relationship, and is often amused by his lack of knowledge and view on women, in particular the way they dress.

Victoria is known for her screaming – indeed her reaction to any monster she meets is to scream. However, in *Fury from the Deep* it is discovered that the weed creatures are susceptible to high-pitched noise and so the survivors on the oil refinery hit on the idea of recording Victoria's screams and using them as a weapon. Ironically she discovers she simply cannot scream on command, but upon seeing a weed creature again scream she does.

She becomes resigned to the random travels early on, but by the time of *Fury from the Deep* she comes to realise that she is tired of the endless travelling and longs for peace and happiness. She decides to remain behind in the 1970s with the Harris family, a decision the Doctor completely understands, although he does insist he remain for another night just so she can be sure. Jamie has a harder time letting go, to the point where he tries to convince her to continue to travel with him and the Doctor, but she knows she cannot. Leaving them is hard, but she knows she must do it. The last we see is an image of her on the TARDIS scanner waving goodbye.

We never hear of Victoria again, save for a mention in *The Two Doctors* when an older Doctor explains to Jamie that she is off studying graphology for a short time, implying that somehow she resumed her travels with the Doctor and Jamie for almost another twenty years.

An astrophysicist from an undefined point in the twenty-first century (*The War Games*) Zoe stated quite specifically that she was *born* in the twenty-first century, although in *The Mind Robber* she explained how she read *The Hourly Telepress* from the year 2000.

Zoe Heriot – Wendy Padbury (The Wheel in Space to The War Games)

Zoe first meets the Doctor and Jamie in *The Wheel in Space* when she is working as a librarian. Highly trained in logic (which, the Doctor points out, only allows people to be wrong with authority), she is considered to be 'all brain and no heart' by her colleagues, especially Leo Ryan. She realises this is true and wants to feel more and not be like the students usually produced by the parapsychology teachers.

Her need to 'feel' expresses itself immediately upon meeting Jamie. She is fascinated by his girl's clothing, having never seen a kilt before. This immediately annoys Jamie, and Zoe realises he is an easy target, setting the scene for much teasing and bossiness for the rest of their association. Her logical approach is called into question as she spends more and more time with the Doctor, who is the most illogical and instinctive person she has ever met. The Doctor intrigues her greatly, and when she learns about the TARDIS her curiosity is taken to a whole new level. So after being refused entry, she stows away as soon as the Doctor and Jamie's backs are turned. The Doctor spots her, and gives her the choice; no doubt because he is still weary of the reasons behind Victoria's departure.

Despite witnessing the Doctor and Jamie's previous encounter with the Daleks by way of thoughts being transmitted to the TARDIS scanner by the Doctor (*The Evil of the Daleks*), Zoe elects to remain and thoroughly enjoys her first trip to the planet Dulkis (*The Dominators*). She is more than happy to assist the Dulcians, encouraging them to resist the oppressive Dominators, although she does make the usual first-traveller mistake of giving away too much information about the TARDIS and how they arrived on the planet.

COMPANIONS

When the TARDIS is removed from regular time to escape an exploding volcano, Zoe has to explain to Jamie the danger they are in, and the concept of 'nothing' being outside the ship is something she has no problem understanding. While there, she sees an image of her home city – a sprawling futuristic metropolis quite unlike anything ever seen on twenty-first century Earth! This image is soon swept away when she finds herself alone in the Land of Fiction (*The Mind Robber*); she reacts with sheer terror at being removed from everything she finds familiar. Her knowledge of history is not very good, but she is aware of some of the classic tales, like Theseus and the Minotaur, Perseus' battle against the Gorgon Medusa and *Gulliver's Travels*, and is also a fan of the Karkus' adventures in *The Hourly Telepress*. She displays some basic self-defence training, and is temporarily turned into fiction by the Master of the Land of Fiction. Her photographic memory also comes into play when she corrects a mistake the Doctor makes as he reassembles Jamie's face, thus altering his appearance for a short time.

Upon arrival in the 1970s (*The Invasion*) Zoe is enticed into a brief stint of model work by fashion photographer, Isobel Watkins, and through the subsequent friendship she discovers a much more normal, fun-loving side of her character. In particular, she finds posing for the camera 'great fun'. Yet she finds it hard to relax while the Doctor and Jamie are off finding Isobel's father and can't help but sense that something is wrong. Isobel and Zoe encourage each other to visit International Electromatics and come up against the robotic secretary. Frustrated by its unwillingness to help, and refusing to be beaten by a 'brainless' box, Zoe sets it an unsolvable puzzle by use of the computer language ALGOL, a chance for her to prove that she is better than a machine. It is Zoe that computes the attack patterns needed to defeat the Cybermen spaceships, which leads to one UNIT soldier remarking that she is, 'so much prettier than a computer', a comment that pleases Zoe greatly.

On the planet of the Gonds (*The Dominators*) Zoe displays

knowledge of geology. She recognises the mica rocks and likens the Gond city to those built by the Incans. It is while there that the Doctor admits that Zoe is something of a genius, which can be irritating at times, while Zoe believes the Doctor to be almost as clever as she is. This appears to be proven when she initially gets a better score on the Kroton teaching machine but she is trumped as soon as the Doctor realises his mistake.

She is an expert in space flight and has total recall, which comes in useful when learning to fly Professor Eldred's rocket in *The Seeds of Death*.

Like Jamie, Zoe is returned to her own time by the Time Lords, and her memory of the Doctor is erased, save her initial adventure with him. She doesn't want to leave him and hopes that they will one day see each other again. It is sad that once she is returned to the Wheel, all that she learned and experienced is taken from her, and so she reverts back to the 'all brains and no heart' Zoe we first met. Although for a moment she can't help but think that she has forgotten something.

We never see Zoe again, except as a phantom, alongside phantom Jamie, produced by the mind of Rassilon in the Dark Tower on Gallifrey in *The Five Doctors*.

The Second Doctor
Expanded Universe

There is a fascination with the companions of the Second Doctor among authors of the Expanded Universe material – what happened to them once they left the Doctor? With the erstwhile companions of the First Doctor, the writers seem more intent on expanding the background of these characters, giving them reasons for acting the way they do on television. Not so with Ben & Polly, Jamie, Victoria and Zoe...

One thing is certain in the minds of the majority of *Doctor Who* fandom, Ben & Polly end up together and most likely get married. Much like Ian & Barbara, writers of the books and comics seem intent on bringing these two characters together.

First of all there is the little matter of Polly's surname. In the original character outline she is named Polly Wright, sharing the same surname as Barbara. It is a name that never makes it to the television screens, but it is confirmed as her surname in the 1995 novel *Invasion of the Cat-People* by Gary Russell. In this story we also learn that both Ben & Polly were born in 1942, a point later contradicted in the 2009 audio book *Resistance*, which tells us that Polly was born in 1943. We also learn that her father is Doctor Edward Wright and her mother the former Miss Bettingham-Smith. Polly later considers that she took them both for granted, spending so much time away from home enjoying herself. Another important point is mentioned – Polly and Barbara are not related, they simply share a common surname.

For Ben's own part, not much of his personal history is revealed; save that when he was fourteen he snuck aboard his father's ship, and as a result of his interest in the sea-faring life, the captain promised him a job when he turned fifteen.

Otherwise, the Expanded Universe stories set during their travels with the Second Doctor do not deviate much from what we already know on television, but a special note must be made of instances from the 1968 *Doctor Who Annual*. In this collection of stories we see a different side of their journeys. These stories are at odds with their television counterpoints, especially the characters inter-personal relationships. In one story the Doctor favours Polly over Ben, considering her sensible and smarter than Ben. This may explain why, in another story, Ben and the Doctor have a very contentious relationship. In yet another, Polly manages to operate the TARDIS, something she never does on television. In the audio book *The Forbidden Time* (2011), we learn that Ben & Polly consider Jamie a 'little brother'.

Much has been made of their lives since leaving the Doctor and once again it is Polly who receives the most attention. In the 2005 comic *The Love Invasion* published by *Doctor Who Magazine* there is a brief moment where the Ninth Doctor and Rose Tyler rush by at the top of the Post Office Tower in 1966 and witness Ben proposing to Polly. In *The Five Companions* Polly takes Ben home to meet her parents, much to their horror. But Ben & Polly each go on to marry other people. However, in the 1998 short story *Mondas Passing* the estranged couple meet up in 1986 – but separate as friends after reminiscing about their time with the Doctor and Jamie.

Polly's life by the turn of the twenty-first century comes under the microscope in Joseph Lidster's short story *That Time I Nearly Destroyed the World Whilst Looking for a Dress* published in 2004. Lidster describes her as something of a music mogul. She regularly features in *OK!*, *Hello* and *Heat* and has been married several times. Her first husband, Simon, is dead and she also, at some point, marries a gay boy-band member. As a result she suffers a few bouts of excessive alcohol dependency and bulimia. She has a son, Mikey, and by the end of 1999 she fears she will mess his life up too. She goes on a rather bizarre journey through time and encounters the First Doctor, Ian and Susan in Sherwood, and later the Fifth Doctor, Tegan, Peri and Erimem – the latter she has a catfight with. Eventually, as 2000 comes to pass, she encounters the Second Doctor and Jamie once again. The TARDIS crew take her to Ben, who is now running a pub in Sydenham, and the two finally admit their love for each other.

Before meeting the Fifth Doctor again in *The Five Companions*, Polly takes to searching the internet to find other companions of the Doctor. Brigadier Lethbridge-Stewart has erased all such information, but they communicate via email and are joined by companion of the Fifth Doctor, Thomas Brewster (*The Three Companions*). The last we see of Polly in the Expanded Universe is in the 2012 play *The Five Companions* where she finds herself in an alternative version of the Gallifreyan Death Zone, coming into contact with several past companions and the Fifth Doctor. She admits to the Doctor that she feels like a useless companion, but he reminds her of how she stood up to the Cyberleader in 1986. She parts company with the Doctor once more, certain she will never see him again, but not before she tells him that she and Ben are, indeed, married.

Other than finding out that Jamie is twenty-two in the 2013 audio book *Shadow of Death* we learn very little that is new about him, save that he knows all about the Doctor's regeneration from Ben & Polly, as revealed in the 1997 novel *The Dark Path*. The more interesting stuff comes after he is returned to Scotland following *The War Games*.

Before we get to that, however, we need to consider his solo adventures with the Doctor in the pages of *TV Comic* from 1968 to 1969. Trying to place these adventures has been a bone of contention among *Doctor Who* scholars for decades, but Jamie does appear to be older than he is on television, which does muddy the waters somewhat. For some unknown reason he is initially living in 1960s Scotland and working at a tracking station in *issue #872*. His final appearance is in *issue #898*, and nothing is said about where he goes; he is just not there from the following issue and never returns.

To explain away the obvious age difference of Patrick Troughton and Frazer Hines in the 1986 adventure *The Two Doctors*, Season 6B was created by the authors of *The Discontinuity Guide* (first published in 1995 by Virgin Publishing). It suggests that before the Doctor was regenerated and exiled by the Time Lords he was, in fact, used as an agent. This is never confirmed beyond the guide until the 2005 novel *World Game* by Terrance Dicks, in which the Time Lords do indeed set him up as an agent – the alternative is his execution (a change from the television series, wherein he is merely threatened with exile). At the end of the novel the Doctor demands to have assistance on his missions. Consequently the Time Lords agree to return an older Jamie to him – albeit with his memory altered to include an awareness of their mission and the 'knowledge' that Victoria is absent studying graphology (as established in *The Two Doctors*). Various short stories have been written, seemingly set during this Season 6B, but mostly they see the Doctor travelling alone, with the exception of the 2007 audio book *Helicon Prime*. It is, in fact, distinctly possible that this older Jamie is the one seen in the pages of *TV Comic*.

An older version of Jamie continues to appear in other Expanded Universe material including a Jamie some forty-two years after he left the Doctor. He appears in *The Glorious Revolution* in 2009 visited by an agent of the Celestial Intervention Agency of Gallifrey, who removes the memory block placed on Jamie by the Time Lords. At this point Jamie is happily married to Kirsty McLaren (who appears in the television story *The Highlanders*) with at least eight children and an unmentioned number of grandchildren. Once the Time Lord agent solves the problem of Jamie's past, Jamie asks for his memory block to be restored since he doesn't want the knowledge of his travels with the Doctor to threaten his happy life.

In another possibly contradictory story, the Sixth Doctor and

Peri reunite with a man the locals call 'Mad Jamie', who claims to have travelled to the moon and beyond. In *The World Shapers* (*Doctor Who Magazine issues #127-129*, published in 1987) it is revealed that Jamie, some forty years after he left the Doctor, remembers his adventures. Following an adventure against the Voord, Jamie sacrifices himself to stop the Worldshaper from evolving the Voord into Cybermen.

The most recent appearance of Jamie, post-TARDIS travels, is in the audio play trilogy produced by Big Finish in 2012 *City of Spires*, *The Wreck of the Titan* and *Legend of the Cybermen*. The Sixth Doctor arrives in the Scottish highlands in 1780 and comes across Jamie who, posing as Black Donald, is the ruthless leader of rebels fighting the Redcoats. Jamie has no memory of the Doctor, but still agrees to travel with him. They soon discover they are in the Land of Fiction, now run by the Mistress of the Land, and become involved in a series of adventures which leads them to Zoe, who Jamie doesn't remember either. Zoe is able to release the Time Lord's block and later discovers that he is not the real Jamie at all, rather a work of fiction created by the Mistress of the Land. Fictional Jamie is not keen on learning that the Doctor never returned to the real Jamie. It is eventually revealed that Zoe is also a work of fiction, and the Mistress of the Land is actually the real Zoe (more on her role on page 60). At the end of the adventure, fictional Jamie makes the Doctor promise that he will one day seek out the real Jamie.

There is one final piece of the Jamie puzzle in the Expanded Universe and that is a comic-exclusive companion of the Tenth Doctor, one Heather McCrimmon, a descendant of Jamie's. More on her on page 328.

Victoria Maud Waterfield, as the 1996 novel *Downtime* reveals, was born in 1852 – meaning she was only fourteen during her travels with the Doctor. Her mother, Edith Rose, died in November 1863 when Victoria was eleven. And she was once photographed by Charles Dodgson, implying she was the physical model of his heroine Alice while writing under the pseudonym Lewis Carroll.

Once again her travels with the Doctor, though covered in many novels, short stories and audio books, remain largely unaffected, although a few authors are keen to explore the fallout of her father's death. In the 2010 audio book *The Emperor of Eternity* she reveals to Jamie that she has forgiven the Daleks for killing her father, and in the novel *The Dark Path* Koschei (later to be known as the Master) offers Victoria a chance to change the past by destroying Skaro, thus ensuring the Daleks will not be around to kill her father. Faced with such a decision, she cries to make it happen, but fortunately the presence of the Doctor is able to prevent this from happening. A further link to the Daleks comes in the comic strip, *The Bringer of Darkness* in a *Doctor Who Magazine Special* published in 1993. In this Victoria is appalled at the way the Doctor destroys the Dalek force and realises she will leave the Doctor and Jamie soon.

Her life in the twentieth century, after leaving the Doctor, has been explored by several authors to varying degrees. In a prelude to the 1993 novel *Birthright,* published in *Doctor Who Magazine issue #203*, the Seventh Doctor visits Victoria when she is with her adoptive parents (one presumes it is the Harrises) and takes her back to 1868 to take care of her father's fortunes before returning her to twentieth century life.

Her father's fortune comes back to haunt her in 1980 (in the video drama and novel *Downtime*) when she is visited by a lawyer with her father's will. At this point in her life she still feels displaced, despite a stint working at the British Museum. Haunted by the voice of her father she returns to Det Sen in Tibet, and once again comes under the influence of the Great Intelligence – manipulating her through the body of her old friend, Professor Travers (from the television stories, *The Abominable Snowmen* and *The Web of Fear*). With her fortune she founds New World University. She hires journalist Sarah Jane Smith – unaware that Sarah was once a companion of the Doctor – to investigate the cover up of the Great Intelligence's previous invasion attempt. This attracts the attention of retired Brigadier Lethbridge-Stewart, who once met Victoria during the previously mentioned invasion attempt (*The Web of Fear*), and eventually helps UNIT to overpower the Intelligence, Victoria escaping in the confusion. It is only later that Sarah realises who Victoria is, having been told about her by the Doctor in the television story *Pyramids of Mars*. At the end of this little adventure, Victoria is visited by the Third Doctor who apologises for not checking up on her sooner. He gives her a letter of recommendation for UNIT, as well as asking her to travel with him again. She refuses, and refuses again when the same offer is made by the Fourth Doctor.

By 2008 she is married and expecting her first grandchild. She has never told any of her family about her adventures or that she was born in the nineteenth century (*The Great Space Elevator*).

The last appearance of Victoria is in the 2012 audio play *Power Play*. Now over sixty years old Victoria is reunited with the Doctor who is in his sixth incarnation. She knows nothing of regeneration and it takes both the Doctor and Peri to convince her that he is the same man she once knew. Not unlike Jo Grant, here Victoria is shown to be fighting for Earth in her own way, by protecting the environment.

Zoe, as one would expect, alters very little in the books and audiobooks, but much is made of her life after the Time Lords return her to her own time, with only the knowledge of her initial adventure intact. These events are difficult to put into chronological order, especially as much is contradictory. For instance, in the 2003 short story *The Tip of the Mind,* Zoe is seen to be working on Space Station XZ49 for UrtiCorp. Although she doesn't remember her time with the Doctor, she can access her memories unconsciously. The Third Doctor visits the station, believing that Zoe holds the secrets to the dematerialisation codes he needs to help him beat his Time Lord-imposed exile. Fearful of the damage such a recall may have, the Doctor knows he must tread carefully, but a spiteful supervisor working on the station brings Zoe into contact with the TARDIS intentionally. This contact unleashes the floodgates – she remembers everything, causing her to fall unconscious. Yet when she wakes it is revealed she has forgotten every single memory of the Doctor, permanently.

In the later *'Companion Chronicles'* released by Big Finish we are told in several stories that Zoe remembers her journeys as detailed dreams and often talks about them with a psychiatric counsellor. And in *The Uncertainty Principle* she is targeted specifically because of her buried memories by a race who wish to unlock them for their own nefarious reasons.

In the 2012 release *Legend of the Cybermen* we discover that only a month after returning home, Zoe had somehow aged two years. From this she deduces that she must has had further adventures with the Doctor that she could not recall.

An attack by the Cybermen leads to some surprising developments. They realise she has above average intelligence and could be a suitable Cyberplanner, but the conversion unblocks all Zoe's memories of her travels. Only partly converted, Zoe takes control of the Cybermen's ship and takes them all to the Land of Fiction. She uses the Land's damaged control computer to create fictional characters to fight the Cybermen. She realises she needs the Doctor to truly defeat them and, unable to create an accurate fictional version, she draws the TARDIS into the Land. It materialises far off course, and Zoe creates a fictional Jamie to protect the Doctor (now in his sixth incarnation) as he finds his way to the control centre. Together, the three manage to defeat the Cybermen, and the Doctor returns her back to the Wheel, but her removal from the Land causes her to lose her memories of the Doctor once more, this time completely.

As with the First Doctor, the Second also has exclusive Expanded Universe companions and once again they are his comic grandchildren, John and Gillian. They travel with him into their teens, making no mention of his change of appearance. The role of grandfather in the First Doctor comic strips in *TV Comic* doesn't really take with the new impish Second Doctor. John and Gillian are soon written out in *issue #872*, when he abruptly enrols them into Zebedee University to keep them safe from the Quarks (even though they had fought the Quarks several times already), before he visits Scotland and reunites with Jamie.

John returns for a cameo appearance in a later issue, now as Professor John Who. And slightly different versions of them are seen later, first in the 1994 novel *Conundrum* in which they are fictional characters from the Land of Fiction, travelling with a man called Dr Who. They meet the Seventh Doctor, who has never heard of them. In a further and final appearance, they appear in the Eighth Doctor's dream in *The Land of Happy Endings* printed in the pages of *Doctor Who Magazine issue #337*.

The Third Doctor
Jon Pertwee

*'A straight line may be the shortest distance between two points,
but it is by no means the most interesting.'*
The Doctor – *The Time Warrior*

For the first time in six years of *Doctor Who* history the new Doctor encountered a new type of companion. The only carry over was UNIT, led by Brigadier Lethbridge-Stewart – a familiar element to reassure the audience that it was still the same show. However, the Doctor's companions reverted to purely contemporary characters with not a single male voice amongst them. From a fully-fledged scientist, to a wannabe secret agent, all the way up to an investigative journalist, the Third Doctor was challenged by a very independent kind of companion.

Liz Shaw – Caroline John (Spearhead from Space to Inferno)

We meet Liz as she is being driven from Cambridge to London at the start of *Spearhead from Space*. Much to her obvious irritation; she is far from impressed with her drafted position as scientific advisor for UNIT. She has important research programmes going on at Cambridge and is an admired member of the scientific community (known, for instance by Professor Lennox in *The Ambassadors of Death*); an expert on meteorites with degrees in medicine, physics and a dozen different subjects. She takes a while to warm to the Brigadier, initially finding him irritating and bemusing, not believing a word he says, 'An alien who travels through time and space in a Police Box?'

She takes great pleasure in belittling him in front of General

Scobie, UNIT's liaison with the regular army and, technically, the Brigadier's superior. When he questions the presence of the TARDIS in Liz's quickly assembled lab, she points out, much to the Brigadier's annoyance, 'It's not just a Police Box – it's a space ship.' Nonetheless she gets on with the job at hand, and starts examining the meteorites, which she realises, are not meteorites at all – but it takes the presence of the Doctor to reveal that they are in fact, containers for an alien intelligence called the Nestene Consciousness.

She finds the Doctor both amusing and charming and soon sides with him in his dismissal of the Brigadier, smirking when the Doctor tells him to go away and let him and 'Miss Shaw' get on with their work. She finds the idea of the TARDIS incredulous, in particular the supposed size of the interior. When the Doctor states that he has an entire laboratory in there, she laughs at him like he is an imaginative child, 'Yes, I'm sure you have.'

Under the pretence of needing specialist equipment to further study the Nestene container, which can only be found in the TARDIS, Liz agrees to ask the Brigadier for the TARDIS key. The Brigadier pays her no attention and she cheerfully steals the key off his desk, reasoning that it is, after all, the Doctor's property. When the Doctor then attempts to escape in the TARDIS, leaving Liz behind, she refuses to accept the Brigadier's assertion that they will never see him again. When the Doctor does return Liz berates him for tricking her. At the end of this first adventure together, the Doctor requests the continued assistance of Liz, who notably doesn't resist – a sign of her growing affection for him. Not to say that this leaves her blind to his inaccuracies – she is quite willing to confront him if she thinks he is wrong, and is quite happy to mock him over Bessie, the Edwardian roadster the Doctor insists on as a part of his agreement to work for UNIT.

She is also not above employing a bit of manipulation to get her own way. For instance when she wants to enter the caves beneath Wenley Moor during *Doctor Who and the Silurians*, she threatens to tell the Brigadier about his planned expedition if he doesn't comply. The Doctor relents easily enough, suggesting he had every intention of letting Liz join him in the first place.

Similarly, she will not be ordered about. She is not a soldier and doesn't believe she is required to follow the Brigadier's orders or indeed the orders of Reegan when he holds her captive in *The Ambassadors of Death*.

Her scientific background is often used to great effect. Whilst working with the Doctor in the lab at the Wenley Moor research centre, very little is said – the Doctor is quite confident in Liz's abilities to help find a cure for the Silurian virus. Later, when kidnapped by Reegan, she works alongside disgraced Cambridge professor, Lennox, to maintain the alien ambassadors, and help him create a device to communicate with them. Once again the Doctor's faith in Liz is shown when, once the ambassadors are safe, he leaves her and Cornish with the task of returning them home.

Liz's doubts regarding the TARDIS continue in *The Ambassadors of Death*. When the Doctor accidentally shifts her fifteen seconds into the future, she is very sceptical, believing he simply vanished. We never see her inside the TARDIS, mainly because the console has been moved into his UNIT lab (but we are not exactly sure how). Later it makes an appearance in a shed at the Inferno drilling station. By this point Liz has learned enough about the console to monitor the Doctor's experimental test flight and return him and the console. When the Doctor disappears completely (in reality to a fascist parallel Earth where he meets Section Leader Elizabeth Shaw) Liz remains in the shed hoping that he will somehow find his way back. When the Doctor does finally return she cares for him, railing against the Brigadier's assertion that a medical doctor should look at him. She checks both his hearts – the first companion to know that he has two, knowledge she presumably gleans from the reports made by Doctor Lomax in *Spearhead from Space*. As the Doctor wakes he is almost in a rage having seen the result of the Inferno project destroy one world. Everyone thinks he is mad, including the

Brigadier, but Liz believes him and sides with him against the Brigadier once more.

Liz remains unique among the Doctor's companions. She never travels in the TARDIS, be it to another world or another time. She is also one of the rare few who are able to hold their own against the Doctor's scientific knowledge – although never his equal, she knows her stuff. We last see Liz as she laughs at the Doctor, who after storming off in a sulk, accidentally lands the TARDIS in a rubbish dump. Before leaving he does, however, make a point of saying to her, 'I will miss *you*.'

In the next story, *Terror of the Autons*, we discover that Liz, for reasons unknown, returns to her research at Cambridge, never to be seen again. However, in 2010, we do finally learn that she is still alive and well, working on the UNIT moonbase in *The Sarah Jane Adventures: Death of the Doctor*.

Jo, in most ways, was the complete opposite to Liz. She had no scientific background (she took general science at A-level, but did not pass). She was clumsy and often got herself into the kind of trouble that tested the Doctor's ability to conduct a safe rescue. In some ways she was a continuation of the type of companion seen throughout the 1960s.

Josephine Grant/Jones – Katy Manning (Terror of the Autons to The Green Death, and The Sarah Jane Adventures: Death of the Doctor)

After Liz leaves, the Doctor asks the Brigadier to find him a new assistant. Enter Jo, barely twenty years old, a recently trained civilian agent who is dumped on the Brigadier by her uncle, a high ranking civil servant who pulls some strings to get her assigned to UNIT. Unsure what to do with her, and knowing the Doctor needs an assistant the Brigadier reaches the obvious conclusion. Initially the Doctor thinks Jo is a tea-lady, and is far from impressed when she botches his experimental work on the TARDIS' dematerialisation circuit. She introduces herself as his new assistant to which the Doctor can only respond, 'Oh no.' He later takes the Brigadier to task over this, who is happy to 'sack' her but only if the Doctor tells her himself. In the event the Doctor finds that he cannot do it, and so he has no choice but to welcome Jo.

Determined to prove herself, Jo goes off to investigate on her own. Her inexperience, and clumsy nature, lead her to not only become a captive of the Master, who arrives on Earth to help the Nestene in their second invasion attempt, but also becomes a subject of his incredible hypnotic power. He sends her back to UNIT headquarters to eliminate the Doctor which she almost does, but is prevented in the nick of time by Sergeant Benton. The Doctor initially finds it difficult to bring Jo around, but eventually succeeds leaving her traumatised by the thought of being forced to do something against her will. But this is not the last time she is hypnotised. In *The Curse of Peladon* she is accidentally hypnotised by the Doctor when she stumbles in and prevents his attempts to placate the royal beast of Peladon, Aggedor. This susceptibility to hypnotism is finally overcome in *Frontier in Space* when the Master attempts to hypnotise her and she reveals that she has learned mental techniques to prevent such a thing happening again.

She develops an early fondness for the Doctor, as seen when she mothers him while he is held at Stangmoor Prison (*The Mind of Evil*) but she doesn't really believe his stories of adventures in space and time, especially when he talks of historical figures in a very matter-of-fact way. However, her fondness and loyalty is not absolute for a while. She is easily convinced that he has betrayed Earth and his friends when he appears to ally himself with the Master, leaving Earth to the mercy of Axos (*Claws of Axos*). As it turns out, the Doctor is merely using the Master to get to Axos so he can trap the space vampire in a time loop for eternity, thus saving Earth. The Brigadier is certain the Doctor will not return, but Jo hopes he will, and her hope is validated moments later when the TARDIS does indeed return – although not by the

Doctor's choice, since the Time Lords wired the TARDIS to return to Earth to prevent him from escaping his exile.

Jo finally learns firsthand the truth of the Doctor's claims when she enters the TARDIS in *Colony in Space* and is whisked off five centuries into the future. She is, as were so many before her, amazed by the TARDIS' interior, but doesn't really believe that they are heading to another world. Indeed, as she thinks about it, fear kicks in, and she only tentatively steps out onto Uxarieus with the Doctor, not willing to stray too far from the relative safety of the TARDIS. Even though she is on an alien world she is still not convinced that they have travelled in time, until Mary, a human colonist she befriends, tells her that the year is 2471.

Jo is a rather superstitious girl, despite the Doctor's attempts at making a scientist of her, and believes in both magic (*The Dæmons*) and ghosts (*Day of the Daleks*). She doesn't hold to the Doctor's thinking that science can explain everything, even though she learns that the satanic creature feared by the inhabitants of Devil's End is actually an alien called a Dæmon and that black magic is just the remnant of the Dæmon's old science. Later, when confronted by 'ghosts', Jo discovers that they are merely echoes of future and past times or time lines crossing over. For instance she and the Doctor are confronted by slightly older versions of themselves in the Doctor's UNIT lab, a result of the Doctor's playing with the time mechanism of the TARDIS console.

She is quick to form opinions, often seeing things in black and white. She considers Anat's time travelling guerrilla force to be criminals (*Day of the Daleks*) even though the Doctor tries to make her see the truth. Later she is easily taken in by the Controller's story of future Earth, despite the Doctor's assertion that twenty-second century Earth is not the free and prosperous society. Indeed, as Jo later discovers first hand, by then humanity has been conquered and enslaved by the Daleks again.

With the Doctor convinced he has the TARDIS working, and Jo dolled up for a night on the town with Captain Mike Yates, he persuades her to join him on a quick joyride. This takes them to Peladon *(Curse of Peladon)* and she is introduced to King Peladon as Princess Josephine of TARDIS. She catches the king's eye, and is quite taken by him, until she realises he is looking for a political ally – failing to see that he is clearly attracted to her. Once again her simplistic view of life interferes with her thinking. She is not, however, above using his interest in her to get him to spare the Doctor's life. Over the course of her stay on Peladon, Jo warms to the king and freely admits she would love to remain behind with him, but she cannot, and is upset when it comes time to leave. She starts to become used to TARDIS travel, and insists on accompanying the Doctor on his next mission for the Time Lords to the planet Solos in *The Mutants*, claiming that he needs her to look after him. While there she discovers the state of the Earth Empire and how bad things have become on Earth by the thirtieth century. It is a key moment for Jo, awakening in her a concern for her home planet; the first seeds of her eventual departure from the Doctor are planted.

Although charmed by the Master while he is imprisoned in *The Sea Devils*, Jo never forgets what he is capable of, and is insistent on going with the Doctor to Atlantis when he pursues the Master in *The Time Monster,* even though she knows it will be dangerous. During this adventure the Doctor appears to die, having been cast out into the time vortex; such is her grief that she doesn't care what the Master intends to do to her. Later, to defeat the Master, she is more willing than the Doctor to sacrifice them both and forces the Doctor to ram his TARDIS into the Master's. As a result of this 'time ram' they end up in a netherworld created by the Chronovore, Kronos, which Jo believes to be heaven – a place she considers groovy. This is not the last time she believes they are in heaven. When she and the Doctor are later transported to Omega's anti-matter world she believes it to be the afterlife.

In *The Three Doctors* she is initially confused by the idea of more than one Doctor, until Benton explains who the Second

Doctor is, and she learns about regeneration. She is also infuriated by the Doctors' inability to work together, and later when they are faced with the might of Omega's will, she convinces them that as two Time Lords they should be able to combat him. At the end of this adventure, in thanks for saving them, the Time Lords finally lift the Doctor's exile. Seeing the delight on the Doctor's face, Jo worries that he will leave her behind. Of course he tells her otherwise and promises her a trip to Metebelis Three to break in the new dematerialisation circuit.

They never quite make it there, however, instead ending up in the Miniscope – a kind of intergalactic zoo (*Carnival of Monsters*) containing a variety of life forms including humans, Ogrons and Cybermen. By this point she is becoming an old hand at time travel and takes most things in her stride, but upon meeting the horrifying Drashigs a new fear is born. It is a fear that the Master later attempts to use against her with his fear-inducing device in *Frontier in Space*; other fears that manifest include a Sea Devil and a Mutt, but Jo is able to combat the device, impressing the Master no end.

Such is her experience with the Doctor that she expects trouble when the Draconian ship docks with the Earth ship the TARDIS has landed on, despite knowing nothing about the political cold-war happening between the two planets. Her instincts serve her well. She ends up stranded on Earth, a 'guest' of the Earth Empire while they decide what to do with her, meanwhile the Doctor is carted off to the Lunar penal colony. She is rescued by an unlikely ally, the Master, and she is not afraid to stand up to him, even though she needs his help to get off Earth and rescue the Doctor. It is a strange alliance, but she is not so easily charmed this time. At the end of this adventure the Doctor is gravely wounded, and Jo helps him into the TARDIS. Such is her concern for him that she appears to have forgotten that he sent a message to the Time Lords to guide the TARDIS to the secret Dalek base on Spiridon (*Planet of the Daleks*).

While on Spiridon, Jo meets a group of Thals, and bonds with one in particular, Latep with whom a slight romance develops. With the Dalek army destroyed, Latep asks the Doctor's permission for Jo's hand. Jo is not consulted on this, but when he finally asks her to return to Skaro with him she declines, preferring to return home where she has her own life, a life she cannot leave behind.

This decision is fortunate as when she is back on Earth a young activist, Professor Clifford Jones, is waiting for her (*The Green Death*). Jo has been following the exploits of Global Chemicals in the Welsh mining town of Llanfairfach. In particular she is interested in the happenings at the Wholeweal Community run by Cliff Jones, who is creating a new fungus based protein. Jones reminds her of a younger Doctor and she is determined to go to Llanfairfach and assist them against Global Chemicals, even if that means she has to resign from UNIT. The Doctor tries to entice her to come with him to Metebelis Three, certain he can get there this time, but Jo is so fired up about Jones' work that she is not really listening. She heads to Llanfairfach with the Brigadier. The Doctor decides to take a trip to Metebelis Three alone. Before he does he ponders the truth of the situation – 'the fledgling flies the coup'. He knows, even before she does, that Jo is going to be leaving him soon.

Jo's first meeting with Jones is not the most auspicious, and she ends up messing up his experiments through a mix of absent mindedness and clumsiness – much like when she first met the Doctor. She is quickly charmed by Jones and a very strong romance develops between them – she simply cannot get enough of his company, and will not stop talking about him. She is completely enthralled by his stories of the Amazon and she confesses to him that when she first got assigned to the Doctor she expected to be holding test tubes and telling the Doctor how brilliant he was – but it did not quite work out that way. In some ways she treats Jones much like she does the Doctor. Jones insists she does nothing, just stay at the Nuthutch safely, but she goes to collect samples of the giant maggots for him to run tests on. He is furious, but still goes after her and comes to her rescue when she is trapped by several of the huge creatures. Later, when Jones is infected by the chemical waste, Jo maintains a vigil, and is still there when Jones finally recovers – he kisses her hand in appreciation.

When it is time to return to UNIT, Jo explains to the Doctor that she is not going with him, but is staying with Jones to explore the Amazon. Jones is very happy about this and reveals they will probably get married along the way – this comes as a surprise to Jo but she readily accepts the offer. Before leaving, Jo and the Doctor talk one last time, and she says she hopes to see him again. He tells her to save him a piece of wedding cake, suggesting that they will indeed meet again. He gives her a blue crystal from Metebelis Three as a wedding gift, and leaves, heartbroken. Jo is very sad to be leaving the Doctor but also overjoyed about her forthcoming adventures with Cliff Jones.

Many months later, in *Planet of the Spiders*, the Doctor hears from Jo when she returns the blue crystal to him in the post as it was offending the natives of the Amazon. In *The Sarah Jane Adventures* story *Death of the Doctor* Jo reveals that after she returned from the Amazon she called UNIT to speak to the Doctor, only to learn that he had left and never returned (which suggests this is some point after *Terror of the Zygons*). Jo continues to wait for him, but he never returns to see her.

We discover in the interceding thirty-plus years that Jo and her husband continue a life of political and environmental activism; she lives in huts, climbs trees, tears down barricades, flies kites on Mount Kilimanjaro and sails down the Yangtze River in a tea chest. At one point she even chains herself to Robert Mugabe. By 2010 she and Cliff have seven children, twelve grandchildren and a thirteenth on the way.

In *Death of the Doctor* when she is invited to the Doctor's funeral at a UNIT installation at the base of Mount Snowdon she brings one of her grandchildren, Santiago. They arrive late, interrupting the service, and much like her initial meeting with the Doctor, the first thing Jo Jones does is trip, smashing a vase of flowers she brought with her to commemorate the Doctor. Despite the sombre atmosphere, she is thrilled to meet the vulture-looking Claw Shansheeth, having not seen any aliens in such a long time. At the funeral she finally meets Sarah Jane Smith, who joins the Doctor shortly after Jo leaves. They have both heard of each other; Sarah, no doubt, from the Doctor and Jo, presumably from someone at UNIT. She is surprised to learn that Sarah has met the Doctor again and is a little hurt, explaining that the Doctor never returned to see her. Sarah's explanation that it was an accident the first time only makes Jo even sadder. Discovering that Sarah and the Doctor have seen each other several times since 2007 obviously affects her. Neither is willing to accept the Doctor's death believing that, should the Doctor die, somehow they would just *know*. As it turns out the Doctor is indeed alive, and Jo is finally reunited with a very young looking Eleventh Doctor – who she thinks looks like a baby. The Doctor responds that it is odd for him too, since when he last saw Jo she had been either twenty-two or twenty-three and now she looks as if someone has baked her.

On the Wasteland of the Crimson Heart, Jo sits watching the banter between the Doctor and Sarah. This only serves to emphasise how useless she must have been for him to never have returned. She is also saddened to hear that the Doctor now travels with a married couple since she only left him because she got married. They have a heart to heart, and she asks him if she was stupid since he never came back to see her: 'I thought... he wouldn't just leave, not forever. Not *me*. I've waited my whole silly life.' The Doctor admits he could not keep up with Jo's life; she moved about so much that he could never hope to find her, but before his last regeneration he had tracked her down, and watched her entire life. Their peace made, she visits the TARDIS one last time (she loves the new look console room and, despite numerous modifications, notes that it still smells the same). Jo admits she is very tempted to carry on travelling with him, but doesn't want him getting into trouble with the Time Lords (not aware that the Time Lords are all dead). Finally able to say goodbye, Jo returns to her life of activism, but not before suggesting to Sarah that she try and find herself a fella.

If Jo was an ideologist, then Sarah was a realist. Jo, although independent, is very much a girl with an eye for the men and developed a very familial relationship with the Doctor. He was the affectionate uncle, she the doting niece. With the arrival of Sarah a new shift occurred. For the first time since Jamie, the Doctor made a new friend – someone who became his best friend.

Sarah Jane Smith – Elisabeth Sladen (The Time Warrior to The Hand of Fear, K9 & Company: A Girl's Best Friend and The Five Doctors)

It is important to note from the outset that, certainly according to Sarah, her full name is *not* 'Sarah Jane'. The only time she is seen to use 'Jane' is when introducing herself as 'Sarah Jane Smith'. We later learn that her family seem to always call her 'Sarah Jane', including her Aunt Lavinia (*K9 & Company: A Girl's Best Friend*) and her parents (*SJA: The Temptation of Sarah Jane Smith*), which might suggest why she later calls herself 'Sarah' – a sign of her independence or maybe to distance herself from her loss. The Doctor, occasionally, refers to her as 'Sarah Jane', a term of affection from him (used, most notably, moments before he 'dies' in his lab). Once her time with the Doctor comes to an end, Sarah takes to calling herself 'Sarah Jane' again, and doesn't allow anyone, except the Doctor, to call her 'Sarah'. It seems that 'Sarah' is a name that she associates with the Doctor and the Doctor only. It says much about her mindset, and the influence he has on her life.

Sarah was just a baby when her parents died and was raised by her father's sister, Lavinia Smith. When Sarah first meets the Doctor she is only twenty-three-years-old (it is later revealed that she was born in 1951, dating *The Time Warrior* [at least in regards to her] as 1974). Although later still, in *Pyramids of Mars*, she states categorically that she comes from 1980, suggesting that she travels with the Doctor for over six years.

Sarah is a journalist working for *The Metropolitan* magazine and investigating the strange disappearance of scientists. She poses as her Aunt Lavinia to get into the UNIT-controlled research base. There she meets the Doctor, who is still working for UNIT – his friendship with the Brigadier the only thing keeping him on Earth. He finds her story amusing, concluding that 'Miss Lavinia Smith' must have been only five when she wrote a paper on the teleological response of the virus. Sarah, accepting she has been found out admits the truth, and introduces herself. A strong believer in Women's Lib, Sarah is incensed when the Doctor promises not to give her away as long as she makes the tea. Sarah initially finds the Doctor patronising and believes him to be a spy. She doesn't trust him; quite certain that he is hiding something. It is only when she stows away in the TARDIS that she discovers the truth. She is immediately transported to Medieval England and finds her way to Irongron's castle. Sarah refuses to accept the authenticity of her surroundings – convinced that she has walked into some kind of pageant or film set – and will take none of Irongron's bile.

When she is confronted by Linx, a Sontaran warrior, she begins to accept the truth. Linx determines that Sarah is from the future. Sarah is rescued by Hal the Archer who takes her to the castle of the Earl of Wessex. She impresses all of them with her fire and her plan to kidnap the Doctor, who she now believes is working for Irongron. Once back at Wessex castle, the Doctor explains the truth (that Linx is kidnapping scientists from the future to fix his crashed spaceship) and Sarah admits she *might* have been wrong. She is bewildered when the Doctor explains he is a Time Lord and his people are keen to stamp out unlicensed time travel ('intergalactic ticket inspectors'). Before leaving the Middle Ages, the Doctor states to Hal that he is not a magician at all, but Sarah is no longer sure of this.

En route back to Earth Sarah gets herself a new haircut, presumably in the TARDIS since it is stated clearly that they have only just left the Middle Ages. Faced with a largely deserted London in *Invasion of the Dinosaurs* she is not entirely convinced that they have returned to her own time. After being arrested for looting they have their mug-shots taken. Sarah is amused by the Doctor's frivolity and soon joins him in making light of the situation. It is the first real sign of affection she shows for him. To help discover the truth behind the strange appearances of dinosaurs in London, Sarah makes use of her own journalistic contacts, despite the danger. She has great interpersonal skills and twists people around her little finger with ease, notably Yates, Benton and General Finch, with a mix of easy charm and forthright cheek. She does, however, have a tendency to allow her enthusiasm to blind her to what is staring her straight in the face – like Sir Charles' duplicity. The idea that the world is a bad place is something that is alien to her; she is a constant optimist and loves the chaos of life. Sarah is quite happy to remain on Earth, but the Doctor entices her with tales of Florana and so the stowaway becomes a chosen companion.

But they never make it to Florana, even though Sarah has her water wings ready ('I can sink anywhere'). Instead the TARDIS lands on the barren plains of Exxilon and she encounters her second alien species (*Death to the Daleks*). At first she is understandably both scared and untrusting of them until she meets Bellal, a friendly Exxilon who wins her over with his gentleness. Conversely she is less fearful of the Daleks, thinking them mere machines, until the Doctor shows her otherwise. Here we also learn that Sarah's natural defence mechanism for dealing with her fear is to make jokes. During their time on Exxilon the Doctor and Sarah draw closer together – a consequence of his determination to save her from being sacrificed by the high priests. When the Doctor realises he must go to the ancient Exxilon city (from which he may not return) the two travellers share a tender moment – more tender perhaps because he is still mourning the loss of Jo.

Sarah's gradual acceptance of aliens continues when they land on Peladon and she meets a whole host of aliens, most notably the Martian Ice Warriors and Alpha Centauri, whom she initially finds repellent until she, once again, learns that not all aliens mean her harm. It is in *The Monster of Peladon* that Sarah once again demonstrates her strong sense of self when, on seeing how Queen Thalira is constantly undermined by the men around her, she teaches her about Women's Lib and how she needs to stand up for herself. It is also on Peladon that Sarah is, for the first time, confronted by the idea that her travels are far from safe when it appears the Doctor has died. She finds it very hard to accept, not because she is stranded on an alien world, but because of her emotional attachment to the Doctor. She finds herself having to carry on without him, working with the Ice Warriors and making the most of a bad situation. She cries over the Doctor's supposedly dead body which wakes him up. This is not the last time she thinks him dead.

Although travelling with the Doctor, Sarah still manages to hold down her job whenever they return to Earth, and is often found to be working on a story. She develops a very good friendship with Mike Yates, mostly off screen, so much so that he calls her in to help when he suspects dodgy goings-on at the monastery he lives in following his dismissal from UNIT after the events of *Invasion of the Dinosaurs*.

On Metebelis Three, in *Planet of the Spiders* she faces the Doctor's apparent death. She is also convinced that he can help the human colonists of Metebelis Three (the 'two-legs') against the giant spiders that rule there – she doesn't know how, but she has complete faith in the Doctor. She is at the monastery when K'anpo, an old Time Lord hermit and former guru of the Doctor's regenerates – an event that helps her to deal with what happens to the Doctor. For three weeks the Doctor goes missing, having returned to Metebelis Three to face his biggest fear. Sarah continues to return to UNIT HQ, but despite the Brigadier's reassurances, she succumbs to the belief that the Doctor has died and will not return. Just then, the TARDIS materialises and the Doctor staggers out – his body all but destroyed by the radiation of the cave in which the Great One of the spiders resides. Sarah attempts to comfort him, but her ministrations prove fruitless. Before he dies in her arms, he feels her tears fall on his face: 'A tear, Sarah Jane? Where there's life, there's...' he says, giving up his last breath, repeating a phrase he previously spoke to her on Peladon. Sarah is devastated, but barely has time to breathe before K'anpo arrives, floating mid-air in the Doctor's lab. Things become too much for her, but she accepts the hope K'anpo brings and watches in amazement as the Doctor regenerates...

The Third Doctor
Expanded Universe

It seems that the writers of the Expanded Universe generally regard the Third Doctor's era with a lot of affection – they just don't seem to want to tamper with it. Most stories hold true to the television series, but unfortunately when they do add to them they often find themselves contradicted by later television episodes – in large due to *The Sarah Jane Adventures*, which often reveals new information about UNIT-related stories.

On TV Liz never travels in the TARDIS. She always seems a little disdainful of the notion that it could do even half the things the Doctor claims. However one of the most common things in the Expanded Universe is to see Liz travel in space and time. Most notably in, *The Wages of Sin*, she joins the Doctor and Jo Grant on an adventure in the past, solving the mystery of Rasputin, and later in the *Companion Chronicle*, *The Sentinels of the New Dawn*, she travels to the year 2014. It is suggested that she even travels alone with the Fourth Doctor for an unknown length of time: *Down to Earth* (printed in *Doctor Who Magazine issue #210*) sees the Fourth Doctor visit to apologise for having never said goodbye to her – in an attempt to make amends, he offers to take her off in the TARDIS, an offer she accepts.

Liz's departure is also the topic of many stories, with several conflicting reasons behind it. In a short story published in the 1994 *Doctor Who Yearbook*, *Reconnaissance*, Liz is visited by the Master who then hypnotises her to discover all she knows about the Doctor. Once he leaves, she is left with no memory of his visit and decides it is time to resign from UNIT. But in the previous *Yearbook* (1993) we witness her departure in *Country of the Blind* when she is offered a position at CERN, a research centre. In that story, unable to get to the Doctor to say goodbye, she quietly slips away. Several years later, in the 1996 novel *The Scales of Injustice,* it is after another disastrous encounter with the Silurians that Liz decides she has had enough and quits UNIT. These accounts, on the surface, seem to be somewhat contradictory, although in the 1997 novel *The Devil Goblins from Neptune,* Liz mentions that she is 'always leaving', which suggests that her involvement with UNIT is not as straightforward as it seems.

Liz's Expanded Universe life scores a first. With the advent of the short-lived *PROBE* series of videos produced in the mid-'90s, Liz becomes the first companion to star in her own live action spin-off series, long before *Torchwood, The Sarah Jane Adventures* and *K9.* In this series Liz heads an organisation called the Preternatural Research Bureau (or PROBE), created at her behest to investigate paranormal activity. Dealing with issues like psychiatric trauma and possession it is not a show for the faint of heart (and definitely not children). This series shows us a harder edge to Liz than ever seen in *Doctor Who,* as well introducing her new habit of smoking pipes (something she is also seen to do in the novel, *Who Killed Kennedy?*).

In *Shadow of the Past* an older Liz is aware of other versions of the Doctor, knowledge she probably gets from the short story *Girls' Night In,* published in the *Doctor Who Magazine Holiday Special* in 1992. In this story she responds to an advert placed in *Time Out* by Jo and Sarah. She enjoys a night of wine and shared memories alongside future companions Tegan and Ace.

Liz's ultimate end is something of a mystery in the Expanded Universe; in the novel *Eternity Weeps* Liz dies on the moon in 2003 from Agent Yellow, a biological weapon, and yet in the audio story *Faithful Friends: Part 3,* Liz attends a special Christmas meal arranged for the Brigadier at some point after his wife, Doris, dies in 2012. The time of her actual death is unknown (despite the events of *Eternity Weeps*), but we do know she is survived by at least one child, her daughter, Elizabeth Holub, who assists the

Seventh Doctor in Prague, 2050.

A few background details are also revealed in the Expanded Universe. She was born in 1943, in Stoke-on-Trent, to Reuben and Dame Emily Shaw, and had one sister, Lucy, who by the time of Liz's association with the Doctor, had two daughters.

Although Jo appeared in many stories in the Expanded Universe the majority of them take place during her travels with the Doctor. Surprisingly little new information is given surrounding her; their relationship is much the same as it was on TV and it is never developed in any meaningful way. However, a few bits of information are given regarding her past and future.

In *The Sarah Jane Adventures* story *Death of the Doctor* the Doctor reveals that he last saw Jo (*The Green Death*) when she was twenty-one or twenty-two. The Expanded Universe instantly contradicts this. *The Doll of Death* states that she was eighteen when she started working for UNIT, and in *Carpenter / Butterfly / Baronet* we are told that she was born in 1951, suggesting that *Terror of the Autons* is set in 1969. Not only is her birth covered in the Expanded Universe, but so is her death; she dies in a house fire in 2028, at the age of seventy-seven. It is interesting to note that at this point she is still a Jones, even though in the novel *Genocide* she is going under the name of Grant again. It may not be stated as such, but it is heavily implied that by this point in the 1990s she is no longer married to Cliff, although they did have one child, a son, Matthew.

Naturally, as we come to expect, the Expanded Universe often offers up contradictory evidence. In *The Doll of Death* she is seen to be still happily married in the 2000s.

In terms of her time with the Doctor, several writers attempt to explain a few story threads that were not really followed up on TV. For instance, the never-quite-romance with UNIT Captain Mike Yates. In *The Curse of Peladon* we learn that Jo is all set to go on a date with Yates, but it never comes about and is never mentioned again. However, in the novel *The Speed of Flight* it is revealed that Sergeant Benton and Corporal Bell set up a blind date for Jo and Mike. The Doctor gets wind of this and offers to take them both to the planet Karfel (which also solves the mystery brought about in the TV story *Timelash* where we are told that the Third Doctor once visited there with Jo and a mysterious second person – even though he never travelled with Jo and a second person during the television series). And in the short story *The Switching,* Yates asks Jo out on a date after receiving what he believes to be the Doctor's blessing – he doesn't know that it is, in fact, the Master who has switched bodies with the Doctor.

The social conscience that leads her to leave the Doctor is explored in the short story *Come Friendly Bombs...* as Jo requests to participate in the original CND (Campaign for Nuclear Disarmament) march of the 1960s, so she can learn why it is so important that such weapons be banned.

One more, somewhat unusual, bit of continuity is apparently cleared up in the short story *The Touch of Nurzah* in which Jo watches the Doctor undergo an almost-regeneration and sees a glimpse of his fourth incarnation. She later explains to the Doctor that he would become all 'teeth and curls', a phrase the Third Doctor says in *The Five Doctors* when he later meets Sarah who mentions his future incarnation.

On television Sarah spends only a season with the Third Doctor, so it is of little surprise that her time with him is the subject of very little in the Expanded Universe.

The biggest curiosity of Sarah's Expanded Universe is that she gets to meet the Brigadier for the first time in a story that flatly contradicts their first meeting on television. The radio play *The Paradise of Death* was written by the producer of the Third Doctor's television run, Barry Letts, but it just adds to the confusion. While she interviews the Doctor for *The Metropolitan* she is sceptical of his stories about travelling in the TARDIS, despite having experienced such travel herself – a fact the Doctor himself draws her attention to.

It becomes established in stories set after Sarah leaves the

Doctor that she ends up writing books. The first instance of this is seen in the radio play *The Ghosts of N-Space* when an exasperated Sarah decides that a career as a best-selling author is better than that of a hardworking journalist – although her attempts at writing do not work out too well for her. She is joined in both these stories, by Jeremy Fitzoliver, an inexperienced office boy from her paper. In many ways the relationship between these characters is almost a template for what will later develop between Sarah and Harry Sullivan, although there is barely the same affection and respect shown to Jeremy.

In the short story *Separation Day*, the Doctor reminisces to Sarah about Jo, completely oblivious to how it makes Sarah feel. In a nice echo, we see shades of these feelings many years later when Sarah and Jo finally meet in *Death of the Doctor* – Sarah even comments that she has heard so much about Jo.

In *Playtime*, a short story from the *Doctor Who Magazine Holiday Special* in 1992, it is revealed that a very young Sarah snuck into a junkyard in Totter's Lane in 1963, where she not only saw the TARDIS but Susan as well (who, of course, she did not recognise at the time). Interesting as it may be, it is hard to reconcile this little moment with all that is later established in *The Sarah Jane Adventures* – she would have been twelve in 1963. Another thing mentioned in a novel that is later contradicted is her father's locality. In *Island of Death* he is from Liverpool yet when he later appears in *The Temptation of Sarah Jane Smith* he is quite clearly a Londoner.

One thing from the television show that is not contradicted, but merely followed up on is the Doctor's attempt to get Sarah to Florana in *Death to the Daleks*. In the short story *Neptune* the Doctor is shown to still be attempting to fulfil this promise and they finally make it there in the year 5968 in the short story *The Hungry Bomb*.

A major alteration does occur during Sarah's time with the Third Doctor in the Expanded Universe, although in this instance it is intentional. In the two-part novel *Interference* Sarah witnesses the Doctor getting shot and, upon dragging him into the TARDIS, she can do nothing but watch him regenerate. Many years later, Sarah's memory of the events on Dust is confused – she remembers the Doctor both regenerating and dying. In the event, it is a deliberate alteration of the timeline by the Faction Paradox, which is ultimately restored in the novel *The Ancestor Cell*.

The Third Doctor's companions are not greatly added to in the Expanded Universe, although he does have a number of one-off companions in the pages of the *Doctor Who Annuals* and *TV Comic* and even, at one point in the 1990s, in a stage show (these companions, Jason and Crystal, are covered on page 174, when they became bona-fide Expanded Universe companions via the Big Finish adaptation of *The Ultimate Adventure* and the sequel story, *Beyond the Ultimate Adventure*).

The first non-TV companion to remain with the Third Doctor for more than one story is a young boy called Arnold. Introduced in the pages of *TV Comic*, he remains with the Doctor for fifteen issues (*#1133-1148*) covering two and a bit stories. On a world run by children the Doctor is sentenced to imprisonment, and one of his jailers, Arnold, is convinced to free him and help him overthrow the regime of Oswald (*Children of the Evil Eye*). He joins the Doctor, having a further adventure against the evil Spidrons in *Nova* before he is returned home at the start of *The Amateur*.

In 1993 we were introduced to Jeremy Fitzoliver in the radio play *The Paradise of Death*. Although he was never intended as an Expanded Universe companion, his later appearances in two anthologies *Short Trips: Repercussions* and *Short Trips: The Solar System* show him travelling alone with the Doctor. Jeremy is an office boy at *The Metropolitan*, the paper at which Sarah works, and is sent along as a photographer to assist Sarah at the grand opening of Spaceworld on Hampstead Heath. From the outset it is quite clear that Sarah doesn't think terribly highly of Jeremy, who is definitely *not* a photographer – Clorinda, Sarah's editor, sends Jeremy as some kind of joke. 'She did her best,' is the message Clorinda gives to Jeremy for Sarah, 'so she sent me. And you're not to laugh.'

He is very much the comic relief in both of his radio appearances, only accidentally joining the Doctor, Sarah and the Brigadier on Parakon – he carries some equipment onto the TARDIS and the Doctor forgets he is on board when he dematerialises it. Jeremy is always polite, constantly amazed and horrified by the events unfolding around him, and, much like Harry Sullivan, he likes to play the role of gentleman for Sarah. It is not a role Sarah appreciates, especially since she proves herself braver than him in every way possible. His mettle is sufficiently stronger when he returns in the 1996 radio play *The Ghosts of N-Space,* although he is still a 'wimp and a wally. And if you can think of anything else that begins with a w, then you're probably that, too,' as Sarah puts it. Nonetheless, he is keen to prove himself and smuggles aboard a boat owned by the gangster Max Vilmio – even when found out, and faced with physical violence, he tries to stand up to Vilmio, with horrible results.

In the short stories *The Dead Man's Story* (2004) and *Sedna* (2006) Jeremy is consistently clumsy and adept at getting himself into trouble. At this point he is travelling alone with the Doctor, although one suspects not at the Doctor's request. In the former story it is Jeremy's clumsiness that leads to an explosion that accidentally throws an innocent bystander, Jake Morgan, into an altered state of being – essentially turning him into a ghost. And in the latter, after landing on Sedna and coming into contact with the Siccati, a race of inter-galactic artists, it is Jeremy's ineptitude at pottery that saves the day. The Siccati, looking for a rare piece of art, are more impressed by Jeremy's imperfect vase than the Doctor's amazing painting – a fact the Doctor is less than impressed with. It is also Jeremy who finds a way to end the war and save both Sedna and Neptune.

Jeremy returns one final time, in the novel *Instruments of Darkness*, as the amnesiac villain, John Doe. At some point in the intervening years, it transpires that Jeremy's memory was wiped after he messed with the Doctor's IRIS machine (seen on TV in

Planet of the Spiders), and he is later used psychically by a race of aliens. Unfortunately 'John Doe' is killed before he comes face-to-face with the Sixth Doctor, and so any chance of redemption is lost.

The Fourth Doctor
Tom Baker

'I have the advantage of being slightly ahead of you.
Sometimes behind you, but normally ahead of you.'
The Doctor – *Pyramids of Mars*

Sarah Jane Smith – Elisabeth Sladen continued … (*The Time Warrior*
to *The Hand of Fear, K9 & Company: A Girl's Best Friend* and *The
Five Doctors*)

Although clearly worried about the Doctor (*Robot*), who has
a bout of rambling madness, Sarah keeps herself busy with
work, visiting UNIT from time to time to check up on him. The
Brigadier finds himself confiding top secret information in Sarah,
simply because the Doctor is not around to be told. After meeting
the new UNIT doctor, Harry Sullivan, who is assigned to look
after the Doctor, she decides he is a bit old fashioned, a view that
continues when he joins Sarah and the Doctor on their travels –
she doesn't care for his insistence on calling her 'old girl'. When
the Doctor attempts to abruptly leave, it is Sarah who convinces
him to stay and assist the Brigadier, which he does while Sarah
continues her own avenue of investigation with the Think Tank
organisation – actually a front for the Scientific Reform Society.
When confronted with the experimental robot, K1, Sarah's
experiences with the Doctor prove valuable as she entertains the
notion that the robot is alive. Her compassion for the robot puzzles
those around her, especially Miss Winters, but these concerns are
proven well-placed when it is forced into performing functions
against its prime directive – to serve and never harm humanity –
and as a result kidnaps Sarah. After the robot is killed because of

the risk it poses to humanity, Sarah is very glum and is not even cheered up by the idea of travelling in the TARDIS. That is until the Doctor rants about the Brigadier's insistence that he talk to the Cabinet and write seventeen reports in triplicate – she points out that he is being childish and he agrees, 'No point in being grown up if you can't be childish sometimes.' After he offers her a jelly baby, Sarah agrees to join him again – she rather likes this new incarnation of the Doctor – but she fails to stop the Doctor teasing Harry, who doesn't believe a word about the TARDIS. She does, however, sympathise with Harry when the TARDIS arrives on Space Station Nerva in *The Ark in Space* and he finds it hard to understand the inside dimensions and the fact that the TARDIS has moved, 'That's how I felt the first time.'

Despite her objections to Harry's old fashioned way, she strikes up a very easy friendship with him during their few travels together, and develops a lot of affection for him, clearly loving the way he fusses over her. Throughout their journeys there is a lot of gentle ribbing and banter between them – indeed, decades later, her affection for Harry is confirmed when she explains that she always loved him – albeit not in a romantic way (*The Sarah Jane Adventures: Death of the Doctor*). After nearly suffocating on Nerva, she is accidentally placed in suspended animation for a short time and upon her revival she has an unusually strong and adverse reaction to the Wirrn. When she gets stuck in a conduit, she exhibits the symptoms of claustrophobia. It is only the Doctor's goading that forces Sarah to drag herself out. She calls the Doctor a brute for being horrible to her, but soon realises she has been had and jokingly hits him. Later, on a war-torn Skaro in *Genesis of the Daleks*, Sarah is the first person to see Davros, secretly observing him test a Dalek gun. Whilst a captive of the Kaleds, she learns that she is being exposed to distronic toxaemia – which will kill her and her fellow captives after only a few hours. She organises an escape, which ultimately fails, but it does reveal her fear of heights (something we see again in *The Five Doctors*) and her suffering of vertigo, which is later exploited by Styre in *The*

Sontaran Experiment. She and Harry are tortured by Davros, who uses them against the Doctor to learn secrets of later Dalek defeats, but despite the intense pain, Sarah demands that the Doctor doesn't give in, knowing full well what such future knowledge could mean in the hands of a man like Davros. She has a very clear view of the Daleks, and believes them to be the most evil race ever created, and urges the Doctor on in his mission to wipe them out before they can spread out into the universe.

In Scotland, in *Terror of the Zygons*, Sarah once again uses her investigative skills to discover the truth behind the mystery of Tulloch Moor, by which time she is so used to Harry that she easily spots something wrong when she encounters a Zygon duplicate of him – who tries to kill her with a pitchfork after she gives chase. Once the mystery is solved, the Doctor asks if she is going to continue travelling with him – both Harry and the Brigadier refuse the offer – and she says only if they go straight back to London. She knows it is very unlikely, but still goes with him.

Her journalistic background surfaces again when they arrive in 1911 in the Old Priory, the building upon which the UNIT HQ was built, and she explains to the Doctor that the Priory was burned to the ground – presumably she researched the site after spending so much time there in recent months. When the Doctor is moody in *Pyramids of Mars* about returning to Earth, she suggests if he is tired of being UNIT's scientific advisor he can always resign, and tries to cheer him up by wearing a dress that once belonged to Victoria, which only makes him more sullen. Fortunately, arriving in 1911 and the mystery presented there does lift the Doctor's spirits somewhat. Cheered on by this, Sarah embraces the unexpected stop-over, and is heavily bemused by Marcus Scarman's incredulity over her telling him that she is from 1980, and enjoys his bewilderment of the TARDIS interior which he claims is like something by HG Wells. When confronted with the unimaginable power of Sutekh, Sarah asks the Doctor to just take them home – after all she knows that Sutekh did not destroy the world in 1911, as she is from 1980. The Doctor shows her the barren ruins that Sutekh would leave; it would take someone with the power of Sutekh to make such a drastic alteration to the future, and that's why they have to stay. Sarah never forgets her encounter with Sutekh, the last of the Osirians, because in 2010 in *SJA: The Vault of Secrets*, with the help of her computer, Mr Smith, she interferes with a NASA probe on Mars to prevent it from transmitting an image of the Osirian pyramid on Mars; she knows the danger should NASA discover such an 'ancient and deadly civilisation'.

Sarah appears to have a strong distaste for fizzy drinks, since in *The Android Invasion* she doesn't like ginger pop and later in *SJA: Invasion of the Bane* she is one of the 2% of Earth's population who doesn't like Bubble Shock!, a new fizzy drink and the front of an alien invasion. When the TARDIS automatically dematerialises from the ersatz village of Devesham created by the Kraals (having gone on to the real Devesham on Earth) she is, oddly, convinced the Doctor has simply left her. It is an unusual reaction from Sarah, who tends to display such unwavering faith in her relationship with him. Indeed, such is their bond that he later states that Sarah is his best friend (*The Seeds of Doom*). She re-meets Harry, who appears to be working against her and the Doctor, and doesn't even consider that he may, once again, be a duplicate (an android duplicate, as it later turns out). Once the attempted Kraal invasion is thwarted, Sarah jokingly states she is going home by taxi this time, but in the next breath agrees to go by TARDIS. Despite the constant visits to her own time, it becomes increasingly clear that neither Sarah nor the Doctor intend to ever sever their contact with each other. Such is her influence that when they arrive on Karn in *The Brain of Morbius* and the Doctor is in a funk because he believes that the Time Lords are manipulating him, Sarah teases him to no avail. But upon discovering a graveyard of crashed spaceships she is able to easily get the Doctor's interest when she finds the detached head of a Mutt.

When temporarily blinded by Maren's ring, Sarah maintains her usual level of sarcasm, although her sudden return to full vision produces something of a shock when she comes face-to-face with the hastily assembled body of Morbius – one of the rare occasions in which Sarah is seen to really scream in terror. The Doctor's love for Sarah is on full display when he later walks into an obvious trap in the hope that he can procure some of the Elixir of Life to restore Sarah's eyesight. When she is taken by the thug Scorbie in *The Seeds of Doom* the Doctor's anger is palpable. In all her travels, like most of the Doctor's companions, Sarah never once questions how she can understand all the aliens and non-English speakers they have encountered, until they are in fifteenth century Italy in *The Masque of Mandragora*. The fact that she does, alerts the Doctor to the influence that the Mandragora Helix temporarily has on Sarah. His explanation, that it is a Time Lord gift he allows her to share, is later explored in *The End of the World* when the Doctor tells Rose that the TARDIS's telepathic circuits get inside their heads and translate languages for them. When they next arrive on Earth in 1976, Sarah is convinced the quarry in which the TARDIS has materialised is an alien planet, having seen so many similar planets in her travels. Although, being possessed by Eldrad doesn't seem to faze her so much, indeed she makes a joke about it, having become so used to such occurrences. When the Doctor heads off into a dangerous situation she sticks by his side, telling him that she worries about him, and he confesses that he worries about her too.

By the end of *The Hand of Fear* Sarah expresses her frustrations, but the Doctor is not really listening to her, more intent on fixing the TARDIS console. She gets in such a strop that she storms off to her room and returns with her things, determined that it is time the Doctor returned her home. Of course, it is an empty threat, but when the Doctor explains that he does indeed have to return her, she is certain he is joking. But, alas, he has been summoned back to Gallifrey and, although Sarah wants to see it, humans are not allowed. The Doctor sadly says that they have to say goodbye.

Sarah tries to put on a brave face when the Doctor tells her that they have arrived in Croydon, but she is clearly hurting. She tells him not to forget her, and he responds with, 'Don't you forget me. 'Til we meet again, Sarah'. Sarah watches the TARDIS dematerialise, and then realises that she is not on her street after all, indeed she suspects she is not even in Croydon. When she finally does meet the Doctor again, some twenty-seven years later, she reveals that he left her in Aberdeen.

We meet Sarah again, just over a year later from her point of view, in Christmas 1981 in the spin-off episode *K9 & Company: A Girl's Best Friend*. We learn she once lived with her Aunt Lavinia in Croydon. Lavinia moves to Morton Harwood and Sarah eventually follows her there, but as Lavinia says she is so hard to pin down and, much like a butterfly, never in one place for long. Once settled in at her aunt's house Sarah discovers a large box addressed to her. She opens it to find K9 Mark III, who is a gift from the Doctor (delivered to Croydon in 1978). K9 has a message from the Doctor; 'Give Sarah Jane Smith my fondest love. Tell her I shall remember her always.' Never before has such an expression of love come from the Doctor, and Sarah whispers, with a smile, 'Oh, Doctor, you didn't forget'. She eventually returns to London with K9, and it is from there that she is scooped to Gallifrey to take part in the Game of Rassilon, where she re-meets the Third Doctor. She is confused at first, wondering why he looks the way he did when she first met him, and his explanation that maybe he has changed, but he hasn't yet, doesn't help her one bit. During the Game, she encounters the Cybermen again, meets Tegan Jovanka, companion of the Fifth Doctor and is briefly reunited with the Brigadier. Between them they attempt to work out which order the four Doctors come in (the first, second, third and fifth incarnations), but ultimately it comes to nothing as when Sarah is returned home her memory of that adventure is wiped clean. This is revealed in 2007 when she meets the Tenth Doctor and she confesses she believed him to be dead, since he never ever returned for her, and in 2010 when she mentions that, 'I can't be sure, but there's a Tegan,' suggesting she doesn't know Tegan. To be continued on page 254...

For a short while the Doctor and Sarah were joined by Harry Sullivan – the first bona fide male companion since Jamie in 1969. At the time it was possible that the Fourth Doctor might have been played by an older actor, and so Harry was created to carry much of the action, in much the same way as Ian did at the beginning of the series, but in the event Tom Baker was cast and Harry seemed surplus to requirements. He lasted only six stories, plus one return appearance, but during his time there he certainly helped create a memorable team, alongside the Doctor and Sarah.

Harry Sullivan – Ian Marter (Robot to Terror of the Zygons, and The Android Invasion)

Harry is quite distinctive as companions go; he only travels in the TARDIS twice (two times more than Liz) and he is mentioned in a story previous to his introduction. When the Doctor falls into a coma, briefly, in *Planet of the Spiders*, the Brigadier puts in a call to Doctor Sullivan, but cancels it as soon as the Doctor is revived by a cup of tea brought in by Benton. Surgeon Lieutenant Harry Sullivan is called in, some weeks later, in *Robot* to attend to the Doctor, who has just undergone his third regeneration.

Harry is quite baffled by his new charge, and attempts to humour him before the Doctor strings him up in a nearby utility cupboard like a pair of old boots. For reasons unknown, despite being the medical doctor at UNIT HQ, seconded there from the Royal Navy, Harry is completely unaware of the Doctor's alien physiognomy, as shown when the Doctor tests his own hearts' rate; 'I say, that can't be right', Harry says, shocked at the double heartbeat. He keeps close to the Doctor during the investigation into Think Tank, and even suggests he should be a spy (a real James Bond, as Sarah puts it), which he does rather successfully, posing as a man from the Ministry of Health, until he is making a report over the phone and is coshed unconscious. When Sarah is also taken captive by the Scientific Reform Society she finds Harry held at gun point and mocks him with 'James Bond'. It is the first of many such moments of light mockery and banter which soon comes to characterise their relationship. Later, once Think Tank is defeated, Harry pops by to see the Doctor and Sarah who are planning a trip in the TARDIS. He scoffs at the idea, thinking the whole concept of the TARDIS is absurd. The Doctor asks him inside, just to prove that it is indeed absurd, and Harry agrees if it will help. Upon entering, his only response is, 'Oh, I say'. The Doctor and Sarah follow him in, and while the TARDIS dematerialises Harry decides to play with the helmic regulator, sending the TARDIS far off course.

At the beginning of *The Ark in Space*, he staggers out of the TARDIS, 'burbling', telling the Doctor that he could make a lot of money from the time machine by selling it to the police; the space inside could contain a lot of bobbies in Trafalgar Square. Harry is sceptical of the idea that they are in the distant future, but soon learns otherwise when confronted with the cryogenic bay of Nerva Station. His twentieth century knowledge of medicine puts him on the back foot for a while, having never encountered anything like the advanced medical techniques of Nerva, but he soon works out the basic principles and is able to perform the resuscitation process on his own. It is notable that from the moment they arrive on Nerva Harry starts addressing Sarah by her first name, and not 'Miss Smith', but begins to fuss over her a lot, taking on a chivalrous attitude that is not entirely appreciated by her. During their time aboard Nerva, the Doctor claims that Harry is improving, although that is entirely down to the Doctor's influence, of course, and Harry must not take any of the credit. He is a strong believer in the sanctity of life; when Vira asks if Sarah is of value (having been accidentally placed in cryogenic suspension), he responds quite abrasively with, 'Of value? She's a human being!' His lack of experience with the Doctor leads him to suggest that they could use the TARDIS to ferry the revived humans down to Earth to begin the repopulation of it; the Doctor balks at the idea, but does agree to go ahead of the humans to make sure the transmat relays are safe. Harry and Sarah go with him, and Harry particularly enjoys the sensation of transmitting his atoms across space. When he finds a man tortured by Styre in *The Sontaran Experiment*, his Hippocratic Oath comes into play and he does his best to save the man, but with little success. Such a wilful loss of life incenses him intensely. Later, on Skaro, Harry shows an amazing level of bravery when the Doctor accidentally places his foot on a landmine in *Genesis of the Daleks*. Despite the Doctor's insistence that there's no sense in them both being blown up. Harry refuses to leave and manages to steady the landmine enough so the Doctor can safely move his foot away.

His humour is demonstrated throughout his association with the Doctor, taking most things in his stride, and keeping up a playful banter with Sarah. He observes much, and learns quickly. Just from watching the Doctor he learns how to operate the transmat controls. He thinks in practical terms, but can be clumsy, at one point causing a rock fall that knocks the Doctor unconscious. Seeing the prone Doctor, with something strapped to him, Harry attempts to remove the strap. Unbeknown to him, releasing the strap will cause the bomb to go off. The Doctor stops him in the nick of time and shouts, 'Harry Sullivan is an imbecile!' Of course, Harry could have no idea about the bomb, so the Doctor's claim is a little unjust. Indeed, Harry proves time and again that he is far from an imbecile, but rather a brave man with a good head on his shoulders, often thrown into situations far beyond his comprehension.

After returning to Earth in *Terror of the Zygons* Harry elects to take the train back to London, rather than continue travelling in the TARDIS. It is unclear why he would make such a decision, since he clearly learns a lot during his short time with the Doctor, and both the Doctor and Sarah enjoy his company. Perhaps it is his duty to UNIT, after all he is standing next to the Brigadier when the offer is made and the Brigadier is Harry's commanding officer. We see Harry once more several stories later in *The Android Invasion*, when he is stationed with UNIT at the Devesham Space Defence Station, and his knowledge of 'space medicine' is of special use. During the course of the story, however, we learn that no one in Devesham is real – they are all android duplicates created by the Kraals, inhabiting a fake Devesham on the planet Oseidon, a testing ground for an eventual invasion of Earth. When the Doctor and Sarah finally get to Earth to warn the administration at the real Space Defence Station Harry is indeed there, serving the same role his android double did. However, we do not see much of the real Harry since he is soon captured and replaced by his android duplicate.

Like Dodo, Harry never gets a proper goodbye scene; Still, he at least gets a goodbye in *Terror of the Zygons*, but it is somewhat voided by his inconsequential return appearance in *The Android Invasion* and then that is it. Never to be seen again. The question, therefore remains, what happened to this strong, but often forgotten, companion?

In *Mawdryn Undead*, when the Brigadier reunites with the (Fifth) Doctor in 1983, they reminisce about their UNIT days and the Brigadier tells the Doctor that the last he heard of Harry was that he had been seconded to NATO and was doing something 'hush hush' at Porton Down. Harry is fondly remembered by Sarah, who considers naming her adopted son after him (*SJA: Invasion of the Bane*), and in 2010 she mentions Harry in the past tense, suggesting that he may be dead; when she tells her friends Clyde and Rani that Harry went on to do great work developing vaccines and saving thousands of lives (*SJA: Death of the Doctor*).

With Sarah's departure it was time for another shift in the companion/Doctor dynamic. Enter Leela, a character who, in some ways, harkened back to Jamie. Like Jamie, Leela appeared to come from an uneducated and often superstitious culture, primitive in many ways. But to think of Leela as stupid was a mistake, often proven to those who she met on her travels.

Leela – Louise Jameson (The Face of Evil to The Invasion of Time)

Leela comes from an unnamed planet in the distant future and is a descendant of a human expedition that settled there. She is a warrior of the Sevateem, a tribe living in a jungle wilderness, one half of a long-term eugenics experiment conducted by the mad computer, Xoanon. Like all her people, and indeed that of the Tesh, the advanced second half of Xoanon's test, she knows nothing of her history. She has been brought up to believe Xoanon is a god. When she is cast out from the Sevateem for heresy she bumps into the Doctor and believes him to be 'the evil one' with whom he shares a resemblance. With the Doctor, she discovers that her ancestors were a Mordee expedition; the Sevateem being descended from the survey team sent out to explore the planet and the Tesh from the technicians, who remained behind in the ship. The Doctor had previously repaired the Mordee computer, but forgot to remove his own personality from it, thus causing an imbalance between Xoanon's personality and his own, resulting in split-personality madness. From the moment we meet her it is clear that Leela has a hunger for knowledge. She may be uneducated, but she has a sharp brain and soaks up information with the sponge-like mind of a child. She is prone to using weapons to solve her problems, notably a knife and her trusty Janis thorns which cause paralysis and then death. The Doctor warns her to stop using them. Leela doesn't agree, but the Doctor takes her silence as such anyway, a fact he mentions when Leela later kills a Chinese coolie in Victorian London. Once the Doctor has solved the problem with Xoanon, he is all set to leave on his own, but Leela pushes past and rushes into the TARDIS. The Doctor barely has a chance to close the door before Leela plays with the controls of the time ship and they dematerialise.

In *The Robots of Death* the Doctor is busy teaching Leela that there is no such thing as magic, merely misunderstood science.

She believes making a yo-yo go up and down helps the TARDIS fly – that it is part of the magic. Still not understanding, she asks him to explain why the TARDIS is bigger inside than out, and he tries to explain using a large and small box. He places the large one at a distance and brings the smaller up to Leela making it appear bigger. He tells her that if you can have the large box at that distance *and* in the same place as the small one, then the large can fit inside the small. Leela calls this silly, which amuses the Doctor, and when the TARDIS materialises inside the sandminer (a large mobile ore processing vessel), Leela asks how one box (the TARDIS) can fit inside another (the sandminer), the Doctor reminds her of his previous explanation, which Leela still doesn't think is very clear. As she goes to leave the TARDIS for the first time, she picks up the laser gun (a Tesh invention), but the Doctor tells her to leave it behind. She shrugs but keeps her knife in its sheaf anyway – a fact that the Doctor doesn't comment on (her knife proves useless when they come up against the murderous Voc robots). Leela displays a sixth sense about danger; can almost predict or feel something is wrong with no external evidence. Having spent a life surrounded by little or no technology, Leela finds herself feeling uncomfortable around the Voc robots, who she calls 'creepy mechanical men'. She is fiercely protective of the Doctor, as Borg learns when he foolishly attempts to attack the Doctor, receiving a gut punch from Leela that floors him. She is also very adept at reading body language, no doubt something that makes her such a good hunter, being able to spot at first glance that Pool is not what he seems.

After the hi-tech sandminer, the Doctor takes her to Victorian London (*The Talons of Weng-Chiang*), almost as if he is showing her the vastly different worlds she can expect to see on her travels – an echo of the smaller world inhabited by the savage Sevateem and the technologically advanced Tesh. She finds knickerbockers very uncomfortable, but it is almost certain she chose them when the Doctor insisted she get out of animal skins – knickerbockers enable a huntress like Leela to hide her blowpipe and Janis thorns

– since walking around in skins in Victorian London would 'frighten the horses'. She believes the Doctor is trying to annoy her, having no interest in the historical teachings the Doctor is trying to impart. She is somewhat indifferent to learning about her ancestors at this point, but later in *Image of the Fendahl* she finds that she doesn't like the way the Doctor tends to insult them. She has very little concern for the intricacies of nineteenth century police procedure, and when a coolie, who attacks the Doctor, is being questioned unsuccessfully, she steps forward, growling, 'make him talk', quite intent on doing so herself. The idea of Victorian propriety is lost on her and she is not fazed even slightly by the autopsy conducted by Professor Litefoot and is amused by the deference he shows her. The Doctor attempts to explain Leela away by saying he found her 'floating down the river in a hatbox'. She is fascinated by Litefoot's pipe smoking; wondering why he makes smoke from his mouth. The Doctor explains they do not have tobacco where Leela comes from, a fact Litefoot finds to be rather dull yet he soon becomes fascinated by the savage girl. He is fascinated when she attacks a joint of meat with a knife and uses her fingers. It is actually her relationship with Litefoot that teaches her about her own femininity – she loves the dress he buys for her, and clearly enjoys being treated as a lady, even though she does still happily jump through a window to give chase when Mr Sin steals the time cabinet from Litefoot's house.

It is a great shame that when they arrive on Fang Rock, much of what she learned from Litefoot is either forgotten or discarded. She starts out in period clothing, but soon changes into more practical clothes (trousers and a jumper) at the earliest opportunity. This she does in front of the young lighthouse keeper, Vince. He is obviously embarrassed saying that such clothes are not made for ladies, 'I'm no lady, Vince,' she tells him. Once more she demonstrates her fierce belief in the Doctor; when he attempts to explain the situation to a group of survivors of a ship wreck, and they do not listen, she warns them to pay attention or she will cut out their hearts. She admits that she once believed in superstition, after Vince tells her about the mythical Beast of Fang Rock, but the Doctor has taught her to believe in science. At the end of *Horror of Fang Rock*, after witnessing the explosion of a Rutan ship, Leela's eyes turn from their natural deep brown to blue – due to pigment dispersal.

The Doctor's education of Leela seems to end at this point, for no discernible reason, as she was clearly developing – both intellectually and socially – and so when we next see her in *The Invisible Enemy* she is back in her animal skins, and both her and the Doctor seemingly accept that she will always be a savage at heart. Nonetheless, somehow she has learned to operate the TARDIS control console, despite never having seen the 'new' console before (up to this point she has only been in the mahogany-based secondary control room, and is introduced to the original [now redecorated] console room in *The Invisible Enemy*). This suggests that some learning happened off screen and later in *Underworld* she is seen to be still learning how to operate that TARDIS's controls. By the time they return to Earth in *Image of the Fendahl* Leela has developed an odd bloodlust, and seems to want to kill everyone – the guards at Fetch Priory and even a man from the council. This new over-aggressive streak extends to firearms, which she is now adept at using, despite having barely touched them before in *The Talons of Weng-Chiang*. She, more than the Doctor, initially responds to K9 favourably, referring to the mobile computer as 'he' before the Doctor ever does.

Leela does score a first in the history of Gallifrey, being the first 'alien' to be allowed there. The Doctor is acting very out of character, even to the point of telling K9 to shoot Leela if she questions him again, but despite this she is convinced he has a plan, and trusts him, even when, as President of the Time Lords, the Doctor casts her out of the Capitol into the wilderness of Gallifrey. Leela's loyalty to the Doctor convinces Rodan – the first female Gallifreyan to be seen on screen since Susan – to join Leela in the wilderness. Rodan is very out of her depth among the Outsiders, who are not unlike Leela's tribe, but Leela protects her and teaches Rodan how to survive. When the Doctor reveals his plan – a trap for the Vardans – things get complicated when the Vardans are unveiled as dupes for the Sontaran invasion of Gallifrey. To remove the Sontaran threat, the Doctor has to assemble the ultimate Gallifreyan weapon, the DeMat Gun and trusts Leela with the Great Key of Rassilon, an almost mythical Gallifreyan artefact. The Doctor's trust in her is a source of disconcertion for others, but shows how much stock the Doctor places in his 'savage'. At the end of *The Invasion of Time* Leela abruptly elects to remain on Gallifrey, having chosen Andred, captain of the Capitol Guards, to be her mate. Andred doesn't seem surprised by this, despite the fact that there is no previous indication of any such feeling between them. K9 also elects to remain behind with his 'mistress', leaving the Doctor to continue on his own (or not, as it turns out since the Doctor has already started building a K9 Mark II).

Nothing is ever heard of Leela again, except a mention in *Arc of Infinity* when the (Fifth) Doctor returns to Gallifrey and enquires after her, having missed her wedding. We learn nothing, save that she is still married to Andred.

As a footnote, it is interesting that in *Resurrection of the Daleks* an android duplicate of the Doctor is created by the Daleks to assassinate the High Council of the Time Lords. The duplicate needs the memories of the real Doctor, and during this memory extraction, images of *all* the Doctor's previous companions are shown on a screen, except for Leela, the only companion who would be on Gallifrey when the duplicate arrives. We never see this attempted assassination, however, and so never learn why the Doctor failed to remember Leela. An intentional omission?

The next companion was completely different to any featured before; a mobile computer in the shape of a dog called K9. There have actually been five versions of K9 in *Doctor Who* and associated spin-offs, but they all had the same basic character. Mark I was destroyed in the first episode of the spin-off series, *K9,* in 2009, only to regenerate into a more advanced (and for the first time ever, physically different) model (see below). Mark II was left in E-space with Romana. Mark III was given to Sarah in the 1981 spin-off episode, *K9 & Company: A Girl's Best Friend* and destroyed in the 2006 episode *School Reunion,* and replaced by a newly built Mark IV. Since neither Mark III nor Mark IV ever travelled with the Doctor, however, they are not considered companions, even though they both refer to the Doctor as 'master'.

K9 Mark I – John Leeson (The Invisible Enemy to The Invasion of Time and K9)

K9 is an advanced computer-shaped dog 'made up' for Professor Marius, to help him conduct advanced medical research at the Bi-Al Foundation in the year 5000. Unable to bring his own dog with him from Earth due to weight restrictions, Marius constructs K9 himself, and considers the dog his best friend. Leela particularly takes to K9, and he soon becomes very protective of her, rarely far from her side. Unable to return to Earth with K9, again due to the weight restrictions, Marius offers K9 to the Doctor, but the Doctor is uncertain about the prospect, although Leela is very keen on K9 joining them. The decision is, however, taken out of their hands, when K9 trundles into the TARDIS of his own accord.

Due to the often impractical conditions of their adventures, Leela is regularly forced to leave K9 in the TARDIS, but that doesn't stop him from exiting the time ship if he believes his help is needed. He is smug in his attitude, believing himself superior to the TARDIS, and the Doctor never seems to quite get on with him. One suspects that the Doctor tolerates K9 for the sake of Leela (or in light of the revelation [in *The Invasion of Time*] that the Doctor has been making the Mark II while travelling with the Mark I, it might be that the Doctor merely thinks he can do a better job creating a K9 unit), who looks on K9 more as her pet than that of the Doctor's. For a machine who claims to have no emotion, he shows a surprising amount of it, including sulking when Leela shouts at him. K9 is equally loyal to both of them, but his mood will often alter the level of his loyalty, sometimes favouring Leela over the Doctor and vice versa.

It is unsurprising that when Leela chooses to remain on Gallifrey at the end of *The Invasion of Time*, K9 decides to remain with her. As soon as the TARDIS leaves Gallifrey, the Doctor unveils a box containing the Mark II – which, as suggested by the following story (*The Ribos Operation*), he simply needs to assemble.

It is unknown how long the Mark I remains on Gallifrey, but he clearly leaves before the Time War, for he ends up in the year 50,000 and meets Zanthus Pia the head of the Galactic Peace Conference. He witnesses the murder of Zanthus by the Jixen, who escape to London in 2050. K9 follows them there and self-destructs to defeat them. Revealing a previously unknown ability, K9 uses a 'regeneration unit' (which is inscribed with symbols that are said to be the Doctor's Gallifreyan name – suggesting the Doctor installed this unit at some point prior to K9's remaining on Gallifrey) to transform his remains into a, confusingly named, Mark Two body (*K9: Regeneration*). He still remains on twenty-first century Earth working for the Department as part of the K9 Unit, defending the planet with Professor Gryffen and his friends, Starkey, Darius and Jorjie.

K9 Mark II – John Leeson & David Brierly (The Ribos Operation to Warriors' Gate)

The Mark II is more advanced than the original version, understandably so, the Doctor having built it. His personality, although essentially the same as before, takes on a few more of the Doctor's values, as well as a much more obvious ironic wit. As a rule this version doesn't kill, only stun with his nose laser, but will kill in defence if necessary. He also responds to a dog whistle, and has the ability to sense danger and the Doctor from a distance. Technologically the Doctor has made some improvements to K9 – including the ability to hover. This is not seen on screen, however, but the Eleventh Doctor, in *The Power of Three*, mentions that he had a robot dog that could hover – presumably it is the Mark II model since he was built by the Doctor.

At one point, in *The Pirate Planet*, K9 remarks that Romana is prettier than the Doctor, which means she is more likely to receive help than he is. The Doctor is not convinced, but K9 is proven right moments later. As with his predecessor, the Mark II insists he feels nothing, but his actions and responses often belie that assertion, as seen when taking pride in correcting the Doctor in *The Ribos Operation*. He finds organic life forms unpredictable, and is glad to have a conversation with the super-computer, Mentalis, in *The Armageddon Factor*. For a short spell he is turned against the Doctor by the Shadow, an agent of the Black Guardian, but the Doctor is able to restore him to normal. K9 assists the Doctor and Romana in tracking down the Key to Time, after which a very strange thing happens to him. K9, a robot, contracts laryngitis! Whether K9 actually possesses a larynx or not is explored later in *The Creature from the Pit* when Erato, the Tyhthonian ambassador, uses K9 as a medium by which to speak – Erato doesn't possess a larynx and can only communicate verbally by using the larynxes of others. Thus, K9 must have a larynx! As a consequence of his laryngitis K9 is temporarily grounded in the TARDIS (*Destiny of the Daleks* and *City of Death*), unable to speak, but when his voice returns it has changed. His usual voice eventually returns in *The Leisure Hive* for reasons unknown, although he doesn't get to use it very much as his lack of waterproofing causes him to malfunction when he chases a beach ball into the sea at Brighton Beach.

Mark II K9 remains in E-space, the Exo-space/time continuum, with Romana. Damaged by the time winds, it is revealed that if K9 were to return to N-Space, the Normal-space/time continuum, he would no longer function, so he remains with Romana to help free the time-sensitive Tharils. It is assumed that both Romana and K9 eventually escape E-space since K9 is left with a complete knowledge of how to build a TARDIS. There has, however, never been any indication of their return shown, or hinted at, on screen.

As one companion remained on Gallifrey, the next came from there. The Doctor still had K9, and for a further three seasons they were joined by another member of the Doctor's own race – in the shape of Romanadvoratrelundar, a young Time Lord (or Lady, depending on the story) who had never left Gallifrey before. For the first time in *Doctor Who* history the TARDIS was over-crowded with intelligence; Two Time Lords and a brilliant dog-shaped sentient computer. Who was going to ask the questions the audience needed answering?

Romanadvoratrelundar – Mary Tamm/Lalla Ward (The Ribos Operation to *Warriors' Gate)*

Romanadvoratrelundar doesn't want to travel with the Doctor, she is quite content to continue her academic life on Gallifrey, but her presence is requested by the President of the High Council of Time Lords, later revealed to be the White Guardian, posing as the president (*The Armageddon Factor*). She is assigned to assist the Doctor in his search for the Key to Time, an ancient artefact that has to be assembled to restore the universal balance of good and evil. After a bit of initial sparring – her haughty attitude is in complete conflict to the Doctor's own bohemian outlook on life – the Doctor decides he doesn't like her name; it is too long. He suggests shortening it to Romana, but she doesn't like Romana.

'It's either Romana or Fred,' the Doctor insists, at which point she says she prefers Fred. That settled, the Doctor calls her Romana. (Curiously, later the Time Lords on Gallifrey refer to her as Romana in *Arc of Infinity* even though the Doctor came up with the name – we must assume, therefore, that this name change was transmitted to them at some point – perhaps just before *Full*

COMPANIONS

Circle, when she is ordered back to Gallifrey?)

It is unclear if 'Time Lady' is a real term, or an invented one, since initially she calls herself a Time 'Lord', and does so on several further occasions. Only once does she refer to herself as a Time Lady, in *City of Death*, whereas in *State of Decay* Aukon calls her a Time Lord, yet in the same story Adric says she is a Time Lady (but then again, what does Adric know?).

During their Key to Time mission, Romana mellows slowly. She starts off with a massive superiority complex. Having graduated from the Time Lord Academy with a triple-first, she is easily irritated by K9, believing academic knowledge is better than field experience, and is rather smug in her ability to land the TARDIS better than the Doctor. For a long while she is bossy, and loves ordering the Doctor around. The one time she goes off on her own to locate a Key segment, she does so in record time, not distracted by the Doctor's usual habit of getting involved in the adventure of their travels. But her encounter with Professor Amelia Rumford and Vivian Fay on 1970s Earth in *The Stones of Blood* helps to ground her – she learns to favour the quaint things of life, bringing her down from her lofty ways. Her sense of superiority comes in useful on the planet Tara (*The Andriods of Tara*) where she is forced by Count Grendel to play the part of Princess Strella, Romana's physical twin. This is not the first time we have seen Time Lords wearing the bodies of other people; notable instances include the First Doctor who was the double of the Abbot of Amboise in *The Massacre of St Bartholomew's Eve*, the Second Doctor and Salamander in The Enemy of the World, and much later, in *The Caves of Androzani*, the Doctor regenerates into a copy of Gallifreyan guard commander, Maxil, who he previously met in *Arc of Infinity*.

It would appear that the idea of being a princess appeals to Romana on a certain level since when she later regenerates in *Destiny of the Daleks* she intentionally takes on the appearance of Princess Astra who she met on Atrios in *The Armageddon Factor*.

She enjoys dressing up, and is often seen to be selecting

clothes suitable for the location in which they land. She particularly appears to enjoy the fashions of Tara and Earth, although in the latter instance the Doctor does point out the impracticality of her shoes.

Although she eventually comes to trust and respect the Doctor, in *The Stones of Blood* she is enticed to a cliff by a vision of the Doctor, who then pushes her over the edge. When he later rescues her, she is very wary of him, but such doubt soon passes and they develop a relationship of mutual respect – almost.

It is never established on screen the reason behind Romana's regeneration, or indeed which regeneration it was. It has always been assumed that it is her first, but there is nothing in the official canon to back this up. She undergoes a most peculiar regeneration, doing so off screen, and it is when she enters the console room that the Doctor realises she has regenerated – although at first he confuses her for Princess Astra. He tells her she can't go around wearing someone else's body (a point he later ignores in his sixth incarnation when he is walking around wearing the body of Commander Maxil) and she has to change it. She does, going through a selection of options before returning in the guise of Astra, now wearing a pink and white version of the Doctor's clothes. The Doctor highly approves of her attire, and eventually gives up on convincing her to change her appearance again. It is only many years later in stories like *The Christmas Invasion* and *Let's Kill Hitler* that we discover that a Time Lord's body remains in flux for several hours after a regeneration, allowing some Time Lords to continually alter their form to fit their personal ideal. This explains, in part, why Romana is able to control her regeneration in such a way (albeit somewhat more extreme than shrinking the arm length or growing a new hand).

The new incarnation of Romana is much more flighty, with a buoyant personality. Witty and relaxed in equal measure, it seems that in some ways she has fashioned herself on the Doctor, even to the point where she is often seen to lie about her age. When she first arrives on the TARDIS in *The Ribos Operation* she states that she is almost 140, but in *City of Death*, now quite settled into her new persona, she says she is 125, and later in *The Leisure Hive* she decides she is 160. The previous friction between them seems to have fallen by the wayside; it is quite clear throughout the remainder of their time together that they greatly enjoy each other's company, to the point where, when she is summoned back to Gallifrey in *Full Circle* (having only been assigned to the Doctor for the Key to Time mission), she spends some time sulking in her room unwilling to return to Gallifrey and give up her life with the Doctor. On the surface there seems to almost be some romantic overtones to their relationship; they're highly flirty and complimentary with each other, like in *State of Decay* when the Doctor tells her, 'You are wonderful' and she responds with, 'Am I? I suppose I am. Never thought about it.' And when she leaves, the Doctor tells her that she is the, 'Noblest Romana of them all.'

Despite all this, she still maintains her superiority to most that she meets, but is scared witless by the Daleks – whom she claims to know nothing about, a clear lie. This fear is often evident when she is alone with the monsters, without the Doctor to support her, or others to lead, notable in such stories as *The Horns of Nimon*. In *City of Death* she, like the Doctor, is aware of time fluctuations and later, in *Meglos*, is aware of the time loop they become trapped in. She prefers the computer pictures of Gallifrey over the hand drawn and painted pictures of Earth – to the point where she states that the Mona Lisa is only 'quite good'. At some point she builds her own sonic screwdriver, which is better than the Doctor's, not that he will admit it of course, but he still tries to palm it and switch it with his own (*The Horns of Nimon*).

In *State of Decay* she is quite horrified by the idea of vampires, and knows nothing of their Great War against the Time Lords. She is endlessly irritated by Adric, who stows away in the TARDIS at the end of *Full Circle*; she is very dismissive of him, constantly casting him dirty looks – possibly an indication of her subtle romance with the Doctor, finding the boy an unwanted intrusion of her perfect set-up with the Doctor and K9. This is, in fact, backed up somewhat when she starts thinking of leaving the Doctor shortly after Adric becomes a permanent fixture aboard the TARDIS in *Warriors' Gate*. Indeed she strongly disagrees with the notion of taking Adric back to N-space with them.

When Adric learns that Romana is thinking of leaving, he doesn't believe her – this only exasperates her more and as a result she shows an even stronger irritation at his constant questions and smug attitude. The boy fails to earn her respect. Initially she is terrified by the appearance of the wounded Tharil, but later shows concern for the way they are being treated by the crew of the *Privateer* – enslaved and used to help pilot through the time winds, being a time-sensitive race. Her concern becomes so great that she decides she will not leave them, and this is a big factor in her eventual departure from the Doctor. Her goodbye is abrupt, leaving the Doctor with no choice but to accept it. Possibly for the best, since it seems likely that it would have been a very painful goodbye for both of them.

Indeed her departure is as abrupt as her arrival, which adds a nice symmetry to her time aboard the TARDIS. Since K9 has been damaged by the time winds, and cannot return to N-space, he remains with Romana to help her free the Tharils. Adric, showing concern for her despite her treatment of him, asks the Doctor if she will be alright. The Doctor beams, his smile belying his sadness, 'Alright? She'll be superb!'

Up to this point the Doctor only ever travelled with humans or, in two instances, people from his own world (Susan and Romana), and so with the introduction of Adric a new run of non-human companions began, continuing up until the penultimate story of the Fifth Doctor (*Planet of Fire*).

Adric was the first male companion since Harry left in 1975, some five years previously. He was one of the most contentious companions in *Doctor Who*'s fifty-year history. But was he all that bad?

Read on…

*Adric – Matthew Waterhouse (*Full Circle* to *Earthshock, Time-Flight*)*

Following his introduction there is no mistaking Adric's two most dominant character traits; immaturity and arrogance. He wants to be one of the Outlers, a small band of teenage rebels on Alzarius (one of whom is his brother, Varsh) but he thinks himself superior to them. He holds a position as one of the elite but has seemingly turned his back on his roots. Arguably Adric is comparable to characters often seen in 1960s kitchen sink dramas – wanting to better themselves but not having the capacity to achieve their absolute goals. His arrogance is slightly more complicated though; he wants to be accepted for his mathematical excellence, but also be one of the 'gang'. In *Full Circle* Adric agrees to steal river fruit, just to impress his brother. He fails miserably. However, when the Outlers threaten Romana he stands up to them, showing an unusual level of loyalty and bravery. On the other hand, in *State of Decay* he betrays the Doctor and Romana to the Three Who Rule and later claims it was a deliberate ploy. This conflicting self-serving attitude continues throughout his run in the series.

Nevertheless, Adric is a very clever boy. For instance, when Romana becomes possessed after being bitten by the Marshspiders, he and the Outlers scarper into the TARDIS, with Adric managing to pilot the time ship into the Starliner – a skill worthy of the Doctor. Adric is not very emotional; his scientific mind doesn't let him shed a tear when he witnesses his brother die at the hands of the Marshmen. He just takes Varsh's string belt, the badge of the Outlers, as a keepsake. However, as he faces his own death in *Earthshock* he clings tightly to Varsh's belt, as though this is his one final act of bravery.

We never discover much about Adric's family life, beyond his brother. Indeed it is not made clear if his parents are still alive in *Full Circle* or if they are actually dead. One can assume that they are dead, since in *Earthshock* he states there is nothing for him to return to on Terradon (the ultimate destination of his people following the events in *Full Circle*). But then again, considering the lack of consideration Adric often displays for others, it could just be that he doesn't consider his parents reason enough to return home. Either way, he never once mentions them.

K9 is the first to discover Adric after he stows away in the TARDIS. At first K9 is keen to stun him, but Adric convinces K9 that since he is a stowaway he should be allowed to leave the TARDIS. Such logic cannot be argued, and so Adric follows the Doctor and Romana onto an unnamed planet in E-space. He arrives at the village sometime later, and is caught stealing food by Marta, a local resident who has recently lost her son to the Three Who Rule – the vampire lords. Realising the woman's sadness, Adric wilfully plays on it and gets himself settled with food, having forgotten about the Doctor and Romana. Despite his forceful and selfish nature, Adric is not as strong-minded as he likes to believe. Aukon, one of the vampire lords, easily enthrals him and takes him back to the castle. At this point, Romana is still rather fond of Adric, or at least feels some kind of duty to him, and when she discovers he is a captive of the Three, she refuses to leave the castle until she has found him. She need not have bothered, since he is very ungrateful for the rescue and betrays her to Aukon the moment she finds him. He later states that he only pretended to want the eternal life offered him, but Romana is not entirely convinced. Indeed, all the evidence suggests that Adric is quite serious about taking the offer, and only changes his mind when he realises the danger he is in. (This is compounded much later when he is equally entranced by another offer of eternal life – this time as an android in *Four to Doomsday*.) As a result the Doctor is determined to return Adric home.

However, when we next see them the Doctor wants to leave E-space. Romana questions the wisdom of taking Adric with them, especially back to Gallifrey. The Doctor suggests to Adric that he flips a coin. He does so and the decision is made. The TARDIS then materialises near the Gateway – a stone structure that intersects E-space and N-space.

Here Adric's selfishness comes into play once again. At one

point in *Warriors' Gate* he is happy to leave the Tharils as slaves as long as he, the Doctor and Romana can return to N-space. Both Romana and the Doctor verbally slap him down for this and he learns a valuable lesson about the right of freedom. Once Romana leaves Adric becomes a faithful student, even slightly mocking the Doctor for not making a lot of sense. Like most young boys he finds it difficult to be around strong women – note that he develops a very easy friendship with Nyssa, who he considers just a 'girl', but clashes a lot with Tegan, who is very sure of herself and is quite a powerhouse of a woman.

Despite experiencing the awesome power of the Keeper of Traken, Adric is still surprised by the science of Traken, clearly taken in by the tranquillity of this idyllic little planet. Adric responds well to Nyssa, working with the young scientist while on Traken to discover the truth behind the Melkur (revealed to be the Master's TARDIS), and find a way to interrupt the source manipulator, the secret of the Keeper's power. When Nyssa is later brought to Logopolis by the Watcher, Adric is delighted to see her again.

In *Logopolis* Adric learns the basics of block transfer computations – a method of mathematical calculation that shapes reality. He helps the Doctor map the exterior dimensions of a real Police Box in preparation for repairing the chameleon circuit. Adric is less bothered about the sudden arrival of Tegan than the Doctor, although he does clearly take a dislike to her, preferring the company of Nyssa. However, all three work together to distract the guards at the Pharos Project, in order to give the Doctor and the Master time to stabilise the CVE (a Charged Vacuum Emboitment – which is akin to a door between different pockets of space). They all watch the Doctor's tragic fall from the radio telescope and rush to the side of his crushed body. It is interesting to note that Adric's voice pulls the Doctor out of his shocked state (during which his entire fourth incarnation flashes before him). Similarly the Fifth Doctor sees Adric during his regeneration, calling out his name (*The Caves of Androzani*). Having already met the Master's newly regenerated form Adric is not terribly surprised to watch the Doctor regenerate before his eyes...

Nyssa of Traken was never intended to be a companion. She was merely one of several characters in *The Keeper of Traken*, the daughter of Consul Tremas. However, she returned in the following story as part of the official companion line-up to oversee the change of Doctors.

Nyssa – Sarah Sutton (The Keeper of Traken, and Logopolis to Terminus)

Ultimately Nyssa is something of a tragic figure. When we first meet her she has already lost her mother, and within two stories she loses both her father and her entire planet to the machinations of the Master; one more orphan for the Doctor to take under his wing.

She is the loyal daughter of Tremas, a consul of Traken, one of the much revered ruling body who guide the Traken Union via the wishes of the Keeper. Everybody seems to know and love Nyssa, including her step-mother, Kassia, although their relationship deteriorates rapidly when the Melkur exerts his influence upon her. She is incensed when Kassia usurps Tremas' position, as Keeper-elect, but is still upset when Kassia dies as a result of the Melkur taking over the Keepership.

On the surface Nyssa appears to be a very gentle soul, always polite and friendly, a great mediator, trying to understand all points of view, but inside she is a strong young woman. When she needs to get into the Grove, she is not above bribing Proctor Neman, and she single-handedly breaks her father and the Doctor out of prison. She is also very intelligent and gifted, an expert in bioelectronics with a good understanding of general scientific principles.

After her father appears to go missing, she contacts the Doctor for help, and the Watcher (an echo of the Doctor's fifth incarnation) brings her from Traken to Logopolis. There she is reunited with Adric and finally finds her father – who appears to be younger and a lot paler. In truth, as she later learns, it is no longer her father but the Master who possesses Tremas' body with the stolen power of the Keeper – effectively killing him. She is easily taken in by the Master's lie, and doesn't question his obvious physical change, accepting his excuse that it is because Logopolis is a cold place. She bonds quite quickly with Tegan, but remains with Adric when the Watcher pilots the TARDIS outside of space and time. It is there that she, with Adric beside her, watches as Traken is consumed by the entropy caused by the destabilised CVE – a direct result of the Master's meddling. It is Nyssa who works out that the Watcher was the Doctor all the time, as he merges with the Fourth Doctor's damaged body to regenerate into his fifth incarnation.

The third in the trio of companions brought in to smooth the transition between the Fourth and Fifth Doctor was Tegan – and she was certainly different from any who had come before. She would turn out to be one of the longest serving companions, continuing for almost the entire run of the Fifth Doctor's adventures (bar the final two, although she still makes a cameo in the very last moments of *The Caves of Androzani*), she was also the first Earth-based companion not be British, and the first companion to have various family members appear in the show – in this case an aunt, a cousin and her grandfather (something that would become very commonplace in *Doctor Who* from 2005).

Tegan Jovanka – Janet Fielding (*Logopolis* to *Resurrection of the Daleks*)

We meet Tegan on the first day of her new job as an air hostess (*Logopolis*). At this point, February 1981, Tegan is living with her Aunt Vanessa in London. Both of them come from Australia, although, after meeting her maternal grandfather in *The Awakening*, we later discover that Tegan's mother's family is English. This suggests that Vanessa is the sister of Tegan's

Australian father.

Aunt Vanessa is driving Tegan to Heathrow when her car breaks down on the Barnet Bypass. Leaving her aunt to wait by the car, Tegan goes to a Police Box standing beside the road to phone for help, only to find the door open. Seeking help, and amazed by the interior of the TARDIS (apparently deserted – the Doctor and Adric now trapped inside a series of recursive TARDISes), she explores beyond the console room, eventually becoming lost in the labyrinthine corridors, discovering another Police Box deeper inside (in reality the Master's TARDIS). By the time she finds her way back to the console room, she is almost hysterical and confronts the Doctor directly who is somewhat stunned by her sudden appearance. He has no idea what to do with her, but it is too late since the TARDIS is en route to Logopolis.

While she is on Logopolis, Tegan learns that her aunt has been killed by the Master and receives very little comfort from the Doctor; he has bigger problems than the grief of one human. When the Master insists on her help, she refuses until he threatens to kill both Nyssa and Adric. Thrown in the deep end Tegan has little option but to deal with her current situation. She remains very close to the Doctor, who is her ticket back home. Even when the Doctor forces them all back in the TARDIS to be taken away to safety by the Watcher, she sneaks back out and follows the Doctor. She travels back to Earth with the Doctor and the Master and finds herself having to rescue Nyssa and Adric from the Pharos Project guards. Alongside her new found friends she watches the Doctor drop from the radio telescope gantry, kneeling by his side when he regenerates into his new, younger body...

The Fourth Doctor
Expanded Universe

If Sarah's appearance in the Third Doctor's Expanded Universe was contentious, then her time with the Fourth Doctor, and life beyond the Doctor, ends up becoming pretty much irrelevant due to the continuation of Sarah's story on television since her return in the 2006 episode *School Reunion*. Nonetheless, the following information, although largely at odds with Sarah's TV adventures, still proves to be an interesting insight into what might have been, had Sarah *turned left* and followed a different path.

As on television, her name shifts between 'Sarah' and 'Sarah Jane' depending on the author of any given story (and sometimes the name even alternates *within* some of the stories – for instance in the prose stories found in the *K9 Annual* of 1983). However in the pages of *TV Comic* she is consistently referred to as 'Sarah-Jane'. It seems her given name will always remain a mystery.

Despite the amount of Expanded Universe material covering her time with the Fourth Doctor, there is very little that is new to be gleaned, except for a few instances that serve to explain some of her post-Doctor appearances. She is kidnapped from her adventure in Takhail, 2086 (in the 1996 *Doctor Who Magazine* comic strip *Ground Zero*, issues *#238-242*) by the Threshold and trapped in a collective consciousness with future companions Peri and Ace. During this adventure she meets the Seventh Doctor, who wipes her memory of this adventure, returning her to Takhail where she continues with the Fourth Doctor and Harry to Loch Ness (*Black Destiny*, *Doctor Who Magazine #235-237*). Later she encounters further incarnations of the Doctor. In this instance the First, Second, Third, Fifth, Sixth, Seventh (again) and Eighth in the 2004 short story *Categorical Imperative*. She also observes, briefly, fellow companions Susan, Jamie, Jo, Tegan, Turlough, Peri, Ace and Charley Pollard. (This knowledge of other companions is expanded on in the 2003 short story, *Balloon Debate*, when she is seen, sometime after leaving the Doctor, to write a short story featuring every television companion in an attempt to defeat writer's block.) One of the strangest things to happen to Sarah during her Expanded Universe journeys with the Doctor is on the planet Tymus in the *Doctor Who Annual 1978* story *The Sands of Tymus*, when the entire planet is repopulated by copies of her. Another curious incident happens in *The Return of the Daleks* in the pages of *TV Comic issue #1217*), in which (contrary to later events in the television series), Sarah is seen to visit the planet of the Time Lords – called Jewel for the first and only time in any medium.

Regardless of what we learn in *School Reunion*, Sarah encounters the Doctor several times after finishing travelling with him. Naturally such accounts conflict in various ways, but chronologically she first re-meets the Doctor (still in his fourth incarnation, and now travelling with Romana and K9) in 1979, in the short story, *Suitors, Inc.* Here she and Harry are investigating a company called Whildthyme Unlimited which is in the process of making DoctorBots, robotic copies of the Doctor. Not only does Sarah meet K9 three years before *K9 & Company: A Girl's Best Friend*, but at the end of this story she, Harry and the Doctor disappear into the time vortex, closely followed by Romana and K9 – one presumes to have further adventures (still untold). At some point after *The Five Doctors* the Fourth Doctor pays Sarah a visit, to give her a proper goodbye in *Farewells*, a short story published in the *Doctor Who Yearbook 1993*. Sarah says that the Doctor is 'the you you', quoting herself from *The Five Doctors* and the Doctor agrees that yes, he's all 'teeth and curls'. In a very conflicting account, the Seventh Doctor visits Sarah in 1990, again to apologise for not saying goodbye properly in *The Hand of Fear*, in the *Doctor Who Magazine* comic strip *Train-Flight*, published in *issues #159-161*. Here Sarah is still very hurt by his abrupt departure, but eventually forgives him with a hug of reconciliation. She meets the Eighth Doctor in 1996 in the two-part novel *Interference*, where she reveals she doesn't know if she was ever on Dust with the Third Doctor at all, and can't quite remember his third regeneration properly (all part of the Faction Paradox's war on the Doctor). At the end of the book Samantha Jones, the Eighth Doctor's companion, elects to remain with Sarah. By the year 2000 Sarah is married to Paul Morely (actually sometime between 1996 and 1998 since they are married in the novel, *Christmas on a Rational Planet* which is set in 1998) and sometime further in the future we have a glimpse of Sarah and Sam still being best friends. The biggest shift in Sarah's expanded timeline occurs in 1997 in the novel *Bullet Time*, wherein she becomes involved in a complex plan set up by the Seventh Doctor, and shoots herself to avoid being taken hostage. Although it is unclear as to whether Sarah survives or not, it is revealed in the 2004 novel, *Sometime Never...*, that Sarah's maybe-death was one of many (others included future companions Harry, Mel, Ace and Sam) orchestrated by the Council of Eight, an organisation created to replace the now-destroyed Time Lords.

Even if we ignore the times she met the Doctor again, her life after leaving him is nothing less than complicated. Following on from *K9 & Company*, many prose stories deal with Sarah and K9's further adventures, some involving the cast of the television story (most notably in the stories found in the *K9 Annual 1983* and the novelisation of the television episode – which curiously changes the location of the drama from Moreton Harwood to Hazelbury Abbas). In the aforementioned annual, Sarah's reputation developed quite a lot, and she has become something of a celebrity. Aunt Lavinia continues to pop up from time to time. She even sends Sarah to Egypt in 1983 in the Comic Strip *City of Devils* (*Doctor Who Magazine Holiday Special 1992*), where she and K9 encounter another tribe of *Homo Reptilia* – or Silurians. Sarah continues to work with K9 for some time, including the time she and Mike Yates investigate a haunted house and find themselves up against the Master in the short story, *Housewarming*, and in the novelisation of the straight-to-video drama, *Downtime*. During this she encounters Victoria Waterfield, not realising Victoria was a former companion of the Doctor's until a later conversation with the Brigadier when they compare notes. In a perfect example of the Expanded Universe contradicting itself, Lavinia dies twice – first in 1998 according to the novel *Millennium Shock* and then just before the start of the 2002 audio play, *Comeback*, the opening story of the *Sarah Jane Smith* series, which begins with Sarah back in Moreton Harwood attending Lavinia's funeral.

The fate of K9 Mark III is also somewhat different to what is later revealed in the television series. In the short story, *Moving On*, Sarah finally comes to accept that she must put the Doctor out of her life and move on – and thus orders K9 to shut down. Later, in the finale of the first CD season of *Sarah Jane Smith* we discover that K9 is in pieces, his parts having been salvaged by Hilda Winters in *Mirror, Signal, Manoeuvre*, who was involved in a personal vendetta against Sarah for her part in Winters' downfall in the television story, *Robot*.

Sarah's friendship with Harry Sullivan carries on for many years after she leaves the Doctor, as seen in stories such as the novel, *Harry Sullivan's War*, and the novel-duology *System Shock* and *Millennium Shock*. In the 2006 season two opener for *Sarah Jane Smith* we discover that Sarah and Harry meet once a year to talk about their time at UNIT and with the Doctor – just to remind each other that it all happened. But in *Buried Secrets* Harry fails to turn up, leading Sarah to wonder what has happened to him, especially when his step-brother, Will, turns up in his place. At the end of this season, Sarah is left alone, orbiting the Earth in the space shuttle *Dauntless*, a bright light fast approaching. The outcome of this cliffhanger has never been followed up, due in part to the commissioning of *The Sarah Jane Adventures* and the unexpected death of Elisabeth Sladen in 2011.

In comparison, Harry Sullivan's Expanded Universe is fairly

straightforward, mostly due to the nature of his television appearances. These stories run in such a tight consecutive order that they do not really allow for other adventures – not that it stops the 1976 and 1977 *Doctor Who Annuals* from depicting various adventures for Harry, Sarah and the Doctor. Neither does it stop Christopher Bulis from writing *A Device of Death* and setting it in between the television stories *Genesis of the Daleks* and *Revenge of the Cybermen*. The only gap that works is before the TARDIS crew arrive in Scotland in *Terror of the Zygons* and it is before this that the comic strip, *Black Destiny* (*Doctor Who Magazine #235-237*) takes place.

As already established, the character was referenced before his actual first appearance during the Third Doctor's final television adventure, *Planet of Spiders*. The Expanded Universe establishes an even earlier involvement with UNIT during the 1998 novel *The Face of the Enemy*. In it we see Harry – while in the Royal Navy – assist UNIT while the Doctor is off to Peladon (as per the television story *The Curse of Peladon*). As mentioned in the television story *Mawdryn Undead* Harry goes on to work with NATO, and one of these adventures is chronicled in the *Companions of Doctor Who* novel, *Harry Sullivan's War*. It seems that some years later Harry would go on to work with MI5, and by 1997 he is indeed a Deputy Director at MI5 in the novel, *System Shock*, finding himself working with the Fourth Doctor once more, as well as Sarah – both of whom have only recently seen Harry some twenty-plus years earlier in the television story *The Android Invasion*. He is reunited with the Fourth Doctor two years later, at the turn of the millennium in *Millennium Shock* – having returned Sarah to Earth after his unexpected summons to Gallifrey the Doctor is now travelling alone. By 2005 Harry has returned to NATO, now holding the rank of commodore, and is called upon by the Brigadier during the audio play *The Wasting*.

As inferred in *The Sarah Jane Adventures* Harry has died by 2010, and indeed in the novelisation of the episode *The Wedding of Sarah Jane Smith* it is said he died sometime before 2009.

However, this contradicts the 1996 novel, *Damaged Goods* (written by the executive producer and creator of *The Sarah Jane Adventures*, Russell T Davies), which mentions Harry living until at least 2015 where he discovers a possible cure for HIV.

It is unsurprising that most of Leela's Expanded Universe focuses on her life after she left the Doctor. She appears in several short stories, comic strips and prose tales in the pages of *Doctor Who Magazine* and *TV Comic*, as well as a handful of original novels, all set during her time with the Doctor. Throughout such adventures she is the same character as seen on TV, although more in keeping with the character-arc seen in the television stories *The Face of Evil* through to *Horror of Fang Rock*, with the Doctor continuing her education. There also seems to be a trend in taking Leela through Sarah's 'greatest hits' – in the Big Finish audio dramas she encounters Daleks and Kraals as well as visiting Space Station Nerva (from *The Ark in Space*), and even in the pages of the *Doctor Who Yearbook 1994* she encounters the Zygons.

In the 1998 novel *Eye of Heaven*, we discover much about Leela's past. Her father was named Sole, and her mother, Neela. She also had an older sister, Ennia, who died at the age of three before Leela was born. The knife that Leela carries is, in fact, the same knife her mother used to defend Ennia. In this story we also learn that Leela would not swear on her mother's grave – suggesting that perhaps she is still alive. However, in the 2008 audio book *Empathy Games*, we learn that Neela died while protecting Leela – doing what she could not do with Ennia.

As it is revealed in several stories across the Expanded Universe, Leela's life in Gallifrey covers several hundred years, during which time she ages very slowly – due to the influence of living in the Gallifreyan environment (in the *Gallifrey* audio series and the audio play *Zagreus*, which tells us she lives on Gallifrey for over five hundred spans [years?]).

The first time we see Leela's life on Gallifrey is in the 1997 novel, *Lungbarrow*, where we learn that she is still married to

Andred and now has an official Gallifreyan name – Leelandredloomsagwinaechegesima. At the end of this novel we also discover that she is pregnant, carrying the first child to be born on Gallifrey for millennia. Whatever happened to this child we never discover in any subsequent stories.

We next encounter Leela in the Big Finish audio play, *Zagreus* (the fortieth anniversary adventure), when she receives a telepathic call from Rassilon and breaks into the presidential suite to see Romana – her successor in the Doctor's long line of companions, and now President of the High Council of Time Lords (see Romana's entry in this chapter for the full story on Romana's appointment to that august position). She is initially considered a 'savage' by Romana, but over the course of both *Zagreus* and the following series, *Gallifrey*, a respectful and trusting friendship is built up between the two former companions (both of whom have a version of K9 with them).

During *Zagreus* she encounters, and ultimately plays a part in saving, the Eighth Doctor. As a result of her strength and loyalty, she becomes Romana's personal bodyguard during the early chapters of *Gallifrey*. Although clearly not a political animal, Leela finds herself more and more drawn into the politics of Gallifrey, not always seeing eye to eye with Romana. Her husband, Andred, goes missing at one point, and she later discovers he has been killed – the person who imparted this information is later revealed to be a regenerated Andred. She never forgives him for his deceit, not even when he does finally die. During the course of a civil war on Gallifrey K9 is destroyed (thus contradicting the *K9* television series) and Leela refuses a replacement unit – unhappy with the loss of her final link to the Doctor. In the chapter, *Fractures*, she is blinded for the second time (she was temporarily blinded in the television story *Horror of Fang Rock*), and her sight isn't returned to her until sometime later in *Annihilation*. By which time she and Romana are stuck moving from one alternative version of Gallifrey to another. Her sight is restored by the blood of a vampire, but not before she is tortured by an alternative version of herself. On another version of Gallifrey she meets an alternative Sixth Doctor, now called the Lord Burner, in *Disassembled*. She and Romana finally settle on a version of Gallifrey that hasn't mastered time travel – and while Romana seeks to bring some time travel ability to the people of that world, Leela finds herself leading the Outsiders (as she did in *The Invasion of Time*) who were once slaves to the Regenerators of Gallifrey.

At some point Leela is sent to London in the 1890s by Romana to investigate 'time breaks'. It is unclear at which point in Leela's own timeline this occurs, but based on the evidence of her being able to recognise the Sixth Doctor (living in 1890s London under the disguise of Professor Claudius Dark), it must take place at some point after Leela and Romana return to the original Gallifrey (series six of *Gallifrey*), as Leela uses the time ring technology previously seen in season twelve of the television series. While in London, she teams up with Henry Gordon Jago and Professor George Litefoot (whom she befriended in the television story, *The Talons of Weng-Chiang*), and remains working alongside them for some time (from the end of series two of *Jago & Litefoot* [*The Ruthven Inheritance*] right through the following two series' until *The Hourglass Killer*). The Sixth Doctor initially hides his true identity from Jago & Litefoot, although Leela knows, while he works to fix the time break and repair the damage made by Payne's time experiments and defeat the Sandmen. Leela returns to Gallifrey after the Doctor repairs the time ring.

On television Gallifrey is destroyed during the Last Great Time War – and as a result the fate of some companions is left unknown. Leela, having been left on Gallifrey way back in *The Invasion of Time* is one such companion – what was her role during the Time War, did she survive it? We may never know. However, a trilogy of *Companion Chronicles* (*The Catalyst – The Time Vampire*) produced by Big Finish do feature an older Leela narrating a few past adventures with the Doctor, and this Leela talks about the Last Great Time War which she did, indeed, survive. At the end of the trilogy, however, Leela, after living for many hundred years, finally dies and moves on to the Great Hereafter.

Romana, especially the second incarnation, has been a popular topic for the writers of the Expanded Universe, and no matter which series you follow (be it the BBC Books or the Big Finish audios), all writers agree on one thing; she escapes E-space and ascends to the august position of President of the High Council of Time Lords. Even Russell T Davies, producer of *Doctor Who* from 2005 to 2010, agrees and states in the *Doctor Who Annual 2006* that Romana was president during the Time War, even though on television, in *The End of Time*, we saw Rassilon as president. The comic strip, *The Forgotten*, does have the Tenth Doctor saying that the Time War did not end well for Romana, so it could be that she was replaced by Rassilon after a coup? Contention among the High Council during her reign is not a new concept.

Romana first escapes E-space in the 1994 novel, *Blood Harvest*, with the aid of the Seventh Doctor and Bernice Summerfield. She is given a seat on the High Council by the time of *Goth Opera* and is president by *Happy Endings* (by this time, K9 Mk II has also been freed from E-space). It is from this point that the timelines seem to diverge, since Romana's time as president in the novels is very different from that witnessed in the Big Finish audios. In the novels published by BBC Books, Romana returns in *The Shadows of Avalon*, newly regenerated into her third body and sets about hunting down the Doctor's companion, Compassion, who has evolved into the first fully sentient TARDIS. There is a war between the Time Lords and an unknown Enemy, and Romana intends to be ready for it. In *The Ancestor Cell*, the Doctor destroys Gallifrey and retroactively erases the Time Lords from history, but Romana is implied to be one of the very few survivors, in the novel *Tomb of Valdemar*.

Things run in an almost parallel way in the Big Finish audios, with Romana making her first appearance as president in *The Apocalypse Element*, having spent some time as a prisoner of the

Daleks. Upon her escape she and the Sixth Doctor work together to repel the Daleks' first attempt at invading Gallifrey. She returns heading the Time Lords battle against the Neverpeople, wishing to kill the Eighth Doctor's companion, Charley, who is a gateway between this universe and the Never-universe. Like the books, Romana is pitted against the Doctor, and the story ends with the Doctor fleeing. She continues on in the series *Gallifrey*, alongside Leela, where we discover that Romana, in her first body, was corrupted by an ancient evil entity called Pandora. She regenerated to free herself of the taint, but in the *Gallifrey* series Pandora returns in the body of the First Romana and claims herself Imperiatrix of Gallifrey, provoking a civil war. Romana succeeds in destroying Pandora, but is deposed of her position and has to flee Gallifrey. She ends up travelling through various alternative versions of Gallifrey with Leela. At the end of the fifth series of *Gallifrey* we are left with something of a cliffhanger – Romana and Leela are about to return to the original Gallifrey when they hear the sound of the Daleks, who are invading every single version of the Time Lord home world...

Adric doesn't have much of an Expanded Universe with the Fourth Doctor, but he does appear in the *Doctor Who Annual 1982* travelling alongside K9 Mk III (before the robot mutt was sent to Sarah in *K9 & Company: A Girl's Best Friend*).

The most notable companion exclusive to the Expanded Universe of the Fourth Doctor is Sharon Davies, who has the honour of being the first black companion in any *Doctor Who* medium. She appears in thirteen comics and prose stories in total.

The Fifth Doctor
Peter Davison

'*There's always something to look at if you open your eyes.*'
The Doctor – *Kinda*

Adric – Matthew Waterhouse continued... (*Full Circle* to *Earthshock*)

Almost immediately after the Doctor regenerates, Adric is kidnapped by the Master. For a long while neither Tegan nor Nyssa realise this, as the Master forces Adric to create a block transfer computation of himself, which proceeds to help them dematerialise the TARDIS from the Pharos Project and then helps guide the Doctor towards the Zero Room, a place in the TARDIS that helps the Doctor recover from his regeneration. The ersatz Adric is quite knowledgeable about regeneration, although this may well be because the Master is feeding him the information, or it could be that the Doctor explained regeneration to him at some point after Romana left.

As a prisoner, Adric's mathematical clarity is used to create *Castrovalva,* another block transfer computation, which in truth is a complex space-time trap used to destabilise the Doctor further. Adric shows an amazing amount of will power in his attempts to resist the Master's control, creating several images of himself to communicate and warn both Tegan and Nyssa. It is almost certain that Adric gives Shardovan (a denizen of Castrovalva, and thus a block transfer computation also) free-will to help the Doctor defeat the Master. As Castrovalva starts to collapse only Adric can see the way out (as he created the place). The strain on him is obvious; by the time they reach the TARDIS, Adric is almost green, looking quite sick.

Once more Adric's fickle and inconsiderate nature comes into play when the TARDIS arrives on the Urbankan ship in *Four to Doomsday*. He is easily taken in by the promises offered by Monarch – being transferred into android bodies that will never wither and die. This produces the first real crack in his relationship with the Doctor, something that is never quite fixed throughout the remainder of Adric's travels. It gets to the point where the Doctor calls him a 'young idiot' and tells him he is not, 'so much gullible, as... idealistic', which in itself is no bad thing, but idealism mixed with Adric's level of naivety makes for a very unfortunate combination. He often speaks too freely, revealing too much to those who enquire, usually with no thought as to the consequences. This could be seen as his need to be accepted; as an outsider Adric is always trying to find a place to belong, but unfortunately his desire to impress often fails and comes across as arrogance.

Adric is often impulsive, as shown when on the *Kinda* world of Deva Loka and he closes the Total Survival Suit (TSS) before the Doctor can warn him not to touch it. As a result they are marched to the dome of the Earth expedition. Still, he is shrewd enough to play along with the unhinged Hindle in order to get a key to free the Doctor from his cell, even though the rescue attempt does ultimately fail. He later panics as he enters the TSS and ends up almost killing Aris, one of the Kinda, but the Doctor is able to eventually talk him down and release him from the metal suit. Later (in *The Visitation*) the Doctor is seen to be berating Adric rather strongly for his carelessness on Deva Loka; such arguments punctuate their relationship from herein, leading to their biggest falling out in *Earthshock* when Adric is insistent on returning to Terradon and plots a course through a CVE, even though the Doctor is certain he will kill himself if such an attempt is made. The Doctor is clearly upset at the thought of losing Adric, despite the abrasiveness of their relationship, and playfully hits him on the head when Adric admits he doesn't really want to go back to Terradon, even though his calculations are correct. 'Well, it proves a point,' is Adric's retort.

Despite his alien origins, Adric does come across as a typical teenage boy at times. At the party in Cranleigh Hall in *Black Orchid* he would rather stuff his face with food than join in, until Nyssa forces him to dance. Although often it is his arrogance that comes across, every now and then he shows moments of cheekiness, which Tegan warms to, even though verbally they spar a lot. Often it is Nyssa who proves to be the calming influence, since the Doctor just seems to be irritated by the continual arguing going on in his TARDIS. Tegan's concern for Adric is strongly displayed when he is forced to remain behind on a space freighter that is heading on a collision course with Earth – she struggles against the Cybermen as they drag her off, and in response Adric can only offer a sad smile. Despite his outward attitude, it seems that Adric does indeed have a fondness for Tegan. Adric is almost saved from the fate of the freighter by Captain Scott, however, at the last moment, as the doors to the escape pod close, Adric jumps out – certain he has worked out the final course correction. He begins inputting the data, unaware that a damaged Cyberman is in the vicinity. Before he can see if his computations are correct the Cyberman destroys the console. Adric can only stand and watch as Earth rapidly approaches, twisting Varsh's Outler badge in his hands, bravely accepting his fate, 'Now I'll never know if I was right,' he says.

Adric's death affects the Doctor, Nyssa and Tegan in very different ways. Tegan is the most vocal, vehemently insisting the Doctor take the TARDIS back to save Adric but the Doctor cannot since the Cybermen damaged the control console. In *Time-Flight* a phantom of Adric appears briefly to warn Tegan and Nyssa away from Kalid's domain, but they spot his badge for mathematical excellence the Doctor had used to destroy the Cyber Leader, and realise it is not really Adric.

It seems the Doctor carries a lot of guilt with him over Adric's death. This is probably what drives him to such extremes to save Peri's life in *The Caves of Androzani* and explains why the very last word to pass through his mind before regenerating is 'Adric'.

Nyssa – Sarah Sutton continued... (*The Keeper of Traken*, and *Logopolis* to *Terminus*)

Nyssa's scientific knowledge comes into play in *Castrovalva* when she shows an understanding of the Zero Room – a room that creates a null interface, cutting off the influences of the outside world, allowing Time Lords to recover from difficult regenerations. Later, when the room is accidentally jettisoned from the TARDIS to save them all from Event One (the creation of the universe), it is Nyssa who hits upon the idea of building a Zero Cabinet (in which the Doctor can safely recover) from the remaining wall of the room. She also shows a good understanding of recursion – where ideas and concepts fold back on themselves. Even though she cannot pilot the TARDIS, she is able to understand many of its controls merely by deduction. She later claims she is also an expert in bio-engineering and cybernetics, once again reminding us of the true level of advancement the Traken Union reached before its destruction. She finds it very difficult to look at the Master – since he is walking around with her dead father's face (yet it seems she has all but forgotten about this the next time they meet in *Time-Flight*).

She is a lot more mature than Adric and always sensible, instilling in the Doctor a great faith in her technical ability. She develops a very strong relationship with Tegan during their initial travels together and is clearly upset by the idea of Tegan leaving at the start of *The Visitation*, although of course this departure doesn't come about since the TARDIS arrives in the wrong century. She learns the Charleston from Tegan in *Black Orchid*. They meet Ann Talbot (Nyssa's doppelgänger) and the two girls play a joke at the fancy dress ball by wearing the same outfit. Her playfulness with Ann brings Nyssa out of her shell somewhat, and she is rather bemused by the initial attention she receives as people try to work out if Nyssa is a member of the extended Talbot family.

She is kidnapped by George Cranliegh, the former fiancé of Ann, demented and disfigured by a tribe of Indians, but she is eventually released to the safe arms of the Doctor once George realises the mistake, and is quite disturbed to watch him fall to his death as a result.

Her experiences on the Urbankan ship such as almost being transferred into an android body proves too much for Nyssa's gentle soul, and she collapses from the stress, later finding it hard to even focus on a game of chess. Thus, the Doctor builds a delta wave augmentor, which induces her into a deep level of sleep so she can recover (*Kinda*). She awakens four days later.

After Adric's death she is very subdued and spends time helping the Doctor rescue the survivors of the space freighter, returning them home. The loss is made worse when, after returning the passengers of Concorde from prehistoric Earth in *Time-Flight*, she and the Doctor rush off in the TARDIS to avoid official questions, accidentally leaving Tegan behind.

It is unclear for how long Nyssa travels alone with the Doctor, but when we next see them in *Arc of Infinity* they do appear a lot closer, with Nyssa having become much more outspoken – almost as if she is filling in for Tegan's absence – pointing out the problems with the TARDIS quite brazenly. Nyssa has become extremely protective of the Doctor, her one last link to her lost life. Her impassioned plea to the High Council of Time Lords on Gallifrey to intercede and save the Doctor's life brings her to tears, and she resorts to violence to try and save him. Like on Traken, she doesn't use a lethal weapon, merely a staser on stun, until the Doctor stops her. She can do nothing but watch as the Doctor is seemingly killed. She is distraught and retires to the TARDIS, unwilling to talk to anyone for a while, but she is easily persuaded that the Doctor is still alive, taking any bit of hope offered to her. When she discovers that the Doctor, via the Matrix of Gallifrey, has been in contact with Tegan who is in Amsterdam, Nyssa is very pleased at the idea of seeing her again, and sure enough when they are reunited the women immediately bond. Once again Nyssa has the two most important people in her life with her – Tegan, her best friend, and the Doctor, the man who reminds her of her father.

In *Snakedance* she makes a huge deal about changing into new clothes, supporting all on-screen evidence that, other than the fancy dress party in *Black Orchid*, she has indeed worn the same clothes since leaving Traken. Perhaps continually being in the clothes from her home has helped her deal with her loss. If so, then changing out of them could be seen as an indication of her finally coming to terms with the loss, and being able to move on. This notion is backed when she departs the TARDIS a couple of stories later.

Also in *Snakedance*, after learning Tegan is still infected by the Mara (a malignant entity that temporarily possesses Tegan on Deva Loka), Nyssa insists her friend put on a device to keep her free from the Mara's influence. In *Mawdryn Undead* Nyssa meets Turlough, a school boy. She decides he seems 'quite nice' despite Tegan's initial distrust of him. She, like Tegan, is convinced that Mawdryn is the Doctor, in a badly mutated regenerated state, even though there is little physical evidence for this. He is clearly not wearing the Doctor's clothes, and has a strange brain mass erupting from his head.

The Brigadier – who is teaching at Turlough's school some six years earlier (in 1977) – offers Mawdryn the benefit of the doubt, but is less sure than either Nyssa or Tegan. For reasons not fully explained, both Nyssa and Tegan become infected by exposure to Mawdryn and his ship, and they cannot leave without being aged to death or regressed to babies. The Doctor, no doubt still suffering from the guilt of Adric's death, decides that he will sacrifice his remaining lives to cure his two friends. Of course, such a course proves unnecessary since the meeting of two Brigadiers (one from 1977 and one from 1983) causes the Blinovitch Limitation Effect, curing Nyssa and Tegan instead (again, as with the infection, it is not explained why the meeting of the two Brigadiers does this).

We never get to see Nyssa develop a relationship with Turlough. In *Terminus,* Nyssa's final episode, the girl from Traken becomes infected with Lazar's disease. But as she deteriorates Tegan and Turlough are not around to offer her comfort.

She eventually finds a way to cure her illness, and believes she can do the same for the other infected. Learning the importance of self sacrifice from the Doctor (and possibly Adric), Nyssa initially tells Tegan about her decision. Tegan is very upset by this – the two of them having only been recently reunited after their unexpected separation – and tries to tell the Doctor to convince Nyssa to remain with them. The Doctor, although clearly not wanting to lose Nyssa, knows she is doing what she feels is right, and he cannot fault her for that. It is a sad, but final farewell, 'Like you, Tegan, I am indestructible.'

When the Doctor is regenerating in *The Caves of Androzani* a vision of Nyssa tells him, 'You're needed. You mustn't die, Doctor'.

Tegan Jovanka – Janet Fielding continued… (*Logopolis* to *Resurrection of the Daleks*)

The Doctor barely has time to get to know Tegan in *Logopolis,* but still assigns her the job of 'co-ordinator' in *Castrovalva.* While he recovers in the Zero Room, Tegan begins to organise the crew.

She quickly learns how to reconfigure the TARDIS, with a few hints from the Doctor, and is quite pleased that she is able to pilot it to Castrovalva – although she is later disheartened to learn that it would have ended up there anyway, since the Master used the captured Adric to pre-set the co-ordinates.

Tegan is very determined to return home and to her job, despite the constant disappointments with false landings, and insists on wearing her stewardess uniform throughout her initial journeys – only changing once, to attend the fancy dress party at Cranleigh Hall. In *Four to Doomsday* the Doctor offers her a TARDIS key, which she doesn't accept immediately, still smarting over the Doctor's inability to return her to Heathrow, but she does take it eventually if only to stop Adric having it.

When she explains to the Urbankans about modern day Earth fashions (*Four to Doomsday*), she does a sketch to demonstrate and proves herself to be an exceptional sketch artist. She also understands the Aboriginal dialect spoken by Kurkutji, even though the language he speaks almost certainly would have changed over the intervening twenty thousand years – presumably the TARDIS' telepathic circuits help Tegan to do this. We discover that the idea of being immortalised as an android horrifies her, but her main concern is always for Earth (whenever Earth is in danger, most other concerns become secondary to her). Even in her panicked state she manages to pilot the TARDIS a short distance, showing some aptitude for it after all.

She is, temporarily, possessed by the Mara on Deva Loka (*Kinda*), after it works its way into her unconscious in the 'place of shared dreams'. She is freed after the Mara transfers to Aris, and for a while she remembers almost nothing of the possession. However when the Mara is contained in a trap of mirrors, Tegan looks at it, wanting to see what possessed her, and a small portion of it is able to escape into her deep unconsciousness. The horror of having her mind controlled by anything remains with her, as witnessed by her response to the Terileptil's attempt at mind control in *The Visitation*.

By the time of *The Visitation* Tegan is close friends with Nyssa, and expresses sadness at having to leave, but she is determined to get on with her life, and is therefore somewhat annoyed when the Doctor fails to get her back to her own time, 'Call yourself a Time Lord? A broken clock keeps better time than you do. At least it's accurate twice a day, which is more than you ever are!'

The Doctor considers her bad-tempered. When they later arrive in 1925, Tegan decides she wants to remain with the TARDIS, yet she continues to wear her uniform, perhaps clinging to her old life. She enjoys her time at the party in Cranleigh Hall, mixing with the guests, calling it a 'hoot'. There she demonstrates her dancing ability by taking part in the Charleston.

Like the companions before her, and despite their earlier differences, she assertively supports the Doctor. When the Doctor is accused of murder, she point blank refuses to accept such an accusation and strives to prove him innocent in her usual argumentative way. In *Earthshock* she admits she is just a 'mouth on legs', but nonetheless is willing to suit up and take the fight to the Cybermen. She is devastated by Adric's death, even though she did not particularly like him, and is furious when the Doctor refuses to go back in time to save him, regardless of the Doctor's reasoning.

The Doctor finally brings the TARDIS to Heathrow in *Time-Flight*, reuniting her with Concorde and prompting her to question if she wants to stay there. It is curious that, for the first time since entering the TARDIS in *Logopolis*, she leaves *with* her handbag (which no doubt contains her personal documentation). It is almost as if she expects to remain behind, which is exactly what happens. By the time she returns to the TARDIS it is no longer there – the Doctor and Nyssa have left without her.

The next time we see Tegan is in *Arc of Infinity* when she visits Amsterdam to spend some time with her favourite cousin, Colin Frazer, who is backpacking with his best friend, Robin Stuart. Colin and Robin arrive a day earlier than Tegan, and as such they can't find a hotel, so spend the night in the abandoned Frankendael mansion – during which time Colin is kidnapped by the Ergon. We never discover how much time has passed for Tegan, although we do learn that she lost her job and returned to Australia. We can infer, however, that since her grandfather is unsurprised to see her in *The Awakening* which is set in 1984, that her visit to Amsterdam is not too long before this, most likely at some point in 1983. Upon arrival she meets Robin who tells her about the disappearance of Colin, and his later zombie-like behaviour. She is annoyed the local police will do nothing to help, and investigates the mansion herself, coming face-to-face with the Time Lord legend, Omega.

Omega is an old adversary of the Doctor, who uses Tegan as leverage. Tegan manages to get a message to the Doctor, telling him that she is in Amsterdam, and although her main concern is for her cousin, this is quickly replaced by her need to help the Doctor. Eventually she telephones Colin to see how he is, before explaining to the Doctor that he is now stuck with her, since she has no job. Nyssa is delighted, but the Doctor is clearly less so.

She probably should have remained on Earth.

Almost immediately Tegan comes under the influence of the Mara and she unknowingly alters the TARDIS co-ordinates for Manussa. The Doctor creates a device to prevent the Mara from taking hold, but the device is removed, and the Mara consumes her. Eventually the Doctor frees Tegan from the Mara, but she is still concerned that it exists within her. The Doctor places an arm around her when she starts to break down and says, 'Brave heart, Tegan.'

Following this ordeal she decides she wants to return to Earth – not to leave, just to be surrounded by familiar things. The Doctor obliges, but the TARDIS becomes trapped in a warp ellipse and materialises aboard Mawdryn's ship (*Mawdryn Undead*). She immediately takes an active dislike to Turlough; she doesn't trust him at all which is wise as it turns out, but she does warm to the Brigadier when she encounters him in 1977 and discovers he knows the Doctor. Nevertheless she does find it difficult to take orders from the old military officer, thinking him a chauvinist. After finding him in a transmat capsule, she, like Nyssa, is oddly trusting of Mawdryn, believing him to be the Doctor, despite the obvious clues. Mawdryn is more concerned about returning to the ship than the whereabouts of Turlough. When the Doctor agrees Turlough can join the crew Tegan is unhappy about the addition.

On *Terminus*, she and Turlough become trapped together in a ventilation shaft, and despite their time together they do not strike up a friendship, but remain abrasive, even though Turlough tries to smooth things over with charm.

In *Enlightenment* the TARDIS arrives on *Shadow*, apparently an Edwardian racing yacht, at the behest of the White Guardian. The Doctor takes Turlough with him to explore, asking Tegan to remain in the TARDIS in case the White Guardian attempts to make contact again. She wants to go with them, but realises the Doctor is placing a great trust in her, so she does as asked. She is quite charmed by Marriner, the first mate, but is later repulsed by his probing her mind (again the taint of her experiences with the Mara lingers). She is also very uncomfortable with the room he has prepared for her – littered as it is with things from her mind, including a picture of her Aunt Vanessa and her air hostess uniform. As she says, it is a strange mix of her room in the TARDIS and her room in Brisbane. She experiences the symptoms of sea sickness, and with the departure of Nyssa finds herself drawing closer to Turlough, although she still doesn't quite trust him. Once Turlough chooses the Doctor over Enlightenment, Tegan begins to become more relaxed around him.

She is less than impressed by their brief stay in thirteenth century England during *The King's Demons*, and discovers her knowledge of British history is not as good as she thought it was – despite her historian grandfather's teachings. This visit ends with the addition of a new travelling companion, the shape-shifting android, Kamelion, who is being used by the Master. Tegan is unimpressed by the idea of the android joining them. This at least explains why she never refers to him again; happily forgetting that he is in the TARDIS.

Later, while they enjoy a well-deserved rest in the Eye of Orion (the most tranquil place in the universe), Tegan is alarmed when the Doctor starts to lose his temporal cohesion (*The Five Doctors*). In the Death Zone she is surprised by the arrival of the First Doctor, recognising that his former incarnations should not exist at the same time (possibly recalling the last time the Doctor's lives overlapped in *Logopolis* with the ethereal Watcher). She is determined to explore the Death Zone with her Doctor and is joined by Susan, the Doctor's granddaughter (although it is never clear if Tegan is made aware of this familial connection, but they do share some time chatting over food, so it is likely Susan would have mentioned it). Both watch in shock as the Doctor and the Master are attacked by a squadron of Cybermen, resulting in the Doctor being transmatted away.

As a result she joins the First Doctor, who heads to the Dark Tower. She finds him a little miserable, but clearly enjoys his company, calling him 'Doc'. This is unusual as she has never really used such a nickname before – perhaps this is Tegan's way of distinguishing the two Doctors in her mind. In the Dark Tower she feels something oppressive, but the First Doctor simply explains it is fear being transmitted from the mind of Rassilon. He tells her to simply ignore it. Once in the Tomb of Rassilon she is reacquainted with the Brigadier and meets Sarah, as well as the Second and Third Doctors.

At the end she, like Turlough, is convinced the Doctor is about to say goodbye after being asked to become President of the High Council once again, but the Doctor explains that he has no intention of returning to Gallifrey. Tegan is amused that he is willing to go on the run in a 'rackety old TARDIS' but the Doctor points out, 'Why not? After all, that's how it all started.'

Following the slaughter at the seabase in *Warriors of the Deep*, it is Tegan's turn to question whether it is her time to say goodbye. She asks the Doctor to return her to Earth to visit her grandfather, Andrew Verney, in 1984. And so, for the first time ever, the Doctor actively sets the TARDIS to take one of his companions to visit a member of their family. Upon arrival in Little Hodcombe in *The Awakening*, they see a man in seventeenth century clothing. Tegan is, once again, convinced the Doctor has got the destination wrong, even though Turlough insists otherwise. When she and Verney finally meet up, he doesn't seem surprised to see his granddaughter, nor he is too shocked by the TARDIS – this might imply that she has told him all about the Doctor during her return to Earth after *Time-Flight*. Tegan forces the Doctor, with the help of a few locals, to remain there for a while, so she can at least spend some proper time with her grandfather, instead of dealing with temporal problems and war games.

While on the human colony of *Frontios*, she comes under the scrutiny of the alien Tractators, but the Doctor attempts to convince them that Tegan is an android, but not a very good one. For one thing there is the funny walk, and then the accent! Even though she knows the Doctor is trying to keep her safe, she is a little affronted by this insult.

They return to Earth in 1984 once more, only to discover that the Daleks are actively seeking the Doctor. During *Resurrection of the Daleks* Tegan witnesses so many people being killed by both Daleks and their android duplicates – including an innocent man by the Thames who she calls to for help when being chased by two duplicate policemen. No doubt she blames herself for his death, and is greatly disturbed by the needless slaughter. It is here that she realises she can no longer carry on; that too many good people have died. In a sudden moment, just as they are about to leave, Tegan tells the Doctor that she is not going with him. The Doctor is shocked. Tegan doesn't blame him for all the deaths. She does, however, take comfort in what her Aunt Vanessa once said; '"If you stop enjoying it, give it up." It's stopped being fun, Doctor.' She bravely shakes Turlough's hand and dashes off, unable to contain the hurt of leaving any more. She returns seconds after the TARDIS dematerialises, and tells herself, 'brave heart, Tegan' reminding herself of her bond with the Doctor. She breaks down, and mumbles, 'I am going to miss you, Doctor'.

The Doctor doesn't forget Tegan, and when he is lying in the TARDIS dying at the end of his fifth incarnation (*The Caves of Androzani*) it is her face that he first sees in his mind's eye, 'What is it you always told me, Doctor? Brave heart?' It is a curious point that Tegan is the first person he remembers, perhaps a sign of his guilt over the way she left.

As for Tegan herself, she never returns to *Doctor Who* although she is mentioned in future stories, most notably in 2010 in *The Sarah Jane Adventures: Death of the Doctor*, when Sarah tells her friends how Tegan now lives in Australia fighting for Aboriginal rights. (Although it does appear that Sarah doesn't remember having met Tegan in *The Five Doctors* – indeed it seems the only companions who remember those events are Tegan and Turlough).

With Turlough we had the last male companion until 2005, and the very last alien companion to date. He was also the only companion to be introduced with the express intention of killing the Doctor.

Vislor Turlough – Mark Strickson (Mawdryn Undead to Planet of Fire)

On the surface Turlough (we do not learn his first name until his very last story) seems like a normal school boy; a bit of a troublemaker, happy to shift the blame of a car accident (after a joy-ride) to his 'friend' Ibbotson. Turlough is sparklingly intelligent, used to talking his way out of situations. It is only when he is lying unconscious beside the car that we learn the truth of his alien background. The Black Guardian promises him a way off Earth if he does one thing for him – kill the Doctor!

At this point it seems Turlough will do almost anything to break free from Earth – a planet he finds beyond tedious. We do not discover exactly why he is on Earth, or indeed what planet he is from, until *Planet of Fire*, but when he does meet the Doctor and foolishly demonstrates an awareness of transmats and alien technology, the Doctor doesn't question it – almost as if the Doctor is wiser to the situation than he lets on. Indeed the Doctor is not surprised by the appearance of the White Guardian in *Enlightenment*, so could it be that the Doctor has been warned already? It would certainly explain the Doctor's distrust of Turlough despite welcoming him on board the TARDIS at the end of *Mawdryn Undead*.

Turlough quickly warms to the Doctor, and starts questioning the Black Guardian, but his will is nothing in comparison and he discovers there really is no way out of the deal he made. So his attempts at killing the Doctor are, at best, lacklustre. He finds his way into the TARDIS in a scene that is almost echoed in the closing moments of his introduction story, and is very evasive of the questions asked by Nyssa and Tegan, sticking to the Doctor's side. The Doctor notices, but again just lets it slide. Once the threat of Mawdryn is removed and the two Brigadiers are returned to their proper times, the Doctor suddenly remembers Turlough, who he believes is still on Mawdryn's ship, which is due to self-destruct. They rush into the TARDIS to find Turlough there waiting for them – he asks if he can join them, and the Doctor says yes. But Tegan is very weary. From the moment she meets him she is instinctively untrusting of him.

He seems to be older than he appears, and derides his peers at Brendon School, glad to be free of the 'children' there, he is also unimpressed at being given Adric's old room – which he considers a kid's room. He notices Tegan's attitude towards him and tries to smooth the way with charm and a choice phrase, but she will not have any of it, so he tells her that he finds her own way of communicating to be more like a sledge hammer. It is wonderfully ironic, therefore, that shortly after arriving at *Terminus* he finds himself trapped with only Tegan for company. Ultimately he has no one but himself to blame, since it was he who sabotaged the TARDIS, at the behest of the Black Guardian, and forced it to merge with the leper ship that docked at Terminus. He initiates a conversation with Tegan about killing, wondering if she could do such a thing. He is trying to work through his morality, his conscience pricking at him, mostly because he genuinely likes the Doctor, but he is an easy liar and deflects Tegan's own questions.

He knows he hasn't completely gained the Doctor's trust and cheerfully joins him in exploring the Edwardian racing yacht, *Shadow* (*Enlightenment*). Initially he is out of his depth with the rowdy sailors, but soon adapts, donning a straw hat and engaging them in loud and raucous conversation. After almost being driven mad by his bargain with the Guardian, Turlough jumps overboard but is rescued by an Eternal called Wrack, captain of the *Buccaneer*, also an agent of the Black Guardian. She reads his mind but finds it hard to do so, since it is divided and confused. She does recognise that greed is dominant though. Turlough is on the winning ship when it crosses the line and is thus offered the prize of Enlightenment, where he is confronted by both the Black and White Guardians. The Black Guardian goads him, reminding Turlough of their bargain – he can now either give up Enlightenment or the Doctor. He casts the Enlightenment diamond at the Guardian, his choice made. Tired, Turlough strangely wants the Doctor to take him back to his home planet – even though, as we later discover, he is a political exile and cannot return there.

As it turns out, the TARDIS crew end up back on Earth (*The King's Demons*), although whether Turlough has changed his mind or not is not known, but he doesn't seem too impressed to be there again. While there he is almost given over to the iron maiden (the medieval torture device, not the rock band). He is somewhat surprised by the Doctor's agreement to allow Kamelion to join them, although like Tegan he seems to forget about the android almost immediately, preferring to focus on helping the Doctor rebuild the TARDIS console while at the Eye of Orion (one can infer this by the fact that Turlough is familiar with the controls of the radically altered control console in *The Five Doctors* even though it is brand new and the Doctor is only finishing work on it at the beginning of the story – this is easily in keeping with Turlough, having already shown some aptitude for the TARDIS console in previous stories).

Being at the Eye of Orion seems to be a changing point in the Doctor and Turlough's relationship. Although there are still occasions when the Doctor doubts him, the two are more relaxed around each other. They are certainly very peaceful in each other's company, with Turlough drawing and the Doctor enjoying the vista. Turlough is very comfortable with the concept of regeneration. He doesn't bat an eyelid at the appearance of more than one Doctor and seems to delight in heightening the tension with Susan as they spot Cybermen planting a bomb outside the TARDIS. One of the most curious incidents in the Dark Tower is when Turlough steps out of the TARDIS, joining the team of companions who are watching the Doctors' activities with interest. Among these old friends is the Brigadier, one of Turlough's teachers from Brendon. It is odd that they do not acknowledge each other's presence, since the Brigadier was at Brendon when Turlough went missing, and certainly showed no love for the young man after Turlough crashed his car.

At the end of *The Five Doctors* Turlough is convinced, although unbothered, that the Time Lords will be sending him home. He is surprised to learn that the Doctor has no intention of going back to Gallifrey and becoming president. It is around this point that Turlough explains that he doesn't want to return to his home planet, but would rather remain with the Doctor, since he still has a lot to learn. The Doctor is a little doubtful, thinking that Turlough will change his mind again.

By this point, not only are the Doctor and Turlough getting on better, but so are Tegan and Turlough; they are slowly developing a friendly bit of rivalry, with Turlough's cynicism proving to be a nice foil against Tegan's passion. At the beginning of *Frontios* he rather enjoys disturbing her when reading about the 'doomed Earth', knowing it will get to her since she seems to care so much about her planet, which, of course, is the complete opposite of Turlough who doesn't care for Earth at all.

Hearing the stories of the ground eating people, and delving into the tunnels beneath the colony, Turlough begins to regress into a primal, almost feral state, the race memory of Tractators turning him into a gibbering mess. This may lead viewers to believe that Turlough is a coward, but in truth he is simply a survivor, as noted in *Resurrection of the Daleks* when he is forced to take up arms rather than die.

He is, surprisingly, sad to see Tegan leave, and finds himself missing her in *Planet of Fire*, although clearly not as much as the Doctor is. When the TARDIS picks up a distress signal, Turlough recognises its origin and instantly disconnects it. Even though Kamelion is responsible for reprogramming the TARDIS co-ordinates, the Doctor grows a little suspicious of Turlough, and is not convinced by his pleas of innocence, suggesting that although their relationship has progressed, the Doctor still reserves a certain level of doubt. While the Doctor is off exploring Lanzarote for the source of the signal, Turlough does everything he can to cancel out the signal, including shorting out Kamelion, but is soon distracted when he sees a woman apparently drowning. He is exasperated, but still goes out and rescues her, bringing her into the TARDIS for safety. In her bag he discovers an artefact from Trion, his home planet, and the source of the signal. The signal takes them to the planet Sarn. Turlough ventures out and discovers a younger man called Malkon – his brother! When Malkon is hurt, Turlough's aggressive side is brought to the fore and he threatens to kill the one responsible. The Doctor is suspicious when Turlough will not at first confide in him. He warns Turlough that if his secrets should end up aiding the Master, then their friendship would be over. Turlough eventually reveals that his family were political prisoners after a civil war on Trion and he was exiled to Earth. After contacting Trion he discovers that the war is over and he, and all his people, are now free to return. Turlough is torn and, in some ways, doesn't want to leave the Doctor, but he knows he must. Before leaving he asks Peri, the girl he saved from drowning, to look after the Doctor for him.

An image of Turlough appears to the dying Doctor in *The Caves of Androzani*, telling him, 'You must survive, Doctor. Too many of your enemies would delight in your death.'

It had been some years since K9 was booted out of the TARDIS, but he wasn't the last robotic companion. Enter Kamelion – a shape-shifting android found on Xeriphas. It seemed like a wonderful idea, an android that could be anyone, but the reality was somewhat different. Introduced in one story, he isn't seen again until six stories later when he is destroyed – the worst treatment of a companion ever in *Doctor Who*.

Kamelion – Gerald Flood (The King's Demons to Planet of Fire)

While trapped on Xeriphas the Master discovers an android called Kamelion. Although sentient, Kamelion is susceptible to strong personalities, and so the Master, being something of an expert at controlling people against their will, uses Kamelion to pose as King John in an attempt to prevent the signing of the Magna Carta. A battle of wills ensues between the Doctor and the Master which ultimately the Doctor wins. He frees Kamelion from the Master's mind and allows the android to travel with them. After this Kamelion seems to just vanish – we must assume he is still in the TARDIS somewhere, but there is no logical reason for everyone to simply forget about him. Certainly Tegan is not happy about him being there, and Turlough is surprised by the Doctor's decision. The fact that none of them mention him again is somewhat odd to say the least. In *Frontios* the TARDIS is torn apart by the force of the Tractators, and scattered throughout the planet. But what happens to Kamelion?

The next time we see Kamelion, he is being manipulated once more by the Master, but this time it is not only the Master whose mind is powerful enough to dominate. Peri, distraught after almost having drowned, starts to affect Kamelion's mind to the point where he takes on the form of her step-father, Howard Foster. Throughout the story a battle of wills ensues between the Master and Peri, until finally the Master is able to gain complete control of Kamelion. However when the Master relinquishes control, Kamelion begs the Doctor to destroy him, not wanting to be used again. The Doctor reluctantly agrees.

Unfortunately due to his lack of screen time, and the fact that when he is on screen he is almost certainly being controlled by someone else, we never got to see any real growth in Kamelion.

That said, the Doctor clearly never forgets about him since he appears to the dying Doctor in *The Caves of Androzani*, along with all the other companions who travelled with the Fifth Doctor, encouraging him to not give in, and regenerate.

By the mid-1980s *Doctor Who* was becoming popular in America, and to that end a decision was made to introduce an American companion. She was also to serve as the transition across Doctor's, since the end of the Fifth Doctor's run was drawing near...

Perpugilliam 'Peri' Brown – Nicola Bryant (*Planet of Fire* to *The Trial of a Time Lord*)

A young student of botany, when we meet Peri she is on vacation in Lanzarote with her mother and step-father. She seems to have a close relationship with her step-father, Howard, but not so much with her mother. She is a bit flighty when we first meet her, opting to cash in her travellers' cheques to travel to Morocco with a bunch of people she has only just met. When Howard asks her how she hopes to pay for her ticket home, she simply says, 'I'll get a job', as though she hasn't really thought about it at all. Howard, quite rightly, is not keen on this idea, and so purposely strands her on his boat to ensure she cannot leave until they can have a long talk about it. Peri reacts in a very spoiled way, and chooses to steal one of Howard's artefacts to get some money to fund her trip. The only problem she has is getting to shore.

As it turns out, Peri is not a very strong swimmer and is soon rescued by Turlough, who takes her into the TARDIS to recover. Her dreams about her recent argument with Howard are so realistic that she accidentally influences Kamelion, who takes the form of her step-father. When she awakes she has no idea where she is, and stumbles into the console room to find Howard there with the Doctor and Turlough. The time travellers go out to explore, leaving the confused Peri with her step-father. It is then that she learns the truth, that somehow this is not her step-father at all, but the Master. Unusually for a companion of the Doctor's, the Master is quite impressed by Peri's force of will, being able to wrest control of Kamelion from him. Despite her continual whining, she does prove to have a very strong sense of self, and is willing to be convinced that they are on another planet. In her short time on Sarn, Peri becomes quite fond of the Doctor and agrees to look after him when Turlough realises it is time he returns home to Trion. The Doctor is not so sure about having her join him, but she explains she still has three months of vacation left, and he almost reluctantly agrees that she can travel with him.

Their first port of call is the planet Androzani Minor – a place Peri is initially very impressed with. As they begin to explore she demonstrates her sarcastic wit, which helps build up a nice sense of friendship between her and the Doctor. For the first time, the Doctor seems to be truly relaxed with his travelling companion, almost as if he has finally found the perfect person to travel with his fifth incarnation. She is, however, impatient to move on to the next place once she tires of talk about fused silica – the Doctor is in full exploration mode so she has no choice but to follow him, 'Is this wise I ask myself?'

The adventure becomes less fun when they are arrested as suspected gun runners, and are scheduled to be executed. Peri has a very hard time on Androzani; she narrowly avoids death by firing squad and then becomes infected by Spectrox Toxaemia, a fatal infection with only one cure. To make matters worse she finds herself under the close attention of Sharez Jek, an insane genius who becomes obsessed by her beauty. The Doctor becomes very protective of Peri in Jek's company, but his flippancy is insufficient to quell her fear. She tries to keep her humour, but finds it very difficult in the face of such horrendous company. The Doctor literally risks his life to find the cure for his young companion (probably a result of his guilt at the loss of Adric, Nyssa, Tegan and Turlough). The Doctor holds back his regeneration, as he too is infected and near to death; he is determined to save Peri.

By the time he returns, the laboratory is in flames, and Jek is dead. The Doctor carries Peri back to the TARDIS, dodging blasts of primordial mud, and spills enough of the bat's milk (the cure) that he only has some to save Peri. Safe in the TARDIS, and away from Androzani he gives her the cure, which works rapidly. Although still weak, Peri finds the Doctor lying on the TARDIS floor, dying. She can do nothing but cradle him in her arms. She is both upset and terrified – upset at the Doctor's death, and terrified that she is being left alone in a ship she doesn't understand, 'Don't give up. You can't leave me now!' she tells him, but it is too late. The Doctor does warn her that he might regenerate, but she has no idea what he means. Scared and alone, Peri crawls away and pushes herself against the console room walls, having no idea what she is going to do. Then something quite amazing happens... the Doctor begins to change. And not a moment too soon...

The Fifth Doctor
Expanded Universe

The Fifth Doctor's companions are a disparate group, often arguing with each other while frustrating the Doctor. Did this change in the Expanded Universe, or did the authors take the opportunity to delve deeper into the characters to find out why they were so aggressive towards each other? And what of Kamelion – the most wasted companion during the 1980s? Without the restrictions placed on him by a 'rubbish' prop, did the authors take advantage of this shape-changing android?

First though, we will take a look at Adric. Often regarded in fandom as one of the least popular companions, did the authors take the opportunity to make him more interesting, or did their dislike for him come across in their stories?

In *Divided Loyalties*, the 1999 novel in which the Doctor, Adric, Nyssa and Tegan battle the Toymaker, we learn that pizza is a mystery to Adric. He also doesn't appear to know what hygiene is as both Nyssa and Tegan suggest to the Doctor that he have a chat with Adric about his reluctance to bathe regularly, a chat that never takes place. Never one for tact, Tegan also thinks that Adric is lazy and generally loathsome, although in the novel *The Sands of Time* she discusses the emotional impact of his death with the Doctor and the reasons why Adric cannot be saved by using the TARDIS.

We also get a glimpse of Adric's earlier years in *Divided Loyalties*; his childhood friend Jiana, with whom there may have been a romantic link, flees when Adric joins his brother Varsh's rebel forces as they fight against the elite. The Toymaker traps Adric in an illusionary dreamscape and uses Jiana's image to try and turn Adric against the Doctor, reminding him of the numerous times the Time Lord has placed his life in danger while fighting against such foes as the Master and the Terileptils.

There is little exploration of his family life beyond this mention of Varsh, but we do learn that Adric's parents are named Morell and Tanisa.

Adric's adeptness at chess is touched upon in *Divided Loyalties*, a skill he uses to repeatedly beat Nyssa at the game in *Hearts of Stone*, a short story in the *Short Trips: Companions* collection. This shouldn't be surprising though as Adric is not only highly competent in astrometrics (*Divided Loyalties* again) but also possesses a badge for mathematical excellence.

Following Adric's death in the television story *Earthshock* he is remembered by Nyssa and Tegan in the novel *Zeta Major* and again in *Fear of the Dark*, by the Doctor. Unsurprisingly Tegan finds it easier to deal with his death than the others but not for the reasons you would think. In *The Sands of Time* she says that she finds it easier to cope because she didn't see him die.

It is following his death that Adric makes perhaps his strangest appearance in the Expanded Universe. In *The Boy That Time Forgot*, the 2008 audio drama, the Doctor and Nyssa are looking for the TARDIS after its theft by Thomas Brewster in *The Haunting of Thomas Brewster* and their search leads them to an Aztec jungle pocket-dimension packed with insects and giant scorpions. There they find that, during a séance, the Doctor unintentionally saves Adric by sending him subconscious Block Transfer Computations. However, the Adric they encounter is not the boy they remember. Alone and isolated for centuries he has become quite insane and seethes with bitterness. The Doctor makes repeated attempts to show him that he has become essentially a very old and resentful teenager.

In the Expanded Universe of *Doctor Who* novels it appears that Nyssa, the aristocratic daughter of Traken, is always being turned into a monster of some kind. *Goth Opera*, a 1994 *Virgin Missing*

Adventure, sees her changed into a vampire; she even bites the Doctor. In *The Sands of Time* she is chosen to become a host for Nephthys, the sister and wife of Sutekh (encountered by the Fourth Doctor in *Pyramids of Mars*) and for most of the book is wrapped up as a mummy, spending four thousand years in a comatose state. This gives her chance to rest, before becoming a feral monster in *Zeta Major*, a *BBC Past Doctor Adventure*, after being implanted with anti-matter – her Trakenite body gives her only partial protection from radiation.

She manages to remain herself through *Divided Loyalties*, and the book provides some more information regarding her character. We learn that Nyssa has a working knowledge of bioelectronics, in addition to her knowledge of biology which is covered in the television series.

According to Big Finish, there is a very large gap between seasons nineteen and twenty, and Nyssa spends quite some time travelling alone with the Doctor before Tegan rejoins them in *Arc of Infinity*. During this time her latent telepathic powers are explored, most notably when she visits Traken's past. She witnesses the creation of the Cybermen on a battered Mondas in *Spare Parts*. She has her first taste of romance in *Circular Time*, and is later joined in her travels with the Doctor by Thomas Brewster.

In *Empire of Death* (a *BBC Past Doctor Adventure*), Nyssa considers, as she has done many times, asking the Doctor to take her to Traken prior to its destruction. She actually asks him in the audio story *Cobwebs* but it will still be a while before he can. Like most people of Traken (often called Trakenites in the Expanded Universe) she has no knowledge of her planet's history since she wasn't taught this as a child, as mentioned in the audio drama *Primeval*.

In *Cobwebs*, an older Nyssa, some years after she left in *Terminus*, rejoins the Doctor, Tegan and Turlough on their travels. And in *Heroes of Sontar* she confides in Tegan that she is married to a man by the name of Lasarti and has three children called Adric, Neeka and Tegan. She implores Tegan to keep this from the Doctor in order to protect the Web of Time as it isn't until shortly before his regeneration that he finds out that she is married (in *Winter*, a story that sees Nyssa enter the Doctor's mindscape mere seconds before he regenerates at the end of *The Caves of Androzani*).

In *The Darkening Eye* Nyssa is subjected to the Dar Traders' cataloguing process which is halted so that the Dar Trader can inform her that, as a Trakenite, death is attracted to her but she should be able to master and calcify it. Before the process is stopped she has a vision of Tegan cradling her in a field of leaves. Later in the story Nyssa is stabbed and dies for three minutes before being brought back to life by the same Dar Trader as part of a trade. She wakes to find herself in a field of leaves being held by Tegan, as the vision prophesied.

During the same story, Nyssa claims she has a familiarity with dimensional transcendentalism that predates her travels with the Doctor. She goes on to add that she probably understands it better than the Doctor. Once again she displays a knowledge that extends beyond her specialist subject of biology. This is explored further in another audio story, *The Deep*, in which she fixes the chameleon circuit. The Doctor claims to have a TARDIS repair manual and is bewildered as to how Nyssa could have even begun to repair the circuit without it.

Doctor: 'Tegan, has anyone told you how nice it is to have y o u around?'

Tegan: 'Not recently, no.'

Doctor: 'No? Hmmm, I wonder why that is.'

This piece of dialogue from *Divided Loyalties* gives you an idea why Tegan, irascible, outspoken and in her own words 'downright bolshie' (*The Children of Seth* – audio), is such a popular companion with both fans and writers of the Expanded Universe. She is referred to as 'the shrieking hell cat' by Dawson in *The Emerald Tiger*, first part of a 2012 audio trilogy, and as 'an Antipodean harpy' by Major Haggard in the same story. In *The Lions of*

Trafalgar, a 2011 audio story, she freely admits to having a big mouth. Being so strong-willed though works to her advantage at times, such as in *Goth Opera* where her temperament supplies her with enough resilience to make her immune to the vampires' attempts to hypnotise her. Rather than religion, Tegan's beliefs lie in the writings of Primo Levi, Quantas, Australian musician James Reyne and the Australian republic.

Tegan's biographical details are covered quite extensively in the Expanded Universe, most notably in *The King of Terror* (a *Past Doctor Adventure* novel), *Divided Loyalties* and *Cradle of the Snake* (a 2010 audio story). Tegan, which is a Cornish name meaning 'lovely little thing', grew up in Caloundra, around seventy miles from Brisbane (*The King of Terror*). Her father, William (*Divided Loyalties*), owned a sheep farm and two thousand head of merino. One of Tegan's most treasured memories is flying with him in his Cessna Skyhawk over the farm (*The Cradle of the Snake*). He understood that Tegan wasn't really cut out for farm life. Other family mentioned are her mother's brother, Richard, and sister-in-law, Felicity. She also has two cousins, Colin and Michael, and Serbian grandparents living in Yugoslavia named Mjovic and Sneshna Jovanka. However, the thirteen-year-old Tegan hated her grandmother, who died of coronary thrombosis, referring to her as a 'mad cow'. The young Tegan was a John Lennon and Abba fan, listening to their records with her friends Fliss, Dave, Susannah and Richard (*Divided Loyalties*).

Scandal shook the family when Tegan's father had an affair with a twenty-year-old woman who worked in a typing pool. They moved up the coast to try and escape the repercussions of this and Tegan's mother sent her away to a boarding school, where she was expelled after only a few terms. At just fifteen she ran away and headed for Sydney where she ended up squatting in King's Cross. Eventually her father tracked her down and decided to send her to England, to stay with her Aunt Vanessa (*The King of Terror*).

The teenage Tegan, as she admits herself, didn't have a boyfriend. Tegan was overweight and extremely sensitive about this. A boy named Gary Lovarik was the only one she had any interest in but her supposed best friend, Felicity Spoonsy, moved in on him first (*The King of Terror*). According to *Divided Loyalties* she had passed through this difficult period by the age of eighteen and she certainly seems more at ease with herself and the opposite sex by the time she embarks on her journeys with Doctor. In *The King of Terror* she has a flirtation with Captain Paynter, who she seems to be both attracted to and infuriated by. They kiss but the relationship doesn't really go anywhere. In the 1996 novel *Cold Fusion*, Chris Cwej (companion of the Seventh Doctor) gets amorous and makes advances but she drenches him with champagne. An inebriated Tegan is supported by Police Sergeant Andy Weathers in the novel *Deep Blue*, later going on a date with him. In a crossroads moment she even ruminates on what life with Andy would be like if she were to stay on Earth.

Tegan's character offers the writers of the Extended Universe a chance to have a little fun and this is no more evident than in her repeated references to western popular culture. In the 2011 audio story, *Kiss of Death*, she asks Turlough if his parents inherited the planet of Enid Blyton – later in *The Emerald Tiger* she comments on a three-piece suit he is wearing, saying that it makes him look more mature. Also in *The Emerald Tiger,* Tegan mentions Tigger from *Winnie the Pooh* and calls Dawon – the one who dubbed her a shrieking she-cat – Pussy Galore, referencing the James Bond novel and film *Goldfinger*. Loki gets the same treatment in Cobwebs, a 2010 audio drama, when she refers to him as R2-D2, the iconic droid from *Star Wars*. Keeping up with popular culture can come in very handy when you are time travelling; in *Cold Fusion*, Tegan is able to deal with the idea of transmats because of what she has gleaned from *Blake's 7,* the cult '80s television show from Dalek creator, Terry Nation.

However, it is not only this that makes the character fun, there is also her wonderful sense of mischievousness as evidenced in *The Sands of Time* when Tegan tries to make a minor change to history just to see if the Doctor's insistence that it cannot be changed is correct. Then there is her repeated use of the word 'rabbits' as an expletive, something she does in *The Emerald Tiger*.

Tegan makes her choice to leave the TARDIS in 1984 but *The Gathering*, a 2006 audio story, sees her reunited with the Doctor twenty years later, on her fourty-sixth birthday (incidentally Tegan has the same birthday, 22nd September, as Billie Piper. This is referenced in the story on a radio show heard in the background). She has taken on the job of running Verney Food Supplies, her father's stock feed company. The name implies that he inherited the company from Tegan's maternal grandfather, Andrew Verney. It is one of the more poignant outings on audio as she and the Doctor explore their past as travelling companions. Having been diagnosed with a fatal brain tumour while at the same time struggling with a number of relationships, Tegan undergoes a process of reconciling herself with the decisions she has made.

Turlough enters the Doctor's life as an assassin sent to kill him so it is really no surprise that his trustworthiness is a matter of ongoing debate between the Doctor and Tegan, most notably in the audio story *Cobwebs*, when Tegan comments that her Aunt Vanessa always said, 'Once a wrong 'un, always a wrong 'un.' They argue over Turlough's loyalty, and his alliance with the Black Guardian is repeatedly brought up by Tegan in an attempt to change the Doctor's mind. In the audio story, *Freakshow*, Turlough strongly believes that the Doctor mistrusts him due to his involvement with the Black Guardian, and is testing him in order to ascertain where his loyalties lie.

Freakshow is also notable for the observation made by the Doctor that Turlough and Tegan are like a pair of bickering siblings, a fractious relationship which plays out on both television and in the Expanded Universe. During the story Turlough gets seriously annoyed with the Doctor for failing to knock before entering his room, pointing out that he wouldn't dare treat Tegan in the same manner. *Freakshow* sees the TARDIS landing in Buzzard Creek, Arizona in the year 1905 and Turlough dons a Stetson, predating the Eleventh Doctor in *The Impossible Astronaut*.

Turlough's time at Brendon Public School on Earth gets a few mentions in the Expanded Universe. In the 1999 audio drama *Phantasmagoria*, Turlough mentions his enjoyment of studying history at the school (something else noteworthy about this particular outing is the gift to Turlough that the Doctor makes of his 1928 Wisden Almanack) and in the 2011 audio tale *The Heroes of Sontar* we learn that the Brendon Public School scroll of honour is inscribed with the Latin phrase *Dulci et decorum est pro patria mori* (it is sweet and fitting to die for one's country). This is dedicated to all the school's former students who have died in wars. It is interesting to note that Turlough actually outranks some of the Sontarans on Samur as he is a Junior Ensign Commander. In *The Emerald Tiger*, the Doctor tells Turlough that he really should have a word with Brigadier Lethbridge-Stewart in regard to the poor emphasis placed on sport at Brendon Public School in the early 1980s, during Turlough's education.

As the title suggests, *Turlough and the Earthlink Dilemma*, the first *Companions of Doctor Who* novel (1986), Turlough gets a story of his own – the only time we get a look at his life after parting company with the Doctor. In it he alters history in order to erase the annihilation of Trion (his homeworld), New Trion and Earth and in so doing thwarts the plans of evil dictator Rehctaht (read it backwards!). However this results in him being unable to return home in case he creates a temporal paradox and he ends up in an alternative timeline, replacing a dead version of himself. On encountering his older alternative self with long hair, Turlough is warned against the folly of blindly trusting his Time Lord friends. The story also reveals the extent to which Turlough has developed as a scientist; through close study of the TARDIS' temporal control mechanisms he has an astounding grasp of time travel (in the 2004 short story *Observations* he is able to operate the TARDIS with enough accuracy to pilot it six months forward in time to collect the Doctor); he is more than efficient in the fields of physics and quantum mechanics and is also in the possession of an almost perfect memory.

Kamelion gets a raw deal on television, but in the Expanded Universe he is treated a little better. In *The Crystal Bucephalus*, a 1994 novel, we learn that he and the TARDIS have probably been chatting for a while. In the same story Kamelion reveals that he finds free will hard to negotiate and is far more comfortable following orders. Being designed for war this is hardly surprising. It is not only the TARDIS that the android can hear though, as in the 2000 novel *Imperial Moon*, Kamelion is able to sense the Time Lord's thoughts, due to their complexity.

Despite being killed in *Planet of Fire*, he returns in the follow-up novel, *The Ultimate Treasure*, his personality having survived due to his interfacing with the TARDIS. The natives of Gelsandor give him a new body, but he once again has to sacrifice himself for the Doctor and Peri. Later we discover, in *The Reproductive Cycle*, the android has a child with the TARDIS, which is raised by Peri and the Sixth Doctor.

Seventeen-year-old daughter of a dead pharaoh, Erimem – Erimemushinteperem is her full name, meaning 'Daughter of Light' – was the first Expanded Universe companion created by Big Finish for the Fifth Doctor in 2001 (and one of several who, as a result, do not reappear to the Doctor during his fifth regeneration in *The Caves of Androzani*), and was introduced in *The Eye of the Scorpion*. Erimem's father was the late Pharaoh Amenhotep II and her mother one of his sixty concubines, Rubak. Erimem's three elder half-brothers died during the previous year and there is some suspicion surrounding these deaths. Later it transpires that the one thing Erimem regrets after stepping into the TARDIS is that she never said goodbye to her mother.

Erimem is adamant that she doesn't believe in Egyptian gods, however, by the 2006 audio outing, *The Kingmaker*, she informs Peri that she now believes in the existence of an afterlife. As an ancient Egyptian she reveres cats and *The Church and the Crown* sees her getting a new pet cat named Antranak. However, in *No Place Like Home*, it turns out that the Fifth Doctor isn't a cat-lover and the feline addition to the TARDIS becomes the subject of a running joke between the Doctor and Erimem, and remains so until Antranak's death in *Nekromanteia*.

As with Turlough and Peri, Erimem gets her own story in the 2005 novel, *The Coming of the Queen*. It's a pre-Doctor adventure which sees the Pharaoh's daughter, who has lived a protected and luxurious life in her father's palace in Thebes, approaching her sixteenth year, a year that will plunge Erimem and her three half-brothers into a dark world of death, betrayal and tragedy.

Erimem's departure from the TARDIS comes in the 2008 audio tale, *The Bride of Peladon*, in which she makes a decision to stay with King Pelleas. Erimem has a signet ring bearing the emblem of Sekhmet which she uses as a talisman to protect her from the gods, once again revealing that she has moved away from her previous agnostic leanings.

Big Finish are not the only company to create non-television companions for the Fifth Doctor, indeed no sooner has he appeared on television, he receives his first 'exclusive' companion in the shape of Sir Justin, in the pages of *Doctor Who Magazine*. A knight from medieval England, Sir Justin gave his life to stop Melanicus. Another part-time companion created for the comics is Shayde, a Gallifreyan construct placed in the Doctor's TARDIS without the Doctor's permission. He returns on occasion to assist the Doctor, later appearing with the Eighth Doctor and merging with future companion, Trey Truscott-Sade. As previously mentioned, the Fifth Doctor also travels for a time with Thomas Brewster, a street urchin from Victorian London who first appears in *The Haunting of Thomas Brewster*. He remains on Earth in 2008 to pursue a romance with Connie, however she is hit by a car and falls into a coma. He re-enters the Doctor's life, now in his sixth incarnation, and demands to be taken back to his own time, holding Evelyn Smythe at gunpoint to convince the Doctor. Another companion created by Big Finish is Amy (later called Abby to distinguish her from the Eleventh Doctor's companion),

COMPANIONS

a tracer given human form to help the Doctor track down the Key to Time in *The Judgement of Isskar*. During her travels she becomes fully human. She later enters the Time Lord Academy, and joins a Zara (her 'twin sister') on further adventures in *Graceless*.

The Sixth Doctor
Colin Baker

'In all my travelling throughout the universe, I have battled against evil, against power-mad conspirators.'
The Doctor – *The Trial of a Time Lord*

Perpugilliam 'Peri' Brown – Nicola Bryant continued... (*Planet of Fire* to *The Trial of a Time Lord*)

From the moment the Doctor sits up, fresh from his regeneration, one thing is abundantly clear – he is not the man that saved Peri's life. As she later states in *The Twin Dilemma*, she finds him rude, self-obsessed and ignorant – it is a wonder why she remains with him really, since it is very clear she no longer likes him. This is not surprising; she is distraught and confused by his change of appearance, but the new Doctor is very dismissive of her emotional state, simply waving it away saying she will get used to it. Gone is the man she considered sweet, replaced by a dangerously unstable stranger. One who even attempts to kill her! The Doctor finds it hard to believe that he would even think of something like that, but when she cowers away from him in fear he realises that she is not making it up, that something has gone dangerously wrong with the regeneration (almost certainly a consequence of the Fifth Doctor having actually died, before the regeneration kicked in).

A short time later, when Peri believes the Doctor had died in a safe house explosion on Titan Three, she breaks down in tears which, on the surface, doesn't really make sense since she has shown nothing but distaste for him since his regeneration – and with good reason. Even the Doctor doesn't understand why she would be so upset. She explains it away as compassion, but it fails to ring true. It seems more likely that Peri's emotional state is heightened; she is more distraught than she realises, being stuck with a man who might kill her at any time. Nonetheless, she remains defiant and refuses to be bullied by the unstable Doctor. Just as they leave Jaconda, the Doctor tells Peri that he is now fully stabilised, and Peri points out that he could do with a crash course in manners. But when he adds, 'I am the Doctor, whether you like it or not', Peri finds his smile infectious and cannot help but return one of her own. And that is all it really is, an infectious reaction, since between then and the next time we see them in *Attack of the Cybermen* things have not improved much. They have spent much time in the TARDIS, although what Peri's been doing to occupy her time is unclear, and she is quite clearly bored out of her mind while the Doctor goes about repairing systems. She is finding it very hard to relate to the Doctor now, and doesn't think he understands her, a far cry from the closeness that had been developing prior to his regeneration.

She is clearly worried about his state of mind; he has called her a number of names, including Tegan, Zoe, Susan and, at one point, Jamie. He calls her Susan once again while they stand outside the junkyard on Totter's Lane, although Peri fails to understand the reason for this slip up. She is merely frustrated that he forgets who she is – again. She bemoans the fact that her first visit to London is to search for a distress call the TARDIS picked up, and wishes she could just visit like a regular tourist, which is perfectly in keeping with the reason why she remained with the Doctor in the first place. She spends most of her time in London on edge, which is not helped by the appearance of the Cybermen, or their threat to kill her if the Doctor doesn't take them to Telos. Still in a state of distress, Peri is initially horrified by the Cryons, but soon overcomes such terror when she realises they are peaceful, although fighting for their very survival. She learns that Lytton, a man they all thought was working for the Cybermen, is really working against them on behalf of the Cryons. It takes her some time to convince the Doctor that Lytton is actually one of the good guys. After Lytton sacrifices himself to save the Doctor, Peri is surprised, although heartened too, to see his remorse. Perhaps there is some hope for this Doctor after all. If nothing else it is a hint of the man she once knew.

Although American, Peri oddly fits into London very well, seemingly something of an expert on British slang. It may be that she learned key phrases in preparation for travelling to the UK at some point, but it is a strange thing that she rarely uses American slang, indeed more often than not she tends to use British pronunciation. For instance, when the Doctor talks down to her she tells him to not '*pat*-ronise' her, instead of saying '*pay*-tronise' as would be expected from an American.

When the TARDIS is out of Zeiton-7 ore in *Vengeance on Varos* and the Doctor explains that they have barely got enough power to reach Varos, she tells him she would rather be stuck there than in the TARDIS, since unlike the Doctor she doesn't have many lives to live, she only has one and doesn't want to spend it alone with him. This is perfectly understandable, since their level of bickering would only worsen after endless hours of being in each other's company. On Varos she meets Sil, an almost slug-like alien from the planet Thoros Beta, and finds him as repulsive as he finds her. When she is put under the transmogrification beam, Sil is delighted to see her start to turn into some bird-like creature. She recovers from the ordeal, but the Doctor jokes much later (in *The Trial of a Time Lord*) that after leaving Varos she cost him a fortune in birdseed – a joke Peri doesn't appreciate. When the Doctor appears to die in the punishment zone, Peri expresses real grief, almost guilt, at his passing, and wonders what she is going to do if she is stuck on such a horrible world. Although still they bicker and squabble, during their time on Varos there are a few moments of levity between them that suggests that somehow they are bonding.

When the TARDIS takes them to the mining town of Killingworth in the 1820s, Peri expresses an interest in ecology, a perfect companion to her botany studies. On the short walk from the TARDIS to the town itself, there is actual banter between her and the Doctor, showing a steady growth in their friendship – despite their continuing bickering. Indeed at the end of *The Mark of the Rani*, when asked what it is he and Peri do in the TARDIS, the Doctor replies, 'Argue, mainly'. She is shocked by the Master's return, having witnessed his death on Sarn. As you would expect, the Master is quite intent on doing her a great deal of harm; after all she did not lift a hand to save him on Sarn. Nonetheless, even though he wishes her dead, he still has a lot of respect for Peri, referring to her as 'Miss Brown'.

She is saved by the Rani, another Time Lord, but not out of compassion rather because she wants to use the chemicals in Peri's brain. After both the Master and the Rani are defeated, it is nice to note that the Doctor and Peri walk away, with the Doctor putting his arm over her shoulders – a level of closeness not seen between them before. They still have a long way to go though, as shown when they are fishing in *The Two Doctors*, but by this point Peri is giving as good as she gets, a tact that begins to have an effect on the Doctor. Even though there have been several times she could have easily left him, Peri clearly thinks it is worth sticking it out.

Having already heard of Jamie, Peri gets to meet him and is rather charmed. Initially Jamie is not completely on form, having been stranded alone on the deserted Space Station Camera. Peri doesn't quite understand how two Doctors can be in one period, nor how the TARDIS can be in two places at one time.

Despite seeing a holographic image of the Second Doctor on the space station, she still fails to recognise him when he is wheeled out before her by Chessene. Evidently, when in danger, Peri thinks of the Doctor, as witnessed when she is confronted by Chessene, who she feels is a threat. As they leave Spain, the Doctor decides that from now on (after the cannibalistic nature of the Androgums) it is a strict vegetarian diet for both of them – which appears to carry on at least until they arrive on Necros much later in *Revelation of the Daleks* at which point Peri's 'enjoying' one of the Doctor's nut-roast rolls.

After these recent events, at the start of *Timelash,* Peri simply wants to go somewhere to relax and the Doctor suggests the Eye of Orion. But Peri wants to go somewhere else, somewhere fun. The Doctor offers to take her back to 1985 but Peri insists she doesn't want to go back; despite everything, she does appear to enjoy her travels with the Doctor or, at the very least, is not ready to give up on him yet. She doesn't care much for Karfel, and is especially not impressed by the Borad, yet another mutated creature who wishes to make Peri his mate. But she is very impressed, when she later learns that Herbert is the young HG Wells.

Although she has heard of the Daleks, by the time they arrive on Necros (*Revelation of the Daleks*), she cannot have seen one as she fails to recognise a Dalek on sight. We also learn that while on her travels she has been collecting exotic alien plants, since she has to wow her teachers with something as her grades certainly will not – either suggesting she has been away longer than the planned three months, or that she has little faith in her academic ability. When a mutant, the result of Davros' experiments, attacks the Doctor, Peri accidentally kills it in her attempts at a rescue. It is the first time she has killed anyone, and she feels overwhelming guilt, especially since the mutant thanks her before dying. During their long walk to Tranquil Repose, the Doctor and Peri engage in much banter which includes such topics as the American's monopoly on bad taste, and the Doctor's weight. She even, while scaling a wall, unintentionally breaks the Doctor's much treasured fob-watch. She promises to buy him a new one, but the Doctor brushes it away with sarcasm, leaving Peri feeling more than a little guilty. When the Doctor is apparently crushed by his own gravestone, Peri is 'consoled' by the grotesque Jobel. She finds him both repellent and weird, and is comforted when the Doctor climbs from beneath the gravestone unharmed. While the Doctor exposes a plot to create a new army of Daleks by Davros, he leaves

Peri in Jobel's care, thinking she will be safer with him than whatever else is on Necros, but Peri is not so convinced and gives him the slip at the first opportunity, instead enjoying the company of the DJ. At first she thinks he is really from America, and is a little disappointed to discover that his accent is false, indeed that he has never even been to Earth. Nonetheless she does find him amusing, and is horrified when he is later killed by a Dalek. After the slaughter at Tranquil Repose she decides she needs a holiday, and the Doctor agrees to take her to...

Something very strange has happened by the time we next see the Doctor. He arrives at a space station controlled by the Time Lords and is put on trial (*The Trial of a Timelord 1-4*). Only he arrives without Peri and has no idea where she is. He soon finds out, but not before he is shown a couple of recent adventures. The first is set on Ravalox, and it is immediately clear that quite some time has passed for both the Doctor and Peri since they left Necros. Peri's hair is much longer, and they now have a close and quite tactile relationship. They think nothing of walking through a damp wood arm in arm, under an umbrella. Even their banter, once snippy and derisive, is now light and good natured. Finally Peri has found her Doctor again. She finds herself uneasy on Ravalox, unable to shake the feeling that she has been there before – the Doctor remarks on the similarities it has to Earth, and he wonders why. Peri is less interested in the mystery, until they come across the remains of Marble Arch Underground Station. She is very upset to discover that somehow the Earth was almost destroyed in a fireball and then shifted halfway across the galaxy, and reminisces about how London should be, as if she has been there before (not in *Attack of the Cybermen*, since the things she describes do not match what she experienced during her brief visit to London in that story). The Doctor attempts to comfort her, explaining that this is over two million years in her future, the Earth she knows is still there, just as she remembers it. This, however, doesn't help and she simply wants to leave, but the Doctor cannot until he discovers what happened to Earth – why was it almost destroyed and shifted half way across the galaxy?

When captured by the Tribe of the Free, Peri is promised several husbands by Queen Katryca, but it is not an idea that amuses her. She is, however, amused by intergalactic con-man Sabalom Glitz.

Her sadness over Earth's fate has a lasting impression on her because later, while on Thoros Beta (*The Trial of a Timelord 5-8*) she expresses a desire to return home, to be surrounded by people she loves, which is a nice bit of progression from the girl who was so willing to escape her home life when we first met her in *Planet of Fire*. But it is not all future hopes on Thoros Beta, for it is there that we discover Peri's own fate – or do we? Unfortunately we learn about this adventure via the Matrix, which the Doctor later discovers has been tampered with, thus much of the adventure did not happen as we see it. This throws up all kinds of doubt as to what we see, but we can assume much of it is true – even if the attraction between Peri and warrior King Yrcarnos is a little odd. It is believable that Peri would be disgusted by the attentions of a 'dirty old war lord' on the planet Thordon, as well as her compassion for the Lukosor, a werewolf-like creature that was once the loyal companion of Yrcarnos. And it is certainly easy to believe that she would be unimpressed, almost disturbed in fact, to discover that Thoros Beta is the homeworld of Sil, and even more so that the Doctor knew and did not tell her. But what is hard to understand is the Doctor's betrayal of Peri – almost from any angle it seems wrong and completely out of character. Had it happened shortly after his regeneration it might be acceptable, but considering the development of their relationship it just makes no sense at all.

For a while the Doctor believes that Peri was killed on Thoros Beta, that her body was used to house the mind of Lord Kiv, Sil's superior, and that the Time Lords then used Yrcarnos as an assassin to destroy Peri's body and everyone involved in the unholy experiments being conducted on Thoros Beta. Later though, after he defeats the threat posed to him and Gallifrey, he is relieved greatly to hear that Peri survived after all, and has been set up on high by Yrcarnos.

How Peri must have felt at the Doctor's sudden disappearance (being taken out of time by the Time Lords to stand trial) we will never learn, but it is unlikely she will have taken it well.

Peri's confused departure was a good indication of the upheaval in the series at time, and it continued with the introduction of Mel – the first companion, since Susan, to not even get an introduction story. She was simply just there. But that was the least of the confusion surrounding this character...

Mel – Bonnie Langford (The Trial of a Time Lord to Dragonfire)

To demonstrate that things improve, the Doctor, while on trial, shows an adventure set at some point in his own personal future (*The Trial of a Time Lord 9-12*). At this point he is travelling with an Earth girl called Mel. They have clearly been travelling for quite some time, since not only does the Doctor state that he would 'trust Mel with my life', but he has always envied her ability for almost total recall. This implies that it has been quite a long association. They have a very easy and lightweight friendship, with Mel looking to the Doctor with great affection. She is polite, bubbly and always charming; clearly excited about the adventure she is on. We never learn how they meet, nor indeed where she is actually from (although all this is mentioned in the character profile on the official documents, nothing is made of it on screen, so it has no bearing on the narrative). She is defiant and will not be cowed by anyone. She is also fiercely loyal to the Doctor, and will not tolerate anyone talking badly about him. During a moment of reflection the Doctor points out that Mel is not known for being subdued and thoughtful; she can only smile at this, knowing the Doctor is quite right. She clearly places a high value on life, and is saddened by the death of the Vervoids, even though she understands why it was necessary.

She is pulled from the Doctor's future and brought to his trial by the Master, as a witness, and the Doctor is not entirely sure what to make of her, especially when she enthusiastically calls him Doc (*Trial of a Time Lord 13-14*). She is rude to Glitz, who has also been called as a witness, and treats him with total disinterest – clearly not as susceptible to his false charms as Peri was. She admits she is 'truthful, honest and about as boring as they come,' which is a little disingenuous since, although the former attributes are true, she proves in her encounter with the Vervoids that she is far from boring.

Once the threat is averted, the Doctor is offered the position of President of the High Council and again he refuses, leaving the Time Lord space station with Mel, a companion from his future that he hasn't actually met yet.

The Sixth Doctor
Expanded Universe

Probably more so than any other previous Doctor, the Sixth Doctor's Expanded Universe is, primarily, focussed on fixing the perceived mistakes the television series made with both Peri and Mel. Peri who, as mentioned in the previous chapter, has a very confused ending, whereas Mel has a very confused beginning. Does the Expanded Universe fix this? Yes... and no.

Before we get to the over-complicated post-*Trial of a Time Lord* Peri, we will take a look at her back-story as revealed in several novels and audios. The only child of Paul and Janine Brown, Peri was born in 1966 (her parents were married on 21st November 1962). When Peri was thirteen her father died in a boating accident. Coincidentally, her parents and her stepfather are all archaeologists.

Peri has a habit of leaving the Doctor in the Expanded Universe stories. After the events of *The Reaping* (2005), Peri leaves in tears, unable to deal with the deaths of her friends. She has barely departed the TARDIS though when, in another tragic turn, her mother is killed, leaving her completely alone on Earth. When the Doctor comes back for her, she returns to his side, not wishing to stay on Earth alone.

In the 2004 short story, *Chaos*, included in the *Short Trips: Past Tense* anthology, Peri becomes homesick for 1980s America and leaves to pursue a life in New York City. However, she grows frustrated with her job there and soon quits before rejoining the Doctor.

On television, in *The Trial of a Time Lord*, we discover that Peri did not in fact die on Thoros Beta, and this is explored in the

Expanded Universe, in such stories as the 1996 novel *Bad Therapy* and audio play *Peri and the Piscon Paradox*. Peri and Yrcanos have three children; two sons and a daughter who go on to sire her at least three grandchildren, a few of whom would meet the Doctor and Frobisher in the 1994 comic *The Age of Chaos*. *Peri and the Piscon Paradox* goes into some detail about what exactly happens to Peri following the events of *The Trial of a Time Lord*. It transpires that as a result of Time Lord interference in her timeline there are five versions of Peri: one is, of course, killed in *The Trial of a Time Lord*, another becomes the wife of Yrcanos and a warrior queen on Krontep, while a third can only recall the events of her introductory story, *Planet of Fire*. The fates of the remaining two are somewhat vague although there is speculation that one returns to Earth in *Bad Therapy*. Another version, possibly the fifth, returns to twentieth century Earth with Yrcanos as depicted in the Target novelisation of *The Trial of a Time Lord: Mindwarp*, in which she becomes the manager of Yrcanos the Wrestler.

Bad Therapy shows a highly dissatisfied and stifled Peri, now Queen Gilliam, on Krontep, as she makes a discovery whilst exploring the archaeological ruins of the first king of Krontep. Her discovery is an opportunity to escape, through time and space, by activating crystal globes left by Petruska; the first king's wife. Smothered by her own relationship with Yrcanos, who is obsessively in love with her, she uses the escape route to flee Krontep and return to Earth, where she comes into contact with the Seventh Doctor – it is not a happy reunion, what with Peri slapping him for never returning to her.

In the 1994 Marvel comic, *Age of Chaos*, the Doctor travels to Krontep and finds himself on a quest to track down Peri's grandchildren (Artios and Euthys – her two grandsons who have plunged Krontep into civil war – and her granddaughter, Actis, who is very much like Peri in her temperament and taste for adventure). This particular outing is especially noteworthy as it is written by Colin Baker. His motivation behind writing the story was, according to him, because he felt somewhat responsible for

Peri, and the mistreatment the character received during the making of *The Trial of a Time Lord*.

An older Peri appears in the 2004 audio story, *Her Final Flight*, although this is a virtual-reality Peri created by an enemy in order to try and trick the Doctor into self-destructing the TARDIS. Although she is illusionary, the story explores the relationship between the two and especially the Doctor's guilt on having to abandon Peri some twenty years before.

According to producer John Nathan-Turner in the 1987 reprint of his book *The Companions* (sound familiar?) the original plan for season twenty-four was to open with a story introducing Mel properly, having Mel meet the Doctor for the first time. However, this never came about due to the unfortunate removal of Colin Baker from the role in late 1986. As a result we are left with a companion who never, technically, meets the Doctor. That is until 1988 when Target released the novelisation of the final two episodes of *The Trial of the Time Lord: The Ultimate Foe*. At the end of the book we see the Doctor, directly after leaving the Time Lord space station, dropping Mel off on the planet Oxyveguramosa where his slightly older self is waiting for her. The post-*Trial* Doctor then heads off to his uncertain future, knowing that one day he will not only meet Mel but also become the Valeyard.

This first proper meeting is chronicled in *Business Unusual*, a 1997 novel by Gary Russell, by which time the Doctor has been travelling both alone, and with various other Expanded Universe companions (see page 172). The Doctor spends a lot of the novel trying to avoid Mel, knowing that to meet her means he is on the path that will lead to the Valeyard, but time conspires against him and meet her he does – although he has to go to great lengths to pretend he doesn't know her.

We learn much more about Mel during her Expanded Universe travels with the Sixth Doctor; more than is ever revealed on television. When she meets the Doctor she is twenty-five years old and not only a computer programmer, but a computer genius with a BSc (Hons) in Computer Science. She comes from Pease Pottage, Sussex, 1989, and her full name is Melanie Jane Bush, daughter of Alan and Christine.

There is further biographical information to be gleaned in *Catch-1782*, a 2005 audio drama, where we learn that Mel had a passion for science from an early age and was encouraged by her uncle, Dr John Hallam. She acknowledges his influence and views him as being largely responsible for her later success in academia at university. Hallam, in 2003, tells a colleague, Professor David Munro, about Mel's gifted proficiency with computers. In *The Juggernauts*, a 2005 audio story, we discover that she has an excellent knowledge of the computer languages BASIC, COBOL and FORTAN.

Her home address, 36 Downview Crescent, is often used by Mel when she writes computer code to create a 'backdoor'. She uses it to great effect in *The Juggernauts*, efficiently overriding the Mechanoids' (the eponymous machines) programming.

Mel, it seems, often gets separated from the Doctor. In *Catch-1781*, a freak accident transports her back to 1781, and it is some time before the Doctor is able to rescue her. In *The Juggernauts* she is accidentally left on Lethe and it is three months before the Doctor can retrieve her. A testimony to Mel's strength of character and sheer pragmatism though is the manner in which she is successfully able to blend into, and become a part of, the societies in which she finds herself stranded.

In the 2001 novel *Instruments of Darkness* Mel encounters Evelyn Smythe for the first time, and again, in a contradictory account, in the 2005 audio drama *Thicker Than Water*. In the audio drama, *The Vanity Box* she says it is her one wish to continue travelling with the Doctor; 'I love all this, our lives, racketing about the galaxy.' Unfortunately such a wish was not to come true, as we'll discover in the next chapter...

The Sixth Doctor fares rather well with new companions in the audio plays, with no less than eight people joining him in his travels, as well as the previously mentioned adventures with Peri and Mel. He is joined by companions from his past, in the shape of both Jamie and Zoe, as well as audio-companion Thomas Brewster who travelled with the Fifth Doctor previously. He also meets future companion Charlotte Pollard (see page 219), as well as two who have their own spin-off series, the eponymous *Jago & Litefoot*.

It isn't just returning faces (or voices!) the Sixth Doctor has to contend with, but two brand new companions created for the audio series. The latter of the two is Philippa 'Flip' Jackson, a girl from 2010 London who slips through a temporal fissure, while on the Tube, onto the sentient world of Symbiosis. Despite the Doctor's offer to return her home, she leaves her boyfriend, Jared, in favour of continuing her travels.

The first original-to-audio companion is Evelyn Smythe, who scores a first by being the oldest travelling companion the Doctor has ever had. When the Doctor meets her in 2000, she is a fifty-five-year-old university lecturer, specialising in Tudor history and politics. She is initially disdainful of the 'young' Doctor, waving away his concerns about her missing history, but she eventually accompanies him to 1555 where she meets Queen Mary I. She continues with the Doctor for some time, encountering Charles Darwin and Silurians on the Galapagos Islands in *Bloodtide*, the Brigadier in Cornwall in *The Spectre of Lanyon Moor*, and Daleks on Gallifrey in *The Apocalypse Element*. Up until this point she shows immense joy and fun in her travels, but it is her encounters with Nimrod and the Forge that change all this. In *Project: Twilight* she befriends the young Cassie who has been turned into a vampire, and with the Doctor they find a cure for her. But later in *Project: Lazarus* they discover Cassie has been brainwashed by the Forge and watch as she is killed by Nimrod. This devastates Evelyn, but still she remains with the Doctor in spite of her developing heart condition and falling in love with Justice Rossiter on Vilâg in *Arrangements for War*. However, a return visit to Vilâg sees Evelyn leaving the Doctor for Rossiter.

The Doctor reacts badly, and does not return for another two years, by which time he is travelling with Mel. The Doctor and Evelyn make their peace. She is visited again, this time by the Seventh Doctor, Ace and Hex, in *Death in the Family*, and dies of a heart attack but not before discovering that Cassie is survived by Hex, Cassie's son 'Little Tommy', first mentioned in *Project: Twilight*. The Doctor delivers a eulogy at Evelyn's funeral.

Strangely for *Doctor Who*, the Sixth Doctor only had one companion during his comic adventures in *Doctor Who Magazine* that was exclusive to the Expanded Universe, and that is Frobisher. A wise-cracking Whifferdill, he first appears in *The Shape Shifter* (*issue #88-#89*), having accepted the bounty placed on the Doctor by Josiah W Dogbolter (who is really more interested in the TARDIS – something that continues in *Death's Head issue #8* when the Freelance Peacekeeping Agent Death's Head [already having his own score to settle with the time traveller] accepts the bounty and tracks down the Seventh Doctor), he infiltrates the TARDIS and makes the Doctor's life hell. At the time he was living as Avan Tarklu, but upon joining the Doctor on his travels he takes the name Frobisher because it sounds British and he thinks the Doctor will like it. He takes on the shape of a penguin, and in *Genesis!* (*issue #110*) contracts mono-morphia which prevents him from shifting out of his penguin shape.

It would appear that at some point Peri left the Doctor, since she is later seen to be travelling with both the Doctor and Frobisher. Frobisher himself left the Doctor at least once, long enough for the Doctor to undergo his sixth regeneration since Frobisher appears in *A Cold Day in Hell*, a Seventh Doctor comic strip. It is in this story that Frobisher finally leaves, citing what happened to Peri as a reason (one assumes he was told about her 'death' in *The Trial of a Time Lord*).

Frobisher's popularity among fans is proven by his many return appearances, not only in the comics but in one novel, *Mission: Impractical*, and two Big Finish audio plays, *The Maltese*

Penguin and *The Holy Terror* – all of which are set during his travels with the Sixth Doctor.

The Sixth Doctor also received a few prose-exclusive companions, most notably Grant Markham, created by Steve Lyons in the 1995 novel *Time of Your Life*. Grant comes from 2191 and is a computer programmer; although living in New Tokyo on New Earth he is originally from an Earth colony on Agora. It is unknown how long he travelled with the Doctor, since he only appears in two novels (the second being *Killing Ground* [1996]). In the second story he witnesses his father's death during an unsuccessful attempt at being converted into a Cyberman. He continues with the Doctor after this story, and a man who appears to look like him is featured in the linking material of the anthology *Short Trips: Repercussions* (2004). If it is him, then he ends up stuck travelling the time vortex in a temporal zeppelin with others who can no longer interact on the linear plane, such as Jake Morgan who encountered the Third Doctor and Jeremy Fitzoliver.

The other Expanded Universe companions to travel with the Sixth Doctor do the rare thing of crossing over mediums; UNIT officers Colonel Emily Chaudhry and Lieutenant Will Hoffman appear in both prose and audio, while Jason and Crystal first appear alongside the Sixth Doctor (*and* the Third) in the stage play *The Ultimate Adventure* (1989). The play is later adapted into an audio adventure by Big Finish in 2008, with a sequel called, with great creative panache, *Beyond the Ultimate Adventure* in 2011. As if a stage play and audio adventures aren't enough, Jason and Crystal also appear in one prose story, *Face Value* in the 2000 anthology, *Short Trips and Side Steps*.

The Seventh Doctor
Sylvester McCoy

> *'Every great decision creates ripples.*
> *Like a huge boulder dropped in a lake.'*
> The Doctor – *Remembrance of the Daleks*

Mel – Bonnie Langford, continued... (*The Trial of a Time Lord* to *Dragonfire*)

In *Time and the Rani*, the Doctor's sixth regeneration goes unobserved by his companion (for the first time since his second regeneration), because for reasons uncertain Mel is on the floor of the TARDIS unconscious. The tumultuous buffeting the TARDIS endures as a result of the Rani's attack not only knocks Mel out cold, but it somehow causes the Doctor to regenerate. It is never made clear at which point in Mel's journey we meet her again – although the Doctor's waistcoat and cravat suggest very little time has passed since *The Trial of a Time Lord*, so whether or not the Doctor returned Mel to her correct point in time and he got to meet her in the right order finally, remains unclear on TV. But when she does leave in *Dragonfire* the Doctor says, 'You're going. You've been gone for ages. You're already gone. You're still here. You've just arrived. I haven't even met you yet. It all depends on who you are and how you look at it,' which does suggest that Mel's timeline is as confused as it appears.

She is left in the TARDIS by the Rani, but is later removed by the Lakertyan, Ikona. While being carried across the surface of Lakertya, Mel has enough sense to feign unconsciousness, until Ikona is the most distracted, at which point she causes such a fuss that he loses grip of her and she is able to make her escape.

Unfortunately, this great escape ends in a shocking face-to-face encounter with another Lakertyan, Sarn, who runs away in shock and ends up dying in one of the Rani's bubbletraps – Mel's sadness at her death is only matched later by Feroon's (Sarn's mother) who shuns Mel's sympathy. Despite Ikona's unwillingness to accept that Mel is innocent of what is happening on Lakertya (his people being enslaved by the Rani), she still saves him from one of the Rani's traps, and he accepts that she *might* be telling the truth. Away from the Doctor, who is being coerced into helping the Rani (at this point his memory is affected by both his regeneration and drugs administered by the Rani), Mel seems to be in a state of total shock – quickly shifting from histrionic to just plain dumb. When Mel finds her way to the Doctor she takes some convincing to believe the clowning oaf before her is the man she knew so well – such convincing includes her showing him some of the basic self-defence techniques she knows, throwing him across the lab. It is only when they finally agree to a truce and check each other's pulse that they realise the truth. Mel, who knows about regeneration from his trial, is fascinated by the Doctor's new appearance and personality, and responds favourably to it.

His presence seems to give Mel back her fire. She is all for the Rani getting a taste of her own medicine, after the callous way she has treated the Lakertyans. Before they leave Lakertya, Mel points out that the new Doctor will take some getting used to, but he promises her that he will grow on her. And he is not wrong, as proven when next we see them in *Paradise Towers*, by which point they have clearly settled into a nice playful banter, with the Doctor very happy to indulge her wish to visit the Towers.

After the promise of the video brochure, Mel is distinctly unimpressed by the run-down Towers, and is even more unimpressed by the Kangs – young girls who live in the Towers. They are the polar opposite to Mel – abrasive, rude, abrupt and quite violent. It is a wonderful irony that later in the story, Mel comes across two Ressies (the older residents who also remain in the Towers, when the in-betweeners went off to fight a war). On the surface Tabby and Tilda are exactly the kind of people you would expect Mel to like – they are very welcoming, friendly, polite and conversational. Mel responds, unsurprisingly, very well to them, but totally fails to see the undercurrent running through their conversation. She is, quite literally, being fattened up. It demonstrates the blinkered world view of Mel, and this is only enhanced later when she is 'saved' by Pex – the would-be champion of Paradise Towers (in reality something of a coward). Mel doesn't think much of Pex's bravado and will clearly dump him given the chance – indeed when she does manage to free herself of his company she finds her way back into the clutches of Tabby and Tilda, and still fails to see the truth of these two women, until they have trapped her in a net, and are all set to cook her. This time she does welcome the rescue of Pex, and develops a slight respect for him, not liking the way the Kangs later bully him. Throughout this adventure, her stubborn nature is on display; she is very driven, determined to make her way to the swimming pool at the top of the Towers, where she has agreed to meet the Doctor, and will not let anything prevent her from achieving this.

It seems Mel just doesn't learn to look beyond appearance, as shown in the South Wales holiday camp of Shangri-La in 1959, in *Delta and the Bannermen*. Despite the obvious joyous atmosphere, she looks on the camp with disdain – although this might just be disappointment at their failure to reach Disneyland. She soon adapts though, and throws herself into the swing of things, clearly enjoying the rock 'n' roll – joining in the dancing and the sing-song atmosphere. But her righteous side is on display once more when Gavrok destroys a bus-load of innocent holiday makers in his search for Delta and her daughter, the last Chimeron princess. Despite the threat to her life, Mel cannot contain her righteous fury and is quick witted enough to make Gavrok believe Delta was on the bus. Her ability to make friends quickly is often on display, although she doesn't always seem to be a very good judge of character as proven with Tabby and Tilda. But people do find Mel to be trustworthy, as Delta demonstrates when Mel witnesses the birth of the Chimeron Princess. Mel's own lack of judgement comes to the fore once more on Iceworld, the trading colony on the dark side of Svartos in *Dragonfire*. There they are reunited with Glitz, who fobs them off with some story about how he lost his ship and crew, and procured a treasure map – Mel believes him, but when the truth comes out that he sold his crew she immediately turns her back on him. It is curious that she believes him at all, having seen how spendthrift he is on their previous encounter at the Doctor's trial, this shows how naive and trusting she can be, even when she knows better.

For the first time since the introduction of Mel, her character is finally given some thought when she is paired with Ace (*Dragonfire*) – a sixteen-year-old Londoner who is stranded on Iceworld. Unlike the clean-cut, healthy living Mel, Ace is a rebel – a very strong-willed character who is out for some fun, regardless of the rules she has to be break. Mel is easily led by Ace's excitement, coming across as a prefect who is being misled by the 'bad girl' of the class, brushing with danger for the first time ever – and developing a taste for it. This is no more evident than when Mel is throwing a can of nitro-9, a homemade glycerine-based explosive of Ace's design. There is a clear joy on her face as Ace eggs her on – 'Yeah, Doughnut!' Nonetheless, there are still moments of friction between the two. When Ace takes Mel to her very messy quarters, Mel is clearly disgusted and struggles for a place to sit, until Ace insists she just sit on the clothes. But later, when stuck with Glitz, she happily joins Ace in tag-teaming him with verbal abuse. Despite all this unexpected edginess to Mel, it still comes as something of a surprise when she decides to take her leave of the Doctor, especially as she decides to continue her travels with Glitz – keeping him on the straight and narrow instead, a prospect that doesn't fill Glitz with joy. She quite clearly doesn't care for Glitz at all, so why does she leave? The Doctor is sad to see Mel go, but realises he has no choice. Before leaving though, Mel does suggest that the Doctor take Ace with him – possibly realising the perfect fit they will be together.

If Mel was one of the most under-developed companions ever, then her successor could not have been more different. For the first time in twenty-four years, we met a companion whose back-story was almost as important as the Doctor's. Not since Tom Baker and Elisabeth Sladen had a paring in *Doctor Who* been so successful...

Ace – Sophie Aldred (Dragonfire to Survival)

The first time we see Ace is just before the Doctor and Mel enter the cantina on Iceworld. Ace is right in the thick of it, arguing with Glitz, or 'bilge bag' as she calls him. She is immediately shown to be both moody and argumentative, character traits that will soften during her deepening friendship with the Doctor, her 'Professor'. She hones in on the conversation that Glitz has with the Doctor and Mel, and lets them know that Glitz won the treasure map in a game of cards. She is not convinced by the promise of treasure, but enthusiastically invites herself on the treasure hunt – a better alternative to working as a waitress in a space bar, that much is true.

She finds herself teaming up with Mel, whom she calls 'Doughnut' (nicknames are a thing Ace often uses – usually derogatory – which is not a surprise, really, since she refuses to accept her own real name and goes by a self-assigned nickname). She doesn't take too kindly to Mel's prim ways, but enjoys the challenge of corrupting such an obviously clean-living person, and finds herself opening up to Mel in a way that is clearly unusual for her. She tells Mel her story; that she is sixteen, from Perivale (almost certainly from a time no earlier than 1987 [one of the many badges that adorn her bomber jacket says 1987], and when they visit 1988 in *Silver Nemesis* she checks up on her football team, Charlton Athletic, which suggests that she is near her own time), and was studying Chemistry A-level (and developed her own brand of explosive – nitro-9); during an experiment a time storm whipped up in her bedroom and whisked her off to Iceworld (the origin of this time storm is later revealed in *The Curse of Fenric*).

Ace doesn't actually believe she comes from Earth, and is certain her parents adopted her since her *real* parents would never have given her a 'naff' name like Dorothy. Ace is a young girl very much looking for a place in which to fit. Consequently she is almost seduced into serving Kane, the cold-hearted ruler of Iceworld, but it is only Mel's voice that prevents her from giving in. Despite their obvious differences, Ace bonds with Mel. While Mel is horrified by the bio-mechanoid dragon that guards the treasure, Ace is merely in awe of it. At the end of *Dragonfire* Ace is all set to go with Mel and Glitz, but at the behest of Mel, the Doctor offers Ace a trip around the twelve galaxies en route to Perivale. Ace is very excited about the prospect, even willing to obey his rules, although the rule of calling him 'Doctor' and not 'Professor' doesn't last very long at all. Of course what neither Ace nor the viewer realises at the time is that the Doctor's reasons for taking Ace with him are much darker than anyone would suspect.

When we next see Ace and the Doctor, they have just arrived in London, 1963, in *Remembrance of the Daleks*, and it is quite clear that some time has passed since they left Iceworld. Their bond is extremely well-defined, an easy student-mentor relationship that was barely hinted at in *Dragonfire*. But it is more than that. The Doctor clearly trusts Ace a great deal, and in return Ace has much respect for him. It is also clear that this is Ace's first journey into the past; she has a complete indifference to walking around the streets of 1963 London with a huge ghetto blaster over her shoulder, pumping music that is over twenty years out of time. When she comes across a jukebox in a nearby cafe, she is amused by the music, and immediately takes to Mike Smith (a sergeant in the Intrusion Countermeasures Group – a pre-cursor to UNIT – who are in the area investigating alien activity), who watches her in fascination as she tries to work out the coinage of the time. Later, while walking back towards Coal Hill School, Mike is trying to teach her the pre-decimal system, and Ace has as much trouble understanding it as Susan did in *An Unearthly Child* (a wonderfully clever piece of continuity, since *Remembrance of the Daleks* is set in the same locations as that episode *and* only a month or so later). Once at the junkyard in Totter's Lane, Ace is itching to get in on the action, highly impressed by the weaponry used against the Dalek, even though she considers it unsophisticated.

The Doctor is fully aware of Ace's nitro-9; that she carries several canisters in her rucksack, even though he told her not to. Ace uses it against the Dalek much more successfully than the contemporary weapons used by the army presence.

She can drive, although does have a problem with the choke (something cars in her day no longer have), and is fascinated by the Doctor's history – even though she finds his explanation of Dalek history somewhat confusing. She does, however, instinctively understand the racist ideals of the Daleks, and is repelled by them; something that resonates deeply with her as we discover in several stories, especially *Ghost Light* when we learn she once burned down an old house because of her anger over a racist attack against her best friend, Manisha. This protective anger is also often on display whenever she feels the Doctor is being attacked, be it verbally or physically, as the headmaster of Coal Hill School discovers after he traps the Doctor in the cellar with a Dalek – for his troubles he receives Ace's head in his stomach.

She seems to have an instinctive understanding of most weaponry, easily handling the anti-tank rocket, with which she destroys a Dalek. One thing she doesn't like, though, is being left behind by the Doctor when he decides it is time to wander the streets of London to 'bury' his past – she wants to go with him, but he tells her, 'It's not your past, you haven't been born yet', a statement that pricks the curiosity of Professor Rachel Jensen, but Ace will not explain what he meant, revelling in the mystery as much as the Doctor. She also doesn't have much time for people protecting her (not surprising, since in *Battlefield* she states that protecting the Doctor is *her* job), or being treated like a housewife – for instance when Mike suggests she has something nice cooked for when he, the Doctor and the rest return from dealing with things at the school, her response is to call him a 'scumbag'. Fortunately the Doctor is able to calm her down, asking her to trust him, this she does and remains behind. Although not for long – boredom soon sets in, and when she spots the 'no coloureds' sign in the window, she is incensed and ready to verbally assault Mike's mother, but realises that she cannot blame them for being a product of their time, and goes out for a breath of fresh air instead.

Her earlier indifference to the web of time has unfortunate consequences for her – when she returns to the school to collect her ghetto blaster and comes against a whole Dalek assault squad. She doesn't shy from them, though. 'Who you calling small?' she yells, lashing out with her baseball bat (turned into a powerful weapon by the Hand of Omega). She is rescued by the Doctor and Gilmore's men, although her ghetto blaster doesn't come out in one piece – a fact the Doctor is glad about since its existence could have caused incalculable damage to the timeline. Later, the Doctor explains to her the importance of the Hand of Omega – a remote stellar manipulator – and how it played a part in the formation of Gallifrey and the Time Lords. He even hints that he was there at the beginning, although when Ace picks him up on his slip he tries to cover it up, but realises it is too late. Ace's impulsiveness almost proves a problem when she and the Doctor go Dalek hunting – he has to hold her back several times – and when she later discovers that Mike betrayed them to the Daleks, she takes it very personally. 'I trusted you. I even liked you.' His excuse of trying to keep the outsiders out repulses Ace; she is disgusted by his bigotry which she feels is no better than the viewpoint of the Daleks.

In *The Happiness Patrol* we discover that Ace hates fake and phoney things – muzak, for instance – which, from someone who is so real and raw in her emotions, is hardly surprising. She is initially unimpressed by the Happiness Patrol's 'fun guns', thinking them toys, but upon seeing their firepower she soon wants to handle one. She cannot play the spoons (possibly explaining her disdain at the Doctor playing them in *The Greatest Show in the Galaxy*), and is not good at telling jokes. She is not the performing type – for such a loud, outgoing kind of girl, she is not someone who likes attention. While on Terra Alpha she easily befriends Susan Q – an ex-member of the Happiness Patrol – finding in her a kindred spirit; like Ace, Susan is not part of the team, and has never been one to fit in.

Unlike Mel, Ace is not a fan of junk mail, and is very much against visiting the advertised Psychic Circus in *The Greatest Show in the Galaxy*. She reveals a fear of clowns – another aspect of her hatred of fake things – but the Doctor, instead of simply understanding, coerces her into going with him to the circus, exactly so she can face this fear (this will not be the last time he does such a thing, most notably later in *Ghost Light*).

She is convinced the Doctor has hidden her rucksack, and thus her supply of nitro-9. However she does find it again by the time they reach 1988 in the following story, *Silver Nemesis*. Once on Segonax, the planet on which the Psychic Circus performs, Ace reveals her thing for bikes after seeing Nord the Vandal's. When the Doctor challenges her about the circus, she states that she is scared of nothing, but her reaction to the Chief Clown belies this. The Doctor is surprised to hear her call him 'Doctor', 'Ah so, "Doctor", you *can* remember', but the fact is she often refers to him as such – often when she is stressed or in danger. Once the Doctor defeats the Gods of Ragnarok (responsible for corrupting the Physic Circus), Ace is very impressed to discover that the Doctor had planned their downfall from the moment the junk mail arrived in the TARDIS. She is equally impressed by his plan to defeat the Daleks in *Remembrance of the Daleks*, and will later be so when he wipes out the entire Cybermen fleet in *Silver Nemesis*.

This awe and respect will wane somewhat, however, when he begins to interfere in her life later on.

Like the Doctor, Ace has a great love of jazz, in particular she is a fan of Courtney Pine and enjoys relaxing in a pub garden on a warm November day – that is, until the Doctor's alarm goes off. She finds this irritating, but not as much as when she later learns that the Doctor somehow managed to forget that the world is due to end on November 23rd 1988.

She enjoys being in the vault of Windsor Castle, but is a little worried about being arrested for treason – she is too young to go to the Tower. While running from security officers in the castle, she and the Doctor come across a painting of Ace in nineteenth century dress – from an adventure they are yet to have. For someone who seems so exposed to death during her travels, she is unusually freaked out when she and the Doctor find the dead mathematician in Lady Peinforte's study. As she did twenty-five years previously, as the chronometer flies, in *Silver Nemesis* she learns a whole lot more about the history of the Time Lords and Gallifrey, and discovers that the Doctor was involved, in some capacity, during 'the Dark Time, the Time of Chaos' (echoing his slip up in *Remembrance of the Daleks*). When Lady Peinforte attempts to use this knowledge against the Doctor, Ace is as unconcerned as he, after all she trusts the Doctor implicitly – although at the end of the story she does want one question answered; 'Professor? Doctor... who are you?' She never does find out, of course.

The concept of the Cybermen disturbs her on a very visceral level, and she takes great pleasure in destroying one of the Cyber warships with nitro-9 (also destroying her much-treasured rucksack in the process), and is horrified when the Cybermen then kill the half-converted 'walkmen' simply because she blew up the ship. This anger fuels her later when she holds back a battalion of Cybermen with a catapult and bag of gold coins while the Doctor and the Nemesis statue prepare the final trap.

Once again, the time between seasons (in this case twenty-five

[1988] and twenty-six [1989]) seems a lot longer on screen than in reality, since when we next see Ace she has grown up significantly. She is still the same young girl we knew in the previous stories, but her clothes show a new maturity, which develops gradually in her final four stories. It is notable that she rarely wears her bomber jacket through the twenty-sixth season, except when cold, but she still carries it with her, almost as if she is unwilling to let go of the 'Ace' identity she has created – the word 'Ace' is embroidered, in large letters, on the back of the jacket. Her age is now unclear, but one gets the feeling she is a long way from sixteen now, despite the Doctor not allowing her to drink alcohol in *Battlefield*. They have a new understanding about her use of nitro-9 and the Doctor actively encourages her to use it to uncover a secret entrance to an underground tunnel, after seeing Gallifreyan writing at an archaeological dig. She is aware of Clarke's Law – that any sufficiently advanced form of technology is indistinguishable from magic – and discovers the reverse is also true after encountering the magic of the parallel Earth, Avallion, a world in which the legend of King Arthur is closer to the myth. She pulls the alien sword, Excalibur, from the stone (in truth part of a control mechanism for an organic spaceship hidden beneath Vortigen's Lake) and becomes the Maiden of the Lake. Mixing with the people of legend doesn't phase Ace too much, although she is confused by the idea that the Doctor will, one day, become Merlin. She also meets a legend of the Doctor's life, in the shape of his lives-long friend, retired-Brigadier Alistair Lethbridge-Stewart. She doesn't respond well to the Brigadier initially, who refers to her as the 'latest one', one of many companions he has met over the years. She finds the Brigadier's closeness to the Doctor something of a threat to her position. She does, however, warm to him gradually. She is especially affected by the Brigadier's apparent death, and the effect it has on the Doctor.

She is derisive of Bessie, the Doctor's old car, but as with the Brigadier, soon comes to love it and is seen to drive it at the end of the story. When protected by the force field from Excalibur, Morgaine tries to play mind games against Ace, but the racist attitude it brings out in her soon wakes Ace up, leaving Morgaine to muse that they 'breed their children strong' on Earth.

After telling him about her fear of haunted houses, the Doctor promptly takes Ace to the house in question, Gabriel Chase, in *Ghost Light*. Once again, while they explore Gabriel Chase, Ace carries her jacket like a safety blanket. She has no idea why they are at this house, the Doctor conducting an 'initiative test', allowing Ace to work things out as she goes along. As she is slowly introduced to the house guests, including a big-game hunter whose mind is clearly gone, a butler who is the last surviving example of the extinct Neanderthals, Ace finds herself being more and more creeped out, and she wants out – she thinks the house is an 'asylum, with the patients in charge'. She is not much fussed that her off-the-shoulder top incenses Reverend Ernest Matthews, and easily befriends Gwendoline, the supposed ward of the naturalist, Josiah Samuel Smith. She enjoys corrupting Gwendoline, in much the same way as she did Mel, to the point where they both dress up in gentlemen's formal wear. She discovers from Matthews that she is in Gabriel Chase and freaks out at the Doctor. She feels manipulated by him, and when he tries to coax more information out of her, she resists for a short while, but eventually concedes – to a point. She wants to deal with her terrors in her own way! She later finds herself wearing a contemporary dress, which she initially finds uncomfortable, not to say restricting when she ends up in a brawl with Control.

Much like in *Silver Nemesis*, the Doctor offers Ace the TARDIS key as a way out, but she refuses to accept it because it *is* the easy way out. Eventually she confesses all; that she burned down Gabriel Chase in 1983 when she was thirteen, after white kids had fire bombed Manisha's flat. She stumbled into Gabriel Chase which was full of the evil left over by the events of 1883; haunted by the memory. She learns much about herself during her brief stay at Gabriel Chase, but admits she wishes she had blown up the house instead. She is clearly joking, and the Doctor responds with a tongue-in-cheek 'wicked', a phrase Ace often uses.

Ace's trust, although mildly shaken by the events of *Ghost Light*, is severely tested when they arrive in Northumbria during World War II in *The Curse of Fenric*. Continuing her developing maturity, Ace chooses a contemporary hairstyle and clothes, although she is a little self-conscious about how she appears. Again she carries her jacket with her, and later adds a military issue rucksack to her ensemble. She understands logic diagrams, having really enjoyed computer studies in school – her mathematical knowledge impresses Doctor Judson, a crippled genius, no end. She loves watching the sea, which makes her feel so small, but despite her usual bravery (shown during her rock climbing with evacuees, Phyllis and Jean) she is not stupid enough to go into the water – a fact that later saves her from becoming a haemovore (a vampire-like creature). However, Ace's level of intelligence is called into question somewhat when she meets WREN Kathleen Dudman, and her baby, Audrey. It seems almost unbelievable that Ace would not recognise her own grandmother – did she never hear stories when she was a child about her grandfather who went missing in action? Yet, somehow Ace doesn't see the link between Kathleen; Ace even states that she hates the name Audrey because it is her mother's name. This is compounded later when Ace reads a telegram to Kathleen about her husband being missing in action. Even later, Ace sends Kathleen and the baby to Streatham, to the future home of her Nan (Kathleen herself!). One can only assume that at some point Kathleen remarried and Ace never learned about this. Ace is confused by her loyalty to both Kathleen and Audrey, and seems to care for the baby remarkably quickly. Even the Doctor is surprised by this turn of events. When she later discovers the truth about Audrey, Ace cannot understand how she can love the baby but still hate her mum – she is sure there is something wrong with her. Indeed when she is lined up to be shot, she screams out, 'Mum, I'm sorry!', but when the Doctor questions her about this she refuses to comment.

Amongst the confusion with her mum, Ace finds herself attracted to Russian *Kapitän* Sorin. The attraction is mutual. Sorin finds in Ace the 'spirit of a fighter' and is impressed that she has the Russian Red Army emblem on her jacket. She tells him it is a not a real one – she bought it cheap in a market – so he gives her a real one, as well as his scarf. Angered by the death of Kathleen's husband, and the fact the Doctor clearly knows what is going on but will not say, Ace confronts him and makes him tell her everything. He tells her of Fenric – a creature he once trapped in the Shadow Dimension, but he fails to tell her everything, as she later discovers when he admits she is a Wolf of Fenric, a descendent of the Vikings who stole the flask in which the Doctor trapped the entity. She discovers that her whole life had been manipulated – indeed, sending Kathleen to Streatham, and thus creating her own future, is the start of this, while her arriving in Northumbria in her own past is the endgame. Sorin, also one of the Wolves, is possessed by Fenric and learns the Doctor's secret from Ace, who thinks she was talking to Sorin. Even then, Ace maintains her faith in the Doctor – in fact it is so strong that it creates a psychic barrier which prevents the Doctor from closing his final trap around Fenric. For the Doctor to see his plan come to fruition he needs to demolish Ace's faith in him, and this he does in the most vicious way possible, calling forth every doubt she has ever had. He calls her an emotional cripple, a social misfit who he would not have wasted his time on had he not had a use for her. It is all lies, of course, and it is a testament to Ace's trust in him that she still forgives him. Nonetheless, the Doctor uses Ace for his own ends – a major departure for any *Doctor Who* companion.

After the drama of Fenric and the Doctor's manipulation, Ace just wants to return home, and the Doctor takes her back to Perivale in *Survival*. However, she is not there to see her mother, but to catch up with her friends.

Sergeant Patterson recognises Ace, and informs her that

Audrey has her listed as missing, but he is convinced that Ace doesn't care; otherwise she would make a simple phone call. He is, of course, right but Ace aggressively ignores him and returns her focus to looking for her mates. One such friend, Ange, points out that people thought Ace was dead, either that or she had gone to Birmingham.

She is quickly targeted by the Kitlings, under the guidance of the Master, and transported to the planet of the Cheetah People. There she meets a couple of her old mates, Midge and Shreela. There appears to be a lot of history between Ace and Midge – a rather aggressive history at that. Midge has spent three weeks skulking in the shadows, avoiding direct confrontation with the Cheetah People, but Ace's appearance brings out his aggression – that later leads to his possession by the planet. Ace, too, ends up being influenced and possessed by the nature of the planet, which brings out her baser instincts. She connects with the Cheetah Person, Karra, who we later learn used to be human as well. Curiously, as the connection develops, Karra goes directly for the badge Sorin gave Ace, possibly sensing the deep feeling associated with the badge for Ace. The Doctor lets Ace's possession continue, knowing he needs it to return to Earth and track down the Master – who now shares a psychic link with Ace via the planet.

Upon returning to Earth, Ace states quite clearly that the TARDIS is the only home she has now – her belonging issues resolved. Later, after seeing the Doctor apparently killed in a motorbike accident, she fights to hold in her rage, unconsciously calling on Karra, who promptly appears to scare off the gang who are about to descend on her. Karra is then killed by the Master and Ace finds herself weeping for all she has lost, clinging to the Doctor's hat and umbrella. However when the Doctor returns unharmed, to remove his hat from Ace's head, she shows no surprise, merely a smile of content. She knows that with the Doctor she will always be fine.

The last we see of Ace on television is at the end of *Survival*, walking off with the Doctor towards the TARDIS – home!

There were many plans for Ace had the series continued, but alas the show didn't return for many years, until 1996 in fact, by which point the Seventh Doctor is travelling alone with no hint as to the fate of Ace.

Luckily in *The Sarah Jane Adventures: Death of the Doctor* we do learn from Sarah that Ace returned to Earth, since by 2010 she is going by the name Dorothy (*something*, Sarah adds, drawing attention to that fact that we never learn Ace's surname) and runs the business A Charitable Earth (ACE).

And so, on 6th December 1989, the original twenty-six-year run of *Doctor Who* ended. The next bona fide companion wouldn't appear until the series returned in 2005, although in the interim *Doctor Who* continued in novels and audio dramas, with a plethora of Expanded Universe companions introduced – none of whom have, to date, been mentioned on television. The only character who could have become a bona fide companion was Grace Holloway, who appeared in the 1996 *Television Movie*. Had a new series been picked up, she would have resumed travelling with the Eighth Doctor, but in the event no series was commissioned and so the Eighth Doctor's television companions amounted to zero.

Since the series returned in 2005 we have discovered the fate of several companions, and there is an interesting point to draw from this. Since 2005 every companion associated with the Tenth Doctor has ended up becoming some kind of warrior – willing to do anything to protect Earth, to the point of destroying it, as revealed in *Journey's End*. As Davros says, the Doctor fashions weapons out of people. This wasn't always the case – all his companions pre-Time War have gone on to do their part, but in productive non-destructive ways; from running an orphanage, to developing an international charity organisation, or fighting for aboriginal rights and the planet's ecology, to developing vaccines that have saved millions. The Doctor's legacy continues on in his companions – the friends he leaves behind...

The Seventh Doctor
Expanded Universe

With the non-cancellation of the television series in 1989, it was only a matter of time before something was done to continue the Doctor's adventures. The comic strips in *Doctor Who Magazine* waited for no man and proceeded with companionless adventures, but what of Ace, who was last seen walking towards that big cup of tea in the sky?

Enter Virgin Publishing!

WH Allen, under the Target imprint, had been printing novelisations of the television stories since the early 1970s, and had often broached the idea of publishing original novels based on the series. Only two ever surfaced under the *Companions of Doctor Who* umbrella title; *Harry Sullivan's War* and *Turlough and the Earthlink Dilemma*. But this all changed in 1991, by which time Virgin had purchased WH Allen, when they got the rights from the BBC to publish original *Doctor Who* novels – and so the *New Adventures* were born.

For several years these were the only ongoing stories to feature the Doctor and Ace (interlinked with comic strips at one point), but Big Finish came along in 1999 and launched a new series of audio dramas featuring the Fifth to Seventh Doctors. At first it was a simple matter of linking the two products together, but as time went on it became quite clear that the tales of the Doctor and Ace performed in the Big Finish dramas no longer gelled with those published by Virgin, and latterly by BBC Books.

Over at Virgin, Ace was replaced by original-to-prose companion Professor Bernice Summerfield (a character who proved so popular that she continues to this day, having adventures with Big Finish, twenty years later). Bernice was the first new companion created for Virgin, while at Big Finish the Doctor and Ace were joined by their own brand new companion, Thomas Hector Schofield (Hex, as he was known).

As later companion, Amy, would go on to say; this is where it gets complicated...

As we saw in the Sixth Doctor's Expanded Universe, the character of Mel is well served, the writers enjoying developing her into a strong and well focused character, in a way she never got to be on television. They also enjoyed delving into how Mel joined the Doctor, and fixing the issue surrounding the final moments of *The Trial of a Time Lord*. The writers of the Seventh Doctor Expanded Universe also take it upon themselves to explore what happens to make her leave so suddenly with Glitz at the end of *Dragonfire*.

Before that, though, there is the small matter of her travels with the Seventh Doctor. She doesn't appear in many EU stories with the Seventh Doctor, only appearing in two novels and a handful of audio dramas. Very little new is learned, however, but she does appear in a story that shares a lot of similarities with the 2008 episode *The Fires of Pompeii* – even the title. *The Fires of Vulcan* was released in 2000, and like in the later television episode, it is set during the moments leading up to the eruption of Mount Vesuvius and the death of all those in Pompeii. Learning that they are stuck in a time paradox, the ash-shell of the TARDIS having been discovered in 1980, the Doctor realises they are destined to die with Pompeii. It is Mel who forces the Doctor to consider a way out of the paradox. In a short story called *Special Weapons*, 1999, Mel meets a young man called Oliver during World War II. Still shocked by the death of Pex in the television story *Paradise Towers*, Mel tries to convince him not to fight the Germans, worried he will die needlessly, but regardless of Mel's words he still intends to join the army the following year.

In *Heritage*, published in 2002, we discover that in another timeline Mel never left the TARDIS with Glitz, but instead she stayed on Heritage where she died in the sixty-first century.

However, in the novel *Head Games*, 1995, we do meet Mel some years after she left with Glitz. She explains she parted company with Glitz after six months, and tried to hitch-hike across space, ending on the planet Avalone where she got stuck. The Doctor tells her that he knew she was there, but he thought she had settled. In truth she tried for Earth again, but got kidnapped by the evil 'Dr Who' who imprisoned her in the Land of Fiction. She is disgusted by the way the Doctor has changed since she left, and even though Ace attempts to explain why they have needed to get 'harder', she refuses to speak to the Doctor again. She discovers that he manipulated her to leave him on Iceworld because he knew she was not the kind of companion he needed. Ace agrees to get Mel back home using her time hopper.

The last we see of Mel is in the two-part short story *Missing* published in 1999. Here we learn that Mel often sent her parents postcards whenever the Doctor brought her near her own time, and that they have missed her dearly. She talks to Detective Inspector Bob Lines (previously in the novel *Business Unusual*), who offers to take her the rest of the way home.

Ace, in the Expanded Universe, becomes one of the most storied companions ever. It seems she lives at least three different lives, which are not always easy to reconcile. Her first Expanded Universe life is in the Virgin *New Adventures*, and for four years in the comic strip of *Doctor Who Magazine* which ran concurrently with the novels (from *Fellow Travellers* to *Cuckoo* [*issues #164 - 210]*), which see her becoming Time's Vigilante, while her second is in the comic strip *Ground Zero* that leads to her death, and the third is her audio adventures in which she teams up with Hex and goes through a very different maturing process to that witnessed in the *New Adventures*. Other than a multitude of short stories, the novel authors seem to be disinterested in exploring her journeys with the Doctor during the television seasons, even though there are plenty of gaps to explore, notably between seasons (see the previous chapter for more information on these gaps). Much like

The New Adventures and Big Finish, the BBC Books tend to explore her life post-*Survival*. This causes a problem in trying to reconcile them with the Virgin material, since the *New Adventures* begin after *Survival* and tell Ace's story in a way that allows for no other material. It is, therefore, probably easier to place the BBC Books with the Big Finish audios that lead up to the introduction of Hex. As such, we shall look at those books after the *New Adventures*.

Before that, though, a very quick look at the two novels that do take place during the television series. The first thing of note is that the earlier book, chronologically at least, *Relative Dementias* (2002), explains the two surnames of Ace. Throughout the *New Adventures* and the Big Finish audios it is accepted that her real name is Dorothy McShane (first established in the 1995 novel, *Set Piece*), however in Prime Time (2000) her name is given as Dorothy Gale. To make some kind of sense of this, *Relative Dementias* has Ace explaining that her first and middle names come from *The Wizard of Oz* (as revealed in *Love and War* this was her grandmother's favourite film), thus making her full name Dorothy Gale McShane. In this book we are also shown that she has learned some basic TARDIS operational procedures, enough to cross her own timeline, and has already learned about regeneration. In *The Hollow Men* (1998) we discover that Ace suffers from hay fever and has a very strong dislike for the countryside (which follows, since in *Relative Dementias* she says that at heart she is not a country girl). She carries with her some putty and a small metal disc which, when combined, form to make a powerful explosive. She also screams, when a scarecrow breaks through a door, for the first time since she was ten years old.

THE SEVENTH DOCTOR

Ace Timeline #1: The New Adventures

Ace's first Expanded Universe timeline, the *New Adventures*, presents a version of *Doctor Who* that has grown up with its audience, and explores her growing mistrust of the Doctor, developing his manipulation of her life – first seen in television stories such as *Ghost Light* and *The Curse of Fenric*, and it soon became a case of sex, guns and lock 'n' load...

Ace's television journey makes it quite clear that there are some major issues between her and her mother. With so many hints it is hardly a surprise that her past is explored in so much detail during the *New Adventures* – some might say in *too* much detail. Her mother didn't care much about Ace's school life, and was absent so much that the school arranged for her to get a social worker. Often her mother's various boyfriends would look after her, which tended to mean Ace being around a lot of booze. She usually calls her mother by her name, Audrey, while Audrey tended to call the young Ace 'Dorry'. At school she was called Dotty, and was the object of bullying from Chad Boyle (in one reality he even kills her). Fourteen-year-old Ace idolised singer Johnny Chess (the son of ex-companions Ian & Barbara Chesterton), and after he rejected her attention she resolved to never like someone again without getting to know them first.

Following on from *Survival*, Ace is initially much the same as she was onscreen, fiercely loyal to her 'Professor' and always the first to throw herself into any adventure. Still her love of explosives continues, and in *Timewyrm: Exodus* she creates nitro-9a, much more stable than the previous brand, but half the weight and half the explosive quality. In that story she also takes up arms for the first time, shooting guns and blowing several Nazis away to protect the Doctor. She considers the Doctor her best friend and only family, but in *Timewyrm: Apocalypse* the first chink in their relationship appears, after Ace learns that the Doctor knew Raphael – a young man befriended by Ace on Kirith – would die, and does nothing to prevent it. She finds herself very angry about this, certain the Doctor could have done something. It is the first of many such actions that will, ultimately, pull them apart. Nonetheless she still trusts the Doctor, after visiting his mind in *Timewyrm: Revelation* and learning how tortured he is by his past lives. At this point she is, apparently, in her early twenties, which possibly ties in with the obvious gap between seasons twenty-five and twenty-six. She is sure she is going to travel with the Doctor forever, but this changes in *Nightshade* when she meets Robin Yeadon in 1968.

She falls deeply in love with Robin, a proper innocent, deeply emotional love, and when she decides it is time to stop travelling and remain with Robin, the Doctor refuses to let her go. He *accidentally* materialises the TARDIS on an alien world instead of back on Earth. Ace later meets a much older Robin again in Cheldon Bonniface 2010, in *Happy Endings*, and learns that he spent five months waiting for her before moving on to London. In an odd twist, by 2010 Robin is dating Audrey McShane, Ace's mother, and the two get engaged.

In *Cat Litter* (in *issue #192* of *Doctor Who Magazine*) Ace finds her bedroom deleted by the TARDIS and a new room appears – she wonders why, and the Doctor warns her that something dangerous is coming. Not long after, on the planet Heaven, in *Love and War*, Ace meets a traveller called Jan Rydd. They fall in love, but unlike Robin it is more of a mad, passionate love (one suspects it could be a rebound on Ace's part – certainly by *Lucifer Rising* she doubts her love for Jan and thinks it was an act of rebellion against the Doctor) and they get engaged. Jan is killed by the Hoothi (supposedly mentioned in *The Brain of Morbius*,but it was misheard by author Paul Cornell – should be the Muthi) – an act the Doctor had a huge part in. Ace is beyond unforgiving of the Doctor, even more so when she discovers he had always planned on sacrificing Jan. She accuses the Doctor of being jealous of Jan and how she was going to leave the Doctor for him. She departs the Doctor's company, taking with her a device called a tesseract to remind herself of Jan. The Doctor keeps Ace's bomber jacket, knowing that she will need it again one day.

For Ace it is three years until she next meets the Doctor in *Deceit*, by which time she has become part of Earth's Spacefleet, Special Weapons division. She is hardened and bitter, violence and sex being her currency. She discovers that the Doctor psychically drove her away from him in *Love and War* because he was infected by a protoplasmic virus which infected him on Tír na n-Óg (*Cat's Cradle: Witch Mark*), and he left the tesseract with her so she could contact him when the time was right to remove the virus. She remains with the Doctor to keep him honest, but Bernice Summerfield (an archaeologist who joined the Doctor on Heaven) is unsure about her. Ace, while travelling with the Doctor, was infected with a virus that boosts her immune system and prevents her from getting ill. She now considers the twenty-sixth century her home. While visiting Haiti in 1915 (*White Darkness*) Ace is made to confront her violent tendencies. She shoots a man called Richmann in self defence and continues shooting, emptying her gun, angry and upset over her wounded friend. She throws the gun away in fear of her own future. The violence gets worse in *Shadowmind* when she wipes out the entire command crew of the *Broadsword*, who are possessed by the Umbra, and considers it the worst thing she has done.

Her nitro-9 is further advanced when she develops neo-nitro, small white spheres that are activated with saliva, and later the nitro-9a smart bombs.

In *Time and Time Again* (*DWM issue #207*) while searching for the Key to Time, Ace finds herself in a sword fight with the Third Doctor, and encounters Adric during a fancy dress party at Cranliegh Hall (from *Black Orchid*); Adric tries to make a move on her, and she warns him to stop or he will end up limping away.

In *Birthright* we see the template for what will become a regular feature in *Doctor Who* from 2006 – the Doctor-lite story. In this book, Ace and Bernice have an adventure in Victorian London while the Doctor is off elsewhere. At the end of this adventure, when they see the Doctor again, he claims to have spent the entire time in one of the TARDIS' rooms, but neither women trust him. This distrust of the Doctor is potent enough to feed the Garvond in *The Dimension Riders*, a creature that lives off fear, hate and suspicion. She realises just how much the Doctor stood between her and Robin and then Jan, and remains only to one-up the Doctor. In *No Future*, she totally fails to charm Danny Pain, the front man of '70s punk band, *Plasticine,* which frustrates her – she is not used to being rejected like that. They encounter the Monk (whose name is revealed to be Mortimus), and he offers to take Ace back and save Jan, trying to steal her from the Doctor. Ace refuses, and sides with the Doctor despite her distrust of him. She cheats time and prevents the Brigadier from dying in 1976. We also learn that she often feels like killing herself and she only drinks to make herself feel vulnerable.

In *First Frontier* Ace finally gets to have her second round with the Master, who has used Tzun nanites to remove his corrupted Trakenite DNA (he has been living in a half-Trakenite body since he merged with Tremas in *The Keeper of Traken*) and restore his Time Lord regenerative cycle. Still infected by the Cheetah Planet (*Survival*), Ace is able to detect the Master, and she shoots him in the back, unintentionally causing him to regenerate – an act that wipes out the Master's connection with the Cheetah Planet. At this point she is almost twenty-seven. In *Falls the Shadows* the Doctor and Ace discuss the way she has become hardened since she left him; he is worried about her but she tells him that nothing touches her, and he responds that 'it should'. Despite her bravado, as soon as he is gone, Ace retreats to her room and cries for hours. We also discover that she was born in 1970, which means she must have left Earth fairly early in 1987, before her seventeenth birthday.

Ace finally leaves in *Set Piece*, and remains behind in 1870s France (as first revealed in the novelisation of *The Curse of Fenric*), and we discover it was during her time there that the painting found in Windsor Castle in 1988 (*Silver Nemesis*) was commissioned. She decides to remain to keep an eye on the time rifts, and defend the Commune to save more lives. She takes one of Kadiatu Lethbridge-Stewart's time hoppers. The Doctor, having taken a look at Ace's timeline, always knew this would happen. The Doctor, shortly after, meets a thirty-seven-year-old Ace who is being courted by Count Sorin, the grandfather of Captain Sorin from *The Curse of Fenric*. In *Head Games* it is explicitly stated that the only companions the Seventh Doctor travelled with are Mel, Ace, Bernice, Chris Cwej and Roz Forrester, thereby setting this range completely apart from the Big Finish stories that introduce other companions. Ace's time hopper cannot take her any further than 2001, however in *Happy Endings* she visits Cheldon Bonniface, 2010, for Bernice's wedding to Jason Kane and sleeps with a clone of Jason (later leaving with him). She is reunited with her mother, and Robin, and finally makes her peace with Audrey, promising to visit more often. By this point she is known as Dorothée Sorina-McShane, although she and Count Sorin are no longer together, and they only pretended to be married. She is thirty-one, six years younger than in *Set Piece* when she was being courted by the count – an apparent contradiction. She returns one final time in *Lungbarrow*, the final *New Adventure* for the Seventh Doctor, and discovers that the Doctor originally wanted to enrol her in the Time Lord Academy on Gallifrey (a reference to the intent of the production team had *Doctor Who* continued on television in 1990 – see *Ace's Timeline #2: The Big Finish*). At this point she hasn't seen the Doctor for a year, and still totally believes in him. They depart company as close as they ever were, although both a lot older and wiser.

Ace's Timeline #2: The Big Finish

The loosely linked pentalogy of books comprising *Illegal Alien*, *Matrix, Storm Harvest, Prime Time* and *Loving the Alien* cover a lot of ground for Ace, and it is quite clearly an Ace that has only recently lived through the television story, *Survival*. Indeed, by the second book it is revealed that it has been several months since she and the Doctor left Perivale – immediately putting it at odds with the *New Adventures*. This incompatibility is later compounded when the Master, still heavily infected by his symbiosis with the Cheetah Planet, returns in *Prime Time*, flatly contradicting events established in *First Frontier*. Throughout these books, and the other Seventh Doctor-Ace novels published by BBC Books, it is established that Ace has many sexual partners (including James Dean in *Loving the Alien!*), which doesn't tie in with the list of sexual partners she gives in *Happy Endings*, at which point we discover that Ace lost her virginity to Glitz (at some point prior to *Dragonfire*) and never slept with anyone else until Jan in *Love and War,* after which she left the Doctor for three years. Placing these books in Timeline #2 is relatively easy, for the purposes of this chapter, because *Prime Time* references the audio play *The Genocide Machine*, and *Dust Breeding* is an audio play set shortly after the novel Storm Harvest.

In *Illegal Alien* we see an Ace who still has her trust in the Doctor, and has never used a shotgun. This is also her first encounter with Nazis (thus contradicting *Timewyrm: Exodus*), and she still uses the ghetto blaster built for her by the Doctor in *Silver Nemesis*. She is pushed to her limits in *Matrix* by the Valeyard, the Doctor's dark future incarnation first introduced in *The Trial of a Time Lord*, when he mentally corrupts her into a semi-Cheetah Person. She becomes feral and eats raw meat and blood, and later confronts a full-Cheetah Person version of herself.

In *Storm Harvest* she makes it clear that she has been travelling with the Doctor for three years, but not for much longer; since in *Prime Time* the Doctor learns that Ace is due to die at some point in the near future. He digs up her coffin to confirm that it is Ace as she appears now. Obsessed with discovering how she died, the Doctor and Ace visit 1959 in *Loving the Alien*. She is shot in the head by a man called George Limb. The Doctor is unable to save her, and at her autopsy he discovers that she was pregnant with James Dean's baby. The Doctor ends up travelling with an alternative version of Ace who is hardly any different from the original (as later revealed Ace's death [and that of Sarah in *Bullet Time* and Mel in *Heritage*] is a part of the Council of Eight's war against the Doctor).

In *The Fearmonger* we see Ace is willing to give her life up for the Doctor; when she is convinced he is host to the Fearmonger, she would rather blow them both up than allow the Fearmonger to carry on turning the Doctor into something he isn't. But when she discovers it is actually inside her, enhancing her own fear and paranoia, she finds a way to control it and send it packing. She continues a trait she began in *Remembrance of the Daleks*, using her nitro-9 to dispatch several Daleks in *The Genocide Machine*. They create a duplicate of Ace to help them secure the Library on Kar-Charrat, but water-based inhabitants of the planet short out the duplicate before it can do any real damage. Once again she is pitted against the Master, in *Dust Breeding*, who has had his Trakenite body destroyed by a device called the Warp Core resulting in his returning to his skeletal form last seen in *The Keeper of Traken*, and further drifting from the *New Adventures* timeline. She impresses the prisoners of *Colditz* so much that they go on protests for her. Her loathing for Nazis comes to the fore once again, but seeing the death of Kurtz inside the TARDIS shakes her up so much that she decides it is time for her to grow up and get away from the Ace persona. From this point on she decides she is going to be known as McShane.

Just as she is reeling from the death she has seen, and attempting to become an adult, the Doctor takes her to Ibiza and a fateful meeting with a young man called Liam McShane, in *The Rapture*. Once again we learn that Ace was born in 1970, only this time we're told it was on 20th August (the real world birthday of Ace actress, Sophie Aldred), which further suggests she left 1987 relatively early in the year. Liam is Ace's younger brother by four years – he was taken from her life by their father, Harry, while Ace was in playschool, after he discovered that Audrey was having an affair with Harry's best friend, Jack. This flies in the face of everything established in the *New Adventures*, where there isn't any mention of Ace's siblings, despite the sheer amount of background covered in those books. Ace promises to visit Liam again one day, after initially trying to deny him and their past.

A new companion is introduced in *The Harvest* in the shape of Thomas Hector Schofield, or Hex as he likes to be known. He is a nurse at St Gart's Brookside Hospital, London in 2021. He and Ace immediately strike up a good friendship, and he refuses to call her 'McShane', preferring Ace. We learn that she always aced the multiple-choice tests at school (presumably from where her nickname was derived?), and she has been with the Doctor for 'a surprisingly long time'. By *Live 34* she has reverted back to being called Ace, deciding that it is the name that is 'her'. It also suggests that she is now in her mid-to-late-twenties. Another titbit of information drifts through when we find out that her Nan, Kathleen, died in 1973 when Ace was only three years old. By the time of *The Settling* Hex has found himself drawn to Ace in a romantic way, and although if Ace notices she doesn't reciprocate, in *No Man's Land* she points out that she considers the Doctor and Hex her only family. In *Enemy of the Daleks* Ace shows an unusual amount of tactical and military knowledge, which is more in keeping with her *New Adventures* persona than the version that has been developing in the audio plays.

Things come full circle for Ace in *Gods and Monsters* with the return of Fenric, who has been manipulating events for a while. Fenric reveals that Ace becoming one of his wolves was pure chance, a flip of a coin, and it could have easily been a 'lovelorn motorcyclist from Wales' (an allusion to Ray from *Delta and the Bannermen*, a contender for replacement companion in season twenty-four). Fenric takes Ace back to Perivale, to the day she originally left, and offers her a chance to change history, but she doesn't take it. In a final confrontation, Fenric possesses a dying Hex, but he is surprised by the faith Hex has in his dead mother. In turn Ace has faith in Hex, further weakening Fenric's hold. Hex, intent on sacrificing himself to stop Fenric, asks Ace to open the TARDIS doors so he can throw himself into the time vortex. Ace will not do it, and has to be held back by Sally Morgan while Captain Lysandra Aristides complies. Ace is shocked by this, and refuses to be comforted by anyone; not even by the Doctor. 'Just… don't say anything, Professor. I don't want to hear another word.'

That is the last we hear of Ace in the ongoing Big Finish range, for now. But she does return in a short series of stories based on scripts that would have been part of season twenty-seven had *Doctor Who* continued into 1990. This season, called *The Lost Stories*, comprises *Thin Ice, Crime of the Century, Animal* and *Earth Aid*. The range was overseen by Andrew Cartmel, script editor of *Doctor Who* from 1987 to 1989, and it followed the basic plan of the proposed season twenty-seven, by introducing a new companion in the shape of Raine Creevy. The only plot line not picked up for this series of audios, though, is the Doctor's intent to enrol Ace into the Time Lord Academy, which is how Ace would have been written out in 1990.

Ace's Timeline #3: Ground Zero

Ace's final timeline is an odd one. After years of featuring in the comic strips of *Doctor Who Magazine* in her *New Adventures* persona, she returns to the strip in a story called *Ground Zero*. In this story she is back to her television persona, travelling with an older Seventh Doctor, looking much as he did in the *Television Movie* of 1996. This creates all kind of placement issues in itself, but none so much as the resolution of the story. In the most dramatic moment of the entire five parts, Ace attacks the alien Lorbi with the Doctor's umbrella and a can of nitro-9. She destroys the Lobri, and in so doing kills herself for her 'Professor', leading to the tragic shot of the Doctor on his knees cradling the dead Ace in his arms.

For a Doctor with such a long life in the Expanded Universe, it is no shock to learn that he has more than his fair share of companions beyond the television show. Some have been mentioned above, but here's a quick rundown of the more interesting among them.

The first Expanded Universe companion is Olla, the heat vampire, who appears in the comic strips *A Cold Day in Hell* and *Redemption*. Over in the books, after Bernice joins, and Ace leaves, rejoins and leaves again, comes Chris Cwej and Roz Forrester, two adjudicators (policemen) from thirtieth century Earth. They remain with the Doctor for the latter half of the *New Adventures*, although Roz dies in *So Vile a Sin* and Chris goes on to appear now and then in Bernice's own *New Adventures* series.

In the audio plays, as mentioned, Ace and the Doctor are joined by Hex. Although he apparently dies, certainly from Ace's point of view, he continues to live on in the netherworld of Elder Gods alongside Weyland and Fenric. Next up are Sally and Lysandra, also mentioned previously, who joined the Doctor in the Black TARDIS while Ace and Hex travelled with the Doctor in the White TARDIS. When the TARDISes were combined back into the normal blue Police Box, Sally and Lysandra remain with

Ace and Hex, and were there when Hex apparently sacrifices himself to stop Fenric.

The Doctor is later joined by Doctor Elizabeth Klein, a Nazi scientist from an alternative Earth. The Doctor insists she travel with him to prevent her causing trouble to established history, preferring to keep an eye on her.

The Doctor's most well-known Expanded Universe companion is, without doubt, 'Professor' Bernice Summerfield. Introduced in *Love and War* in 1993, she went on to travel with the Doctor until *Happy Endings* in 1996. She returns several times after, most notably in *The Dying Days* and becomes the first companion to meet the Eighth Doctor; at the end the Doctor drops her off to the planet Dellah where she finally becomes a real professor and begins teaching archaeology in *Oh No It Isn't!* – that is, when she is sober enough. This series of *New Adventures* continues until October 1999 with the publication of *Twilight of the Gods*. But even the cancellation of that series does not keep Bernice down, and Big Finish picks up her story. They had already been adapting some of the books since 1998, but in December 2000 a brand new series of adventures began with *The Secret of Cassandra*. The series still continues today, occasionally featuring other *Doctor Who* elements, including the regular character of Irving Braxiatel, who was first introduced in the novel *Theatre of War* in 1994. Braxiatel is noteworthy because not only is he a Time Lord, a younger version of him appearing in the Big Finish *Gallifrey* series alongside companions Leela and Romana, but he is mentioned in the television series obliquely in *City of Death* in 1979. Like her or hate her, no one can deny the popularity of Bernice Summerfield. She is to the Expanded Universe what Sarah Jane Smith is to the television series; the longest running and, probably, most commercially successful companion ever. Twenty years on, Bernice continues…

The Eighth Doctor
Paul McGann

'I love humans. They always see patterns in things that aren't there.'
The Doctor – *Television Movie*

Not unlike the Seventh Doctor, the Eighth's life existed primarily in print and audio. After the failed *Television Movie* of 1996, starring Paul McGann as the Eighth Doctor, the BBC decided to take back the licence they had given to Virgin Publishing since 1991.

And so, from 1997 to 2005, they published an ongoing series of novels collectively known as the *Eighth Doctor Adventures*. Initially they appeared to be a little 'dumbed down' from the more mature tone of the *New Adventures* published by Virgin, but soon much of the *New Adventures* continuity continued forward into the *Eighth Doctor Adventures* and the tone returned to the previous level of maturity. Due to copyright issues, Grace Holloway, the would-have-been-companion from the *Television Movie* was unable to be used and so the BBC had to create brand new companions for the Eighth Doctor – the first of whom was Samantha Jones. Four more companions followed. But this was only the beginning. Over at Big Finish Productions, things were moving in place to bring Paul McGann back to perform further stories as the Eighth Doctor, and new, exclusive to audio, companions would be needed, but more on that later.

In Prose

First we shall take a look at the initial three print companions, to demonstrate the differing extremes the Eighth Doctor was faced with. There seems to be a trend, at the beginning of the *Eight Doctor Adventures*, to echo the origins of the television series. Sam Jones, for instance, bumps into the Doctor in the junkyard at Totter's Lane and goes to Coal Hill School, much like Ian, Barbara and Susan in the very first television episode, *An Unearthly Child*, while the next companion, Fitz Kreiner, comes from 1963, the year *Doctor Who* began. The third companion, however, breaks the mould, in more ways than one and, intentionally or not, paves the way for concepts that will be seen in the revived series launched in 2005...

Samantha Jones (*The Eight Doctors* to *Longest Day*, and *Dreamstone Moon* to *Interference, Book Two*)

The first companion of the Eighth Doctor (in prose, at least; Izzy Sinclair beat Sam by eight months, appearing in October 1996 in the comic strip of *Doctor Who Magazine*), Sam first appears in June 1997 and departs in August 1999, featuring in twenty-five novels. In many ways she sets the bar for all female companions that will follow, especially those featured in *Doctor Who* since its revival in March 2005.

Sam first comes to the Doctor's attention when she is trying to hide from school drug dealers who believe she has grassed on them; she hides in the junkyard at Totter's Lane and the Doctor arrives, saving her from the criminals. Before she really speaks to him he rushes off in the TARDIS, to appear moments later. Sam enters the TARDIS to avoid questions from the police, and the Doctor tells her he will take her on one trip only. At this time Sam is only sixteen, and a bit of an activist, having taken part in campaigns to save whales, to stop animal experiments and defend gay rights. She is also a vegetarian. A clean living girl, she is initially a bit out of her depth in the Doctor's world, and he drops her off at a Greenpeace rally while he travels for a further three years (with other companions). She remains with the Doctor for ten to eleven months initially, and is faced with the reality of war when she meets the Daleks in *War of the Daleks*, forcing her to re-think her own ideals, 'It's easy to be anti-war when you're not stuck in the middle of one.' Sam always maintains a strong sense of right and wrong throughout her early travels, but finds holding onto such ideals more and more difficult the longer she is with the Doctor (not unlike Donna during the 2008 series). For example, in *Longest Day,* she beats herself senseless rather than shoot two rebels on the planet Hirath. During her initial travels she finds herself falling in love with the Doctor – building on a concept initially hinted at with Grace in the *Television Movie*, and further explored in the Big Finish series with Charley Pollard, and later in the revived television series, in particular with Rose, Martha and Amy.

In *Longest Day*, while performing CPR on the Doctor, Sam finds herself kissing him passionately. Worried about what might happen between her and the Doctor, Sam runs from him. She returns a couple of novels later, but misses the Doctor by a hair's breath, and ends up on the planet Ha'olan in *Seeing I*. She spends three years there, working out her feelings for the Doctor. When they finally meet again, Sam, now aged twenty-one, kisses the Doctor but feels no passion or need to do it again – it seems that she is over him. Nonetheless they continue travelling together, first just the two of them, but later with Fitz Kreiner, who develops his own thing for Sam. She doesn't reciprocate, but in *Unnatural History* this changes for a short while when Sam is erased from history and replaced by 'Dark' Sam. It transpires that Sam was never meant to travel with the Doctor; indeed she should have remained on Earth living a hard life from a London bedsit – a life of drugs, sex and work, the complete opposite to the Sam the Doctor knows. This Dark Sam continues to live while Sam is off with the Doctor. A dimensional scar tears through San Francisco, a result of the events seen in the *Television Movie*, and when Dark Sam falls into it the scar's biodata is split in two, rippling back in time to create another version of Sam. In effect, Sam creates herself.

Intentionally or not, Sam continues to have links to the various other media of *Doctor Who*. In the novel *Revolution Man* she uses the alias 'Evelyn Smith', which is curiously close to the name of Big Finish companion Evelyn Smythe, who does not appear for another year. Her contact with her parents is another interesting link, later echoed in the revived television series. For several years she sends them postcards to reassure them she is OK and well, simply travelling. And, in *Interference* she works alongside Sarah Jane Smith, eventually leaving to live with Sarah a year before she even meets the Doctor. It echoes, in some respects, Sarah's offer to Rose in the television episode *School Reunion*, only in the book series Sam and Sarah remain life-long friends. Sam even attends Sarah's funeral at some point in the future. There is one final link between Sam and the revived television series, in the shape of Martha Jones. Not only do they share the same surname, but when Martha goes undercover to the Pharm in the *Torchwood* episode *Reset*, she uses the alias Samantha Jones.

Fitzgerald 'Fitz' Kreiner (The Taint to Ancestor Cell, and Escape Velocity to The Gallifrey Chronicles)

Not only is Fitz the second companion of the Eighth Doctor, he features in fifty novels, from February 1998 to June 2005, making him the longest serving companion of any medium. Between him and Sam, they cover all but six of the *Eighth Doctor Adventures*. Such is his popularity that he even appears in one Big Finish audio play in the 2009 collection, *The Company of Friends: Fitz's Story*.

When the Doctor meets Fitz, he is twenty-seven years old and working as a florist in his native time of 1963, having dodged National Service. In his spare time he is a guitarist – a very good one – and plays as Fitz Fortune, in an effort to hide his German ancestry (his father is of German descent). He plays on the role of a struggling artist with a 'gammy' leg to gain the sympathy of his audience. He is a heavy smoker, although he does give up once or twice, but never for long, and loves his tea and coffee. His mother, Muriel, lives in a care home but dies as a result of the Benelisa programme, which the Doctor has a hand in. Fitz initially holds this against the Doctor, but eventually comes to terms with it and joins the Doctor and Sam (Sam is not too happy about this at first), as he is now a fugitive wanted for a murder he did not commit. When first meeting Sam he tries to seduce her, and his interest continues for some time, until he is eventually able to bed Dark Sam in *Unnatural History*. His strong libido stays with him throughout his travels and he has many liaisons with several women, but only falls in love with one – Filippa in *Parallel 59*, who he always considers his one true love.

He has little understanding of such things as quantum physics and matter transmitters. Very much a man of his time, he is often out of his depth when visiting future times, but doesn't find 2002 all that different, and is disappointed that it is a far cry from the future promised in the '60s – no flying cars or moving pavements in the sky. Nothing like *The Jetsons* at all, just more of the same. This disappointment eventually turns into a blasé attitude, as he starts to consider himself a seasoned time traveller, a fact he likes to lord over Anji Kapoor, after she joins him and the Doctor in *Escape Velocity*.

He leaves the Doctor's company for two years in *The Revolution Man*, and is brainwashed into becoming an agent for the Chinese Communist Army from 1967 to 1969. Although he overcomes this eventually, he faces a bigger problem in *Interference* when he is stored in The Cold in 1966 and removed from it on the colony world, Ordifica in 2593. With little choice, being so far from the Doctor, he and the survivors of Ordifica join the Faction Paradox. He becomes one of their agents, the Remote, after an attempted suicide at the age of thirty-three fails. He eventually teams up with a woman called Laura Tobin, who he nicknames Compassion, while he is given the name Code-Boy due to his affinity with computer systems. Before leaving Anathema, a planet-sized warship, he places his memories in a Remembrance Tank which eventually creates a replica of him called Kode. Fitz eventually becomes a Father in the Faction Paradox, and lives to become the oldest of the Remote. Father Kreiner, twisted and distorted after hundreds of years, hunts down and kills many Time Lords, and even tries to kill the Third Doctor on Dust. He is eventually trapped in IM Foreman's universe-in-a-bottle. After he is freed in *The Ancestor Cell,* he is convinced to help the Doctor. The Doctor explains that he did not mean to abandon Father Kreiner, he truly believed Fitz had died. He asks the Doctor to change time and stop Fitz from meeting him in 1963, but the Doctor (now travelling with a 'remembered' Fitz) refuses. Father Kreiner is brutally killed by Grandfather Paradox, the ultimate Faction-induced corruption of the Doctor.

Kode, one of the Remote, is recognised by the Doctor as a copy of Fitz, and with a mixture of persuasion and a link to the TARDIS, is 'remembered' back to his Fitz identity, who is just shy of thirty at this point (again). He retains much of Fitz's old memories, but there are gaps. He doesn't always trust his memories, as a result. He finds it difficult to talk to Compassion, his old Remote co-agent, and misses both versions of Sam. He becomes good at anagrams and puzzles, though he never used to be and often wakes up uncertain of his identity. As a result of the TARDIS' part in 'remembering' Fitz, he has a great affinity with the time ship, and often finds himself talking to her – she in turn talks to him through vibrations. He is understandably shocked when the TARDIS is destroyed in *The Shadows of Avalon*, and finds it somewhat awkward when Compassion later becomes the first fully sentient TARDIS. The prospect of travelling *inside* her takes a while to process. Sometime later in *The Ancestor Cell*, when they discover the Edifice – in truth the TARDIS which has rebuilt itself – Fitz finds himself confronted with Father Kreiner, his real self. Kreiner lets Fitz live, to see the truth of the Doctor for himself. To stop the Faction Paradox, and indeed his twisted self, Grandfather Paradox, the Doctor destroys Gallifrey – both he and Fitz are rescued by Compassion. The Doctor, now with no memory of who is or what he has done, is taken to the late nineteenth century to recover for a hundred years. Compassion takes Fitz to 2001, where he has to wait for the Doctor to find him again. He only has to wait a week, while the Doctor lives through over a hundred years of history. When Fitz is reunited with the Doctor he is somewhat unsettled by the fact that the Doctor still has no memory of what he has done. Until his memory is restored, Fitz finds himself in the unusual position of knowing more about the Doctor than he does, and so goes to great lengths to protect him.

He is nervous around strong women, and is not interested in new companion, Anji. He is often looked down on by Anji, because he is from the 1960s and she is from 2001, and so he plays up the role of 'seasoned traveller', which comes across as more patronising than the parting of wisdom. Fitz develops a very deep love for the Doctor over the course of their journeys, becoming very like brothers, something Anji notes on many occasions. Such is the length of time that he spends with the Doctor, that by *Eater of Wasps*, Fitz no longer considers Earth his home, but rather thinks of himself as a 'citizen of the universe', echoing a description the First Doctor once used for himself in *The Daleks' Masterplan*.

He turns thirty-three in *History 101*, the age his original self decided to join the Faction Paradox, and doesn't believe he will make it to forty because of his dangerous life with the Doctor. But he is OK with this. He is, at least, near thirty-five when we last see him in *The Gallifrey Chronicles* by which point Anji has left and Trix MacMillan has joined. While travelling through various alternative realities and watching them be destroyed, Fitz makes a documentary in an effort to try and cope. We later learn that he is actively blocking out many of his pre-remembered memories.

Unfortunately the *Eighth Doctor Adventures* in prose comes to an abrupt end in June 2005, when the final book is published, due to the revived series on television and an upcoming series of ongoing novels featuring the Ninth Doctor. As a result of this, we never reach the end of Fitz's story. We are left with him, now in a relationship with Trix (the first proper couple to live in the TARDIS – foreshadowing Amy & Rory in 2010), and they are both thinking of leaving the Doctor after he has defeated the Vore. Do they leave, do they die? Does Fitz make it to forty? Questions to which we may never know the answer. Although Fitz does return for a one-off audio adventure in 2009, it is set during his travels with Anji, and so tells us nothing that we did not already know. But one thing we do know is that Fitz's influence on the Doctor is far reaching, the first proper male companion since Turlough, and the longest serving companion in any medium – seven years! That alone assures his place in the annals of *Doctor Who* lore, and he ought never be forgotten.

Compassion (Interference, Book One to *The Ancestor Cell*, and *Halflife)*

Never destined to be a straightforward companion, Compassion's influence on the future lore of *Doctor Who* is unmistakable. In many ways she becomes the prototype for what we discover in *The Doctor's Wife* in 2010. Although the idea of fully sentient TARDISes is first introduced in *Alien Bodies* (1997), it is not until Compassion comes along that we discover the origin of these enigmatic machines...

Originally a woman called Laura Tobin, from the human colony on Ordifica, Compassion is the result of Laura's personality and biodata being copied into the Faction Paradox's Remembrance Tanks. She joins the Doctor and Fitz because of her previous connection to Fitz, when he had been her partner in the Remote as Kode. She is very resistant to the Doctor, and refuses to allow him to change her, believing that people can do without his interference. She doesn't believe the Doctor understands the concept of having friends, thinking he treats his companions as pets. Ironic, really, since it is the Doctor who suggests she spends three months on Earth to learn more about humanity.

As a member of the Remote, Compassion always wears an

earpiece through which she receives various signals and media. Upon joining the Doctor, she is told she no longer needs it, but despite the Doctor's advice she continues to wear it. This works out very badly for her, since over a short period of time the connection between her earpiece and the TARDIS has unforeseen effects on her biodata. And in *The Shadows of Avalon* (2000) it is warped along Block Transfer Computations, which turns her into the first sentient TARDIS – a type 102. The President of Gallifrey, Romana, wants Compassion so that the Time Lords can breed a new race of sentient TARDISes for the forthcoming war, but the Doctor, Fitz and Compassion go on the run. The Doctor fits Compassion with a Randomiser in *The Fall of Yquatine* (2000), without telling her, which causes her a great deal of pain initially. She eventually forgives him, and gets used to not being able to control her travels through the time vortex. Due to her chameleon circuit she can take on the form of any species she wishes, however more often than not she appears in her 'default' form, the body of Laura Tobin. Although she is now, technically, immortal, she feels she is dead since becoming a TARDIS. She only sticks with the Doctor and Fitz because she doesn't want to run alone, but that changes when the Doctor destroys Gallifrey and she is no longer hunted by the Time Lords.

She meets Nivet in *The Ancestor Cell* (2000), a technician from Gallifrey, and after he repairs her she decides to travel with him, since she will need an engineer. She returns the Doctor to Earth, with his TARDIS, and deposits Fitz a hundred years in the future.

She continues on her travels with Nivet, and both reappear in *Halflife* (2004). Compassion goes under the guise of Madame Xing and restores a portion of the Doctor's memory; giving him a device that will do the rest of the job should he wish to. She is last seen just before she leaves Espero, disappointed and hoping for another chance to restore the Doctor's memories. Perhaps so she can tell him what he did to her. Either way, as with Fitz, Compassion's story is never finished due to the termination of the *Eighth Doctor Adventures* in 2005.

Other prose-exclusive companions include the aforementioned Anji Kapoor, Trix MacMillan and, in only two short stories, Bazima.

Anji appears in twenty-six novels (*Escape Velocity* [2001] to *Timeless* [2003], returning briefly in the 2005 novel, *The Gallifrey Chronicles*), and one short story, *Notre Dame du Temps* (2003). She is a stockbroker, and a third generation British-Asian. She joins the Doctor after her boyfriend, Dave, is killed during a Kulan invasion of Earth, and leaves when she becomes the legal guardian of the young time-sensitive (and ex-Time Lord, now trapped in the body of a young girl), Chloe. Anji gets engaged to a man called Greg, and keeps in contact with her replacement-companion, Trix, who feeds Anji stock tips.

Trix appears in fifteen novels (*Time Zero* [2002] to *The Gallifrey Chronicles* [2005]). She is a con artist working for the Doctor's rival, Sabbath. The Doctor refuses to allow her into the TARDIS, but she stows away and remains undetected for some time. She is still with the Doctor and Fitz when the Doctor restores Gallifrey, and she and Fitz agree that after the Doctor defeats the Vore they will leave him. Whatever happens to Trix is unknown, since no further novels feature her.

Bazima appears in two short stories, *Nettles* and *Transmission Ends* (both 2008). She is a fashion genegineer and travels with the Doctor on a few adventures, before returning home. She works on a plan to alter the DNA of her own people so they can defeat the Gati, who occupy her planet.

On Audio

Big Finish have been producing audio plays based on *Doctor Who* since 1999, but it isn't until 2001 that Paul McGann makes his first appearance as the Eighth Doctor, for the first time since the 1996 *Television Movie*. For a long period his main travelling companion is Charley Pollard, who stays with him until December 2007. In 2006, however, Big Finish made a new series of Eighth Doctor plays for BBC Radio 7, and for this they needed a new companion. Enter Lucie Miller...

In many respects, because she appears in a co-production with the BBC and is featured in adventures broadcast by the BBC, Lucie carries with her a degree of 'canonicity'. She is as close as the Eighth Doctor gets to having an officially recognised companion (although, like every other companion created for the Expanded Universe she hasn't been referenced on television), and as such it is to her we turn the spotlight next.

Lucie Miller – Sheridan Smith (Blood of the Daleks to To the Death)

Both Lucie's arrival and first scene are not too dissimilar to those of Donna Noble in the television stories *Doomsday* and *The Runaway Bride*. (An unintentional coincidence it turns out, as told by author Steve Lyons, who knew nothing of Donna's first scene until he saw *The Runaway Bride*, which was transmitted barely a week before episode one of *Blood of the Daleks* in December 2006.) Lucie appears suddenly in the TARDIS, with no idea how she got there. She thinks the Doctor has kidnapped her, although he claims himself innocent. As it turns out, she does know why she is there. She makes a slip by calling the Doctor a Time Lord before he reveals this fact to her, at which point the Doctor recognises a perception filter placed around her, to block out some of her memories (a trick Time Lords often use). She tells him that the Time Lords sent her to him for protection, because she saw 'something' that she can't remember. It takes a while for Lucie to warm to the Doctor, who she thinks is a 'patronising git', and only stays with him because she has no choice. But she does promise him that she will leave at the earliest opportunity, something the Doctor looks forward to.

She is nineteen and from Blackpool, 2006. She doesn't smoke, although seems very knowledgeable about indoor lamps, of the sort used for growing cannabis. She has always been close to her Aunt Pat, and when it is revealed in *The Zygon Who Fell to Earth* that the Pat she knew is in fact a Zygon, who used to be Pat's dead husband Trevor, the Doctor keeps it from her. This secret comes back to haunt both the Doctor and Lucie in *Death in Blackpool*, and is the sole reason she leaves him.

The reason behind her placement in 'temporal witness protection' is revealed in *Human Resources*, when Straxus, a Time Lord working for the High Council, explains that he is the one who placed Lucie in the TARDIS after having learned that the CIA (the Celestial Intervention Agency of Gallifrey) have been manipulating her life, believing she will eventually become a dictator in Europe. It turns out, though, that they are mistaken and it is in fact Karen, another young woman who goes for the same job as Lucie. Once this is all revealed, Lucie isn't sure she wants to remain with the Doctor, but comes to the realisation that she actually enjoys his company, and the somewhat irreverent relationship they have. However she only agrees to continue their travels after he first admits that he, too, enjoys her company.

Lucie parts from the Doctor for several weeks after he apparently plummets to his death from the balcony of Morbius' palace. She returns home, believing the Doctor to be dead, crying for days as she tries to accept this. She is targeted by an alien Headhunter, and meets the Doctor again on the planet Orbis – six-hundred years having passed for him and he has forgotten who he is. A slap from Lucie restores his memories, due to the chronon particles on Lucie's fingertips. They resume their travels, once again falling into their usual banter and mutual teasing.

On their travels Lucie encounters many foes from the Doctor's past, especially those who encountered him during his first three incarnations, including Daleks, the Monk, Cybermen, Morbius, the Krynoids and the Giant Spiders of Metebelis Three. It is in encountering the latter that Lucie shows her real strength when her body is taken over by the Eight Legs' Queen (much like Sarah was in *Planet of the Spiders*). She struggles against the Queen and learns of her secret link to a Gallifreyan remote stellar manipulator, inside which the Queen has created a virtual space.

Lucie is able to take her own mind there, and use it to contact the Doctor. To save Lucie and stop the Eight Legs, the Doctor transfers Lucie's mind into the TARDIS' telepathic circuits, before using a blue crystal from Metebelis Three to return Lucie's mind to her own body.

Lucie's faith in the Doctor is shattered when they spend Christmas 2009 in Blackpool with her Aunt Pat. She finally discovers the truth about Pat. Although she understands the reason behind the deceit, after Zygon-Pat dies, Lucie finds she cannot forgive the Doctor for the lie and leaves him, deciding to travel around Europe for a time.

At some point in 2010 Lucie joins the Monk (last seen on television in 1965's *The Daleks' Masterplan*), after responding to an ad he placed in a paper for a new companion for the Doctor. It is uncertain how much time they spend together, but she goes on record as saying he is a 'homicidal maniac' and he kicks her out after she refuses to allow him to retroactively kill someone by ensuring said person is never born. She joins the Doctor once again, but only because he promises to give her a better Christmas than the one she had the previous year.

They spend time with Susan, the Doctor's granddaughter, and Alex, his great-grandson, whom Lucie becomes particularly fond of. Lucie returns to Alex's native time, the late twenty-second century, and travels Europe with him to see how humanity has rebuilt following the defeat of the Daleks in 2164 (*The Dalek Invasion of Earth*). While in Thailand a sickness breaks out, engineered by the Daleks. Lucie contracts the sickness, and although it does not kill her, it does cause her to lose an eye and cripples her. Realising she needs the Doctor's help, she summons him back to Earth but he arrives too late – Earth is once again occupied by the Daleks and Lucie, Alex and Susan have joined resistance fighters. Alex is killed by the Daleks while placing a bomb – an incident that leads Lucie to commit herself to a suicide mission that will save the Earth. She flies a Dalek saucer to the core of the planet and destroys the Daleks' time warp engine –

killing herself in the process. Her death drives the Doctor to realise that he has always been too easy on the Daleks, and is determined to take the war to them (possibly leading to the Last Great Time War – the results of which are felt throughout the revived television series from 2005 onwards). He vows that one day, regardless of the Web of Time, he will travel back and prevent Lucie's death...

Other companions created for Big Finish audio plays include Charley Pollard, C'rizz, Gemma & Samson Griffin, Mary Shelley, Tamsin Drew and Molly O'Sullivan.

Charlotte 'Charley' Pollard features in twenty-eight radio plays with the Eighth Doctor (*Storm Warning* [2001] to *The Girl Who Never Was* [2007] and returns for *Solitaire* [2010]), and again with the Sixth Doctor (*The Condemned* [2008] to *Blue Forgotten Planet* [2009]). She is a self-professed Edwardian Adventuress, and is saved from the destruction of the airship R101 by the Doctor in 1930. It transpires that she was supposed to die, and as a result she becomes a temporal anomaly, and is used by the Neverpeople of the Anti-time Universe to break through into the normal universe. The Doctor refuses to sacrifice Charley in order to save the universe. Charley develops a deep romantic love for the Doctor, but learns to accept that these feelings will never truly be reciprocated. For a time she travels with C'rizz, and after his death she asks the Doctor to take her home, however she becomes stranded in the year 500,002. She holds onto the hope that the Doctor survived, and will return for her, but when the TARDIS does finally arrive it brings with it the Sixth Doctor. To preserve the Web of Time, Charley has to pretend not to know him. They travel together through several adventures before Charley is infected with a virus which enables an entity called Mila to shift Charley out of phase and take her place by the Doctor's side. After Mila sacrifices herself to save Earth, Charley reveals her secret to the Doctor. Still believing that he will ultimately die as a consequence of knowing her, she uses memory-altering technology to convince the Doctor that he only ever travelled with Mila and not Charley.

C'rizz travels with the Doctor for fourteen adventures (*The Creed of the Kromon* [2004] to *Absolution* [2007]). He is a Eutermesan from Bortresoye in the Divergent Universe, and joins the Doctor and Charley after he is forced to kill his wife who has been genetically altered by the Kromon. He is still with them when they finally break free into the real universe again, and continues with them for a further series of adventures, all the while seeking the Doctor's help in fixing his emotional wounds. Like all Eutermaseans he is an emotional chameleon, and is subject to the moods of those around him. He dies after being granted incredible psychic powers, which exhaust him and turn his body to dust.

Gemma and Samson Griffin only actually appear in one audio story (*Terror Firma* [2005]) and a couple of short stories. They meet the Doctor in Folkestone Library and follow him into the TARDIS. They have several adventures, and are left in 1816 while the Doctor investigates a distress call. They resume their travels with the Doctor, after he travels with Mary Shelley, until they arrive on the time cruiser, Nekkistani, where they meet Davros (who takes control of their minds). He attempts to use Samson against the Doctor, but once beaten, the Doctor frees Samson from the Daleks' control. The Doctor continues his travels with Charley and C'rizz once Samson and Gemma have been reunited.

Mary Shelley appears in four audio adventures (*Mary's Story* [2009] to *Army of Death* [2011]). She meets the Doctor in 1816, seeing him apparently coming back to life (no doubt inspiring aspects of *Frankenstein*), and joins him in his travels for an unknown period of time. She leaves him eventually after an encounter with the Bone Lord, and realises she is fearful of the Doctor's one constant companion, death.

Tamsin Drew appears in seven audio adventures (*Situation Vacant* [2010] to *To the Death* [2011]). She meets the Doctor by answering an ad for a new companion. We later discover that the ad has actually been placed by the Monk. She fails in her audition, but is later saved since the other contenders want to join him for nefarious purposes. They have several adventures together before arriving on the Martian moon, Deimos. She leaves the Doctor because he will not sacrifice Lucie to save thousands of humans on Mars, and takes up travelling with the Monk who convinces her that the Doctor is evil. During the Daleks' second invasion of Earth, she discovers the part the Monk plays in the invasion and sides with the Doctor, Lucie, Susan and Alex. Like so many of the Eighth Doctor's companions she, too, is killed, after sacrificing her life to save the Earth.

Molly O'Sullivan features in the four audio adventures that comprise the *Dark Eyes* tetralogy on 2012. Hailing from Ireland, Molly is a Voluntary Aid Detachment nursing assistant in France during the First World War. She calls the TARDIS a Tardy-Box, and constantly refers to the Doctor as 'the Doctor' instead of simply 'Doctor'. Following an old running gag from television, Molly believes Gallifrey is in Ireland, and constantly refers to it as 'Galilee'. She is something of a mystery initially, having eyes darker than anyone on Earth, and recognising the TARDIS interior the first time she enters, as if she has been in there before.

In Comics

Although the novels and audios are largely regarded as the primary source material for the Eighth Doctor's adventures (even though both have gone to great lengths to say that each range exists in parallel universes to each other), there is, as with all the other Doctors, a third source of material. The comic strip from *Doctor Who Magazine* which ran from 1996 to 2005.

Throughout this run the Doctor is accompanied by a plethora of companions, including the first legitimate LGBT companion, Izzy Sinclair, who is introduced in 1996 – nine years before the arrival of Jack Harkness on television. For a period she switches bodies with Destrii, an amphibious alien, but is eventually restored to her human form and returned to Earth in the exact same moment she leaves. Like Fitz, she also appears in one audio play from Big Finish, in 2009's *The Company of Friends: Izzy's Story*.

Fey Truscott-Sade is an undercover agent for the British government, encountering the Doctor off-panel, and is later used by the Threshold against the Doctor. Along the way she temporarily merges with the alien entity called Shayde, to become Feyde. She resumes her service for the British government, often working alongside Shayde. There is also a short-lived romance between Izzy and Fey, but it is never made clear if she is a lesbian or bi-sexual.

Kroton is one of the more unusual companions ever – a Cyberman who has retained his emotions. He first appears in a back-up strip of *Doctor Who Weekly* in 1979, returning once the following year. This soulful Cyberman is never forgotten, however, and he returns again in 1999 in *Doctor Who Magazine* in a story that sees him battling Sontarans. He joins the Doctor and Izzy later that year in *The Company of Thieves* in *issue #284*, and remains with them until *issue #296* and the final instalment of *The Glorious Dead*. He left the Doctor and Izzy to become the new centre of the Omniversal Spectrum.

The only other comic companions that count, in so much as they cross stories, are Stacy Townsend and Ssard. They begin their lives in the pages of *Radio Times* (1996-1997), and later feature in the 1998 novel *The Placebo Effect*. Stacy meets the Doctor after the Cybermen have attacked her space haulage freighter and converted her fiancé, Bill. She joins the Doctor on his travels, and later meets Ssard on Mars, who, after dealing with the treachery of High Lord Artix, accepts the Doctor's offer of a holiday. Stacy and Ssard leave the Doctor at the same time, and eventually become engaged. Later, they invite the Doctor to their wedding, and he attends with Sam Jones.

The Ninth Doctor
Christopher Eccleston

'You were fantastic. And, you know what? So was I!'
The Doctor – *The Parting of the Ways*

Suffering from survivor's guilt, a battle-hardened Doctor returns after having disappeared during the Last Great Time War. Sad and lonely in ways he has never been before, the Doctor has lost touch with his emotions; along with the reason why he travels. He is in need of a new companion, someone who can remind him of what he used to be. Enter Rose Tyler...

Rose Tyler – Billie Piper (Rose to *Doomsday* and *Partners in Crime,* and *Turn Left* to *Journey's End,* plus *The End of Time)*

On the surface Rose appears to be a very different kind of companion from those we have been used to, but when you consider her character, she is essentially a combination of Tegan and Ace. Much like Tegan she is given a TARDIS key; we see a lot of her family; and we see her leave and return. Much like Ace she develops a deep love for the Doctor, she is from a London council estate and her back-story is almost as important as the Doctor's, driving much of the ongoing narrative of the 2005-2006 series. In the pitch document, partly printed in the *Series One Companion* (*Doctor Who Magazine Special*), we are told that 'she loves [the Doctor], and he loves her. Simple as that. Not a kissy-kissy kind of love, this is *deeper*'.

Rose actually meets the Doctor earlier than she knew. In *The End of Time*, just after midnight on 1st January 2005, she is walking home from a party with her mother and notices the Tenth Doctor

223

standing in the shadows. She confuses him for a drunken party goer and tells him the year. He tells her that it will be a fantastic year – knowing full well that in March they are due to meet for the first time.

When we first meet Rose in the eponymous episode, she is working as a sales assistant in a department store called Henriks, living at home with her mother and dating Mickey Smith (although judging by the dismissive way she is with him, it does comes across as if she is merely making do, waiting for something better to come along). Upon finding the mannequins in the basement of Henriks coming to life, Rose thinks she has become the victim of a student prank, until they start attacking her – at which point a hand reaches out and grabs hold of hers. She is immediately running with the Doctor, barely having a chance to find out who this mysterious man is before he blows up her place of work. Rose resigns herself to losing her job very quickly and ends up loafing around home with nothing better to do. Even Mickey's enthusiasm over a football match fails to excite her, until the Doctor appears at her house, having followed an Auton arm there. She drags him into the flat, wanting to know more about the night before, but his answers only confuse her more. They are both attacked by the Auton arm, and she follows him out of the flat. The Doctor is impressed by her curiosity, and the ease with which she handles his answers, but he still remains distant from her. She, however, cannot get him out of her head and tries to find out more about him on the internet. This leads her to a man called Clive who collects stories about the Doctor. She becomes totally distracted and doesn't notice that Mickey is very clearly a plastic replica. The Doctor reappears and, amidst the chaos, removes the Auton-Mickey's head. Rose manages to activate the fire alarm, thus evacuating the restaurant safely. She realises that Clive is right; the Doctor is clearly a dangerous man, yet still she follows him into the TARDIS, after a moment's hesitation, and is stunned by the interior. Despite her shock, she is still concerned that Mickey may now be dead. She is annoyed that the Doctor doesn't seem to care about this. The Doctor confronts the Nestene Consciousness, and it is Rose who actually saves the day. He then offers her the chance to travel with him, but she refuses, feeling obligated to look after Mickey, who is now a gibbering mess after his Auton encounter. The Doctor says goodbye, and Rose is left alone with Mickey, clearly already regretting her decision. However, when the TARDIS returns seconds later, and the Doctor mentions it travels in time, Rose barely hesitates and runs inside, no longer giving Mickey a second thought.

The Doctor takes her to the year five billion and Platform One to witness *The End of the World*. She appears to take the plethora of alien dignitaries in her stride, at least initially, but she is quite obviously overwhelmed at the same time. While the Doctor goes off with the sentient tree, Jabe, Rose takes a bit of time out on her own to acclimatise. Her attraction to the Doctor is obvious in this story – there is a hint of jealousy when the Doctor goes off with Jabe (a sign of things to come). Rose can be quite scatty, making very bitchy and sarcastic comments when she feels she is under attack – a good example can be seen during her encounter with Cassandra, the so-called last human. She also encounters, in this story, someone who would go on to become very important to her: the Face of Boe (see the entry for *Jack Harkness* page 280). At the end of this first journey she is saddened to learn that no-one noticed the end of her planet because of the machinations of Cassandra. To cheer her up the Doctor returns to her own time to demonstrate the nature of time travel. With billions of years of life left on Earth they go and get some chips; something Rose later refers to as their first date.

After taking her to the future, the Doctor promises her a trip to the past. Naturally the Doctor gets the time and place wrong, but Rose doesn't care. She is simply amazed that it is Christmas Day all over again. Upon stepping out of the TARDIS in *The Unquiet Dead*, after taking great pleasure in changing into nineteenth century dress, she carefully places her foot into the snow, amazed by the idea of travelling into the past. With her usual bravery she chases after Sneed and Gwyneth, who appear to be stealing a dead body from the Palace Theatre, but Sneed is really an undertaker and the body has been reanimated by a Gelth, a gaseous life form.

For her troubles she is chloroformed and shoved into the hearse, only to later awake in the undertakers being menaced by a zombie, another Gelth reanimated corpse. Although clearly in fear for her life, she responds with sarcasm and gusto. She meets Charles Dickens, who is now assisting the Doctor, but barely acknowledges him – although she is aware of him, she is clearly not a fan and is unfamiliar with his works. She bonds quickly with Gwyneth although, much like Ace in *The Curse of Fenric*, she displays quite a degree of social ignorance when talking about boys – Gwyneth thinks Rose talks like a 'wild thing', a remark that Rose is clearly insulted by initially. Rose brings Gwyneth out of her shell a little, but Gwyneth's psychic abilities (enhanced by the Time Rift that runs through the heart of Cardiff) enable her to see into Rose's mind and she gets more than she bargained for, including the knowledge that Rose considers her stupid. Gwyneth also sees in Rose 'the Big Bad Wolf', an allusion to her forthcoming encounter with the time vortex in *The Parting of the Ways*. Her own sense of morality comes into play later when the Doctor suggests that allowing the Gelth to use dead bodies to save them just might work. Rose tells him that this is wrong, until he confronts her with the analogy of a donor card, 'It's a different morality', the Doctor responds. Despite this Rose insists that Gwyneth should not be used to mediate with the Gelth. As they are surrounded by the animated corpses Rose and the Doctor make their peace. Rose tells him that she is so glad she met him, and he returns the sentiment.

The Doctor takes Rose home in *Aliens of London*, promising that she will arrive twelve hours after she left. This amazes her – to think she has experienced so much in only twelve hours – but upon returning to the flat she is met by a stunned Jackie (her mother), who bursts into tears. Rose doesn't understand such a reaction; it is as though she hasn't stopped out before.

Then the Doctor enters the flat and explains that it hasn't been twelve hours, rather twelve *months*. It is now March 2006! Rose has been gone a whole year.

In the intervening months Mickey has been accused of murdering Rose, and is now something of a pariah on the Powell Estate. The police arrive to question both the Doctor and Rose, who can only explain that they have been travelling together. Everyone suspects a sexual relationship, but this idea clearly embarrasses Rose, but not as much as Jackie who slaps the Doctor. Later when she finds out that the Doctor is nine-hundred years old, Rose comments that her mother is right; it is quite an age gap.

It is now becoming clear that the Doctor is also falling for Rose – her passion and enthusiasm reminds him of the man he used to be. Unfortunately such a connection has a price, one that becomes more evident as time progresses. Considering that Mickey waited a whole year for her, Rose is incredibly dismissive of him. She is much more concerned that the Doctor might have left her (even though he gave her a TARDIS key to prove that he will return) than the fact that Mickey has learned all about the Doctor in the intervening year. Mickey calls the Doctor Rose's new 'boyfriend', but Rose says the Doctor is more than that – he is much more important. In a quiet moment in the TARDIS, while the Doctor observes the news of the supposed first alien contact, Rose admits that she did miss Mickey, and although Mickey buys it, it is clear she is lying. She has never given Mickey a second thought once she stepped in the TARDIS at the end of *Rose*. She doesn't much care for Mickey being involved – when he is explaining about the Doctor's past with UNIT, Rose throws him a look of derision. He is definitely not welcome in Rose's new world. Despite this, Rose's concern for others is on display when she reaches Downing Street and sees how upset Harriet Jones, MP for Flydale North (yes, you know who she is), is over witnessing a Slitheen kill and skin a man. After Rose suggests blowing up Downing Street to stop the Slitheen, Harriet points out that she is a very violent young woman, but Rose doesn't care, she has faith that the Doctor will do whatever is necessary to save them all; even if it means sacrificing them in the process. Jackie implores the Doctor to consider Rose, but Rose is adamant that her life is unimportant. Once the Slitheen are defeated, and Rose is enticed back to the TARDIS, Jackie points out how infatuated she is with him. Rose denies it, but is soon packing her bags to continue her travels. Once again she leaves Jackie and Mickey to worry – they both know now how dangerous life with the Doctor can be.

In the next story, *Dalek*, we see a blatant example of how fickle a girl Rose really is. In this, she meets a young genius, Adam Mitchell, working in Henry van Statten's underground base in Utah, 2012 (six years in her future). She finds that Adam reminds her somewhat of the Doctor, and draws close to him (*The Long Game*). It seems that Rose is still not entirely certain about her feelings for the Doctor – or perhaps she doesn't think they are being fully reciprocated – and as a result she hooks on to the closest alternative. As with Mickey, she appears to be settling for second best until she can have the man of her dreams – the Doctor. Such a mercurial trait is further expanded upon when she meets Jack in *The Empty Child*.

Still, her sympathetic nature is on display when she hears the sound of the 'Metaltron' being tortured, and demands that Adam take her to see it. At this point she knows nothing of the Daleks and their part in the Last Great Time War (but she soon discovers it all), and fails to realise that the Dalek is manipulating her when it talks of its pain. She reaches out to comfort it, and in so doing gives it the chronon energy (a safe radiation picked up through travelling in the time vortex) it needs to rebuild itself. Later when she is trapped by the Dalek, and the Doctor blames himself, Rose tells him 'it wasn't your fault', a further example of her concern for the emotional well-being of others. The Dalek gets more than it bargained for by sampling Rose's DNA, and picks up some of her compassion, to the point where she is able to talk the Dalek out of killing, and even assists it in committing suicide, rather than live on as the last of its kind. When the Doctor confronts the Dalek, armed with a gun, Rose is shocked by what the Doctor has become – the Dalek merely wants to feel the warmth of the sun on its skin (it has opened up its outer casing to show the mutated Kaled form inside), but the Doctor is determined to kill it. Rose thinks it is the Doctor who has become the monster. Her horror and shock snaps the Doctor out of his rage, and he is unable to express himself clearly, such is the emotional damage done to him by the events of the Time War.

With Adam in tow they arrive on Satellite 5 (*The Long Game*). Rose initially finds Adam's awe amusing, until he faints at the site of Earth as seen from an observation window. The Doctor points out that Adam's *her* boyfriend, and Rose looks at the unconscious Adam dismissively; 'not anymore,' she says.

A curious, and almost inexplicable, thing happens at the end of this story. Adam is found to be using technology from the year 200,000 to profit himself when he returns to 2012 – the Doctor is greatly angered by this and promptly returns Adam home, complete with the cranial port that opens a hole in his forehead to his brain. The Doctor claims he only takes the best, a moment of pride for Rose. She seems uncertain about leaving Adam behind, but the Doctor's comment settles it for her, and she rather smugly returns to the TARDIS with the Doctor.

It is odd that the Doctor should treat Adam in such a way, since what Rose does in the next story (*Father's Day*) is arguably much worse than trying to make a quick buck with knowledge of the future. Rose tells the Doctor the story of her father's death in 1987, and asks him to take her back there so that he will not die alone. The Doctor is a little unsure, but soon agrees – an unusual move for him, since it must be clear to him what is going to happen. In the first instance Rose freezes, and is unable to do anything but watch Pete Tyler get mowed down by a car, but once she has recovered from the shock she asks to try again. The Doctor warns her against this. It will be even more dangerous this time as there will be two versions of Rose. Rose says she understands, but that doesn't stop her from running out and pushing her dad out of the way – watched by the earlier Rose and Doctor, who promptly vanish from existence. The Doctor is very angry at her, since she has made a radical alteration to the timeline, but Rose fails to see how having Pete alive is a bad thing. The Doctor confronts her, accusing her of planning this as soon as she learned the TARDIS was a time machine; she refutes the accusation of course, saying that the Doctor just doesn't like the idea that there is someone else more important to her than him. It is a scathing comment, born of anger and hurt, probably because the Doctor is right. Nonetheless, when the Doctor storms off, having taken the TARDIS key from her, Rose pushes aside her hurt in favour of the joy of being with her dad. Seeing the reality of her parents' marriage is a shock to her – they are not the happy, hopelessly in love couple Jackie always told her about, but rather two people who are lumbered with each other, constantly arguing, her mother bitter at Pete's get-rich-quick schemes. Pete's existence threatens the timeline and calls forth the Reapers, creatures who eat the chronon energies created by the rupture in the timeline. The Doctor returns. Rose is so happy to see him and there is no doubt how much she loves him. It takes Pete a while to work out who Rose is, and when he does, Rose is overwhelmed at finally meeting her dad properly – just calling him 'dad' brings her to tears. Pete realises the only way to fix things is for him to die – despite Rose pretending he is still alive in the future; the story she tells him is of a man that he will never be – and so he runs out in front of the car, restoring the timeline. Rose holds his hands while he dies, watched from a distance by Jackie who, we later learn (in *The Parting of the Ways*), doesn't remember any of the events of this story save that a strange blonde girl held Pete's hand while he died.

Arriving in 1941 at the height of the London Blitz, having followed a Chula spaceship to Earth, Rose is disappointed that the Doctor will not give her a 'bit of Spock' and scan for alien tech, instead of doing his usual hands-on kind of search. It seems a bit odd that she should be so concerned about such a thing at this point in her travels, having seen how effective the Doctor's standard method is. She finds herself hanging from a barrage balloon, having wandered off to follow the cries of a child in the darkened back allies, with a Union Flag t-shirt on full display. Fortunately, as the planes come towards her, she is saved by Captain Jack Harkness, a former Time Agent from the fifty-first century, who is responsible for throwing the Chula ship at them in the vortex. She responds to Jack's easy ways with some outrageous flirting; she even unintentionally prints his psychic paper with '*very* available', even though she considers Mickey an occasional boyfriend. Once more she is uncontrollably fickle. It is easy to see why in this instance, since Jack's charm and easy nature completely bewitches her – such is the way of this fifty-first century guy. While discussing terms of sale (in truth a con run by Jack – as he later admits once the Doctor explains to him the reality of what Jack's unleashed on Earth) – they share a dance atop Jack's invisible Chula ship which is tethered to Big Ben. When Jack uses his multi-purpose vortex manipulator to scan for alien technology Rose is impressed – finally a professional. She is amused later when, after the Doctor and Jack meet, they argue over the Doctor's sonic screwdriver and Jack's sonic 'squareness' gun – sonic envy – but it is Rose that saves the day, using Jack's gun to create a hole by which they can escape. The Doctor displays a little jealousy over Rose's appreciation for Jack, and is annoyed that she assumes he doesn't 'dance' (a euphemism for being sexually active), but is later amused by Rose's dismay at learning that Jack 'dances' with everyone regardless of gender or species. Among all this innuendo and flirting, Rose shares a quiet moment with Nancy, a young woman who helps the homeless kids of London, and reassures her that the future will work out fine – indeed, that Germany will lose the war. It is a nice moment and somewhat reminiscent of a moment between Ace and Wainwright in *The Curse of Fenric*, also during World War II, when Wainwright worries about the outcome of the war. After saving everyone, the Doctor and Rose save one final person – Jack, and invite him to join them, which he does, standing aside laughing as the Doctor and Rose dance around the control console in the TARDIS.

When we next see her, in *Boom Town*, it is quite clear that some time has passed since they rescued Jack. The three of them have settled into a camaraderie that only comes from much time spent together – indeed, so strong is it, that when Mickey arrives at the TARDIS in Cardiff Bay he is very much an outsider and out of his depth. Later, Rose confirms the passage of time with stories of the places she visited with the Doctor (and possibly Jack), places we have never seen or heard about. Mickey only comes to Cardiff because Rose has asked him to bring her passport, but she later reveals that she wanted to see him. Once again she is keeping him on hold, the 'occasional boyfriend'. After listening to her rabbit on about the Doctor, and their adventures together, Mickey blurts out that he is dating Trisha Delaney. Rose reacts as if she has been slapped and accuses him of lying. He would never be attracted to such a girl, she says. It turns out Mickey is lying; trying to make Rose jealous, but when it doesn't work out, he tells her that she 'makes [him] feel like nothing, Rose. Nothing.' Rose promptly confirms his accusation by running straight back into the TARDIS when an earthquake strikes Cardiff Bay – really the Rift becoming violently active. It is only after Blon Fel-Fotch Pasameer-Day Slitheen is defeated and the Rift is closed that Rose thinks of Mickey again. She rushes off to find him, but in the chaos around the Bay she cannot see him, although he watches her from a distance. He walks away before she can notice him, finally accepting the truth of the situation. For her own part, Rose realises that Mickey deserves better than her, a fact that upsets her and she tries to hide a tear.

After a couple more off-screen adventures Rose is hijacked from the TARDIS by a transmat beam of unknown origin (revealed to be Daleks) in *Bad Wolf*, and ends up at the Game

Station, the former Satellite 5. There she takes part in a distorted version of *The Weakest Link* wherein after the immortal line, 'you are the weakest link, goodbye' is uttered by the Anne Droid, the loser is apparently vaporised. At first, after some initial confusion, Rose is amused to be on the game show; bombarded by questions she cannot possibly know the answers to. Her amusement continues, until the loser of the first round reacts in utter terror – Rose doesn't understand the problem, until she sees the loser vaporised before her. Horror soon sets in, but Rose has no choice other than to continue and manages to survive until the final head-to-head round with fellow contestant Roderick, which she loses. The Doctor, Jack and a young woman called Lynda Moss join Rose only to see her vaporised in front of them! The Doctor and Jack are convinced she is dead. The Doctor is shocked, while Jack responds with anger and rage, threatening to kill those responsible. In truth, Rose has merely been transmatted to the Dalek mothership, one of two hundred ships on the outer-most limits of the Solar System. The Daleks try to intimidate Rose with fear, but she is resolute that the Doctor will save her. The Daleks attempt to use her against the Doctor, and after a direct confrontation with the Emperor, Rose is stunned to see the defeat on the Doctor's face. She is disconsolate about the presence of Lynda; she sees her as a rival and is annoyed by Lynda's obvious enthusiasm for the Doctor. When the Doctor explains how he will build a Delta Wave and use the Game Station as a transmitter to wipe out the entire Dalek fleet, Rose is resentful of Lynda's response. 'What are you waiting for?' she says, a split second before Rose. Jealousy and distaste vie for dominance on Rose's face.

Later the Doctor convinces Rose to get into the TARDIS and he returns her to 2006. She is angered and hurt by this apparent betrayal, and tries everything to stop the TARDIS, but it doesn't respond to her, and she finds herself stranded back home, 'enjoying' chips with Mickey and Jackie – both of whom are happy to be reunited with her. Rose finds it difficult to just sit there while the Doctor is fighting to save them all. Mickey doesn't understand this, until she tells him that there is nothing left on Earth for her. For Mickey this is the final nail in the coffin, and he accepts his relationship with Rose finally is over. Having a quiet moment with her mother, Rose discloses that she met her dad in the past. She also reveals that *she* was the unknown blonde girl Jackie remembers seeing by his dying body, 'That's how good the Doctor is,' she says. This convinces Jackie to help Rose get back to the Doctor.

Fortuitously Rose realises the true meaning of the words 'Bad Wolf' and is convinced it is a link between her and the Doctor. As messages go it is obscure, but Rose's guess is correct; staring into the heart of the TARDIS she absorbs the time vortex and becomes Bad Wolf, scattering the words throughout time and space, and thus creating a message that only she can decipher. Using the power of the time vortex, Rose returns to the future and disperses the atoms of the entire Dalek fleet, thus ending the Time War. However the pain burns in her mind – she can see *everything* that has ever happened. She defies life itself and brings Jack back from the dead (having been killed during the Dalek assault on the station). The Doctor removes the vortex from her, saving her life, and dispelling it safely. As Rose awakes in the console room, she finds the Doctor talking about how he is going to change. She remembers nothing about being Bad Wolf – the last thing she recalls is looking into the heart of the TARDIS. Rose is then shocked to see the Doctor regenerate before her...

Adam Mitchell, although not technically regarded as a companion, is designed to show why not everyone can work as a companion, to *prove how wonderful Rose is. And how wise the Doctor is, not selecting his crew cos he fancies them* (from Russell T Davies' pitch document). Ironically, based solely on what we see on television, he proves the direct opposite. He is intelligent, inquisitive and uses his initiative – all key elements of a companion. His only crime is trying to make money from the knowledge he has gained while visiting Satellite 5. Does this actually warrant the Doctor dumping him back on Earth? Based on the evidence presented in *Father's Day*, during which Rose's actions almost destroy all life on Earth, the answer would be 'no'. Rose gets a slapped wrist whilst Adam gets dumped with no chance to improve. What would have become of Adam had he remained is something we will never know, since the Doctor doesn't seem to regard him even worthy of mention again. As a result Adam's not so much the companion who couldn't, rather the companion who didn't get a chance.

Therefore the next companion is Jack Harkness, one of the earliest conceived characters for the 2005 revival of *Doctor Who* (according to *The Inside Story* [written by Gary Russell and published by BBC Books in 2006] he was conceived and cast before the outline of the series was even confirmed). He is created to be the soldier and do things the Doctor will never ordinarily do. His travelling days with the Doctor, however, are slightly different to what was originally planned, due to the creation of spin-off show *Torchwood*, for which he became the lead character.

Jack Harkness – John Barrowman (The Empty Child to The Parting of the Ways)

Destined to be one of the most complex and long-serving characters in *Doctor Who* history, Jack begins simply enough. He is introduced into the series under an assumed identity, stolen from RAF Captain Harkness (as revealed in *Torchwood: Captain Jack Harkness*). Jack is an ex-Time Agent from the fifty-first century, who for some reason had two years of his life stolen from him. No longer working for the Time Agency, Jack is now a conman using his knowledge of Earth's history for his own personal ends. Jack is happy to flirt with everyone he meets; indeed flirting is often his way of saying hello. It is inferred that Jack is having a secret sexual relationship with Algy, a British

Army Officer. Yet he is also very impressed with Rose, but mistakes her for a Time Agent, until he later meets the Doctor whom he calls 'Mister Spock' initially due to Rose's use of the name. Despite his sizeable knowledge of Earth history, it seems Jack has some curious gaps – popular television and terminology being most prominent. Jack has a carefree attitude, with much joking and sarcasm, never taking anything too seriously. His biggest character flaw, as he later mentions to the Doctor in *The Parting of the Ways*, is his cowardice.

However, as Jack spends time with the Doctor he draws upon bravery he did not know existed. This is evident in his first story (*The Empty Child / The Doctor Dances*) when he discovers he is responsible for the plague spreading throughout London (in fact a plague of nanogenes rewriting human DNA that escaped from a crashed Chula ambulance he sent to Earth). This shakes him up, but he sticks around to help the Doctor and Rose. To make amends, he returns to his own ship and stops a bomb from falling on the Chula ambulance, but unfortunately, as he heads from Earth he discovers there is no way for him to escape the explosion. He accepts his fate with dignity and good humour, enjoying an alcoholic drink and engaging the onboard computer in conversation. The Doctor and Rose arrive in the TARDIS to take him away from the bomb, and he accepts the Doctor's invitation to join them on their travels.

He remains with the Doctor and Rose for an undefined period of time, and when we next see him, in *Boom Town*, he is answering the TARDIS door to Mickey. Jack has settled into a very easy, and highly flirtatious, relationship with both the Doctor and Rose. He is out of uniform and now dressed in contemporary clothes. He enjoys winding Mickey up, not unlike the Doctor. They spend some time in Cardiff (long enough for Margaret Blaine's photograph to appear in *The Western Mail*), with Jack enjoying being the centre of attention, telling his tall tales of past exploits as a Time Agent. Already, elements of the Doctor's personality seem to be infecting Jack (something that develops even more when Jack takes over Torchwood, and he clearly begins to model himself on the Doctor – name dropping, his sense of dress, etc). When they go to Cardiff Town Hall to confront Blaine, now Mayor of Cardiff, Jack automatically assumes command, giving out instructions, until the Doctor queries who is in charge. Jack apologies, but the Doctor points out that it is a good plan, and they proceed as Jack suggested. He is very excited by the pandimensional surfboard, and instantly recognises it as technology far beyond the inhabitants of Raxacoricofallapatorius and Blaine (Blon Slitheen) had procured it by nefarious means. He seems to be very aware of the Time Lords and their technology – he easily operates the TARDIS console.

Like Rose he is hijacked by the Daleks' transmat in *Bad Wolf* and deposited on the Game Station. He finds himself in a version of *What Not to Wear* and is at the mercy of the robotic Trine-e and Zu-Zana. They instruct him to try on various clothes before deciding he would be better without a face. Being naked in front of a television audience amuses Jack, but it doesn't prevent him from hiding a gun about his person. He uses this to destroy both robots.

He is outraged by the apparent death of Rose, but is the first person to work out where Rose really has been taken. He assists the Doctor in rescuing her, and arranges the defence of the Game Station against the oncoming Dalek fleet. He has heard of the Time War and knows why the Daleks disappeared, but is unaware the battle involved the Time Lords. When the Emperor Dalek challenges the Doctor's resolve in using the Delta Wave, Jack's faith in the Doctor is absolute. Such faith is misplaced since, in the event, the Doctor proves unable to use the Delta Wave. The sacrifice of every life on Earth is too great a price for the Doctor. Jack, while the Doctor is admitting defeat, fights to the last man. Cornered, he accepts his fate and is exterminated by a Dalek. He is later resurrected by the Bad Wolf version of Rose; only she gets it wrong (more on that on page 275). He is shocked to find himself alive, and rushes towards the sound of the TARDIS dematerialising. The last we see of Jack is on the Game Station, seconds after the Doctor and Rose leave, upset at being abandoned.

It is some time before Jack meets the Doctor again – indeed, for him, a *lot* of time passes. Over a hundred years. But more on that on page 275.

The Tenth Doctor
David Tennant

> *'Once upon a time there were people in charge of those laws, but they died. They all died. Do you know who that leaves? Me!'*
> The Doctor – *The Waters of Mars*

Regenerated and healed, the Doctor found himself drawn ever closer to Rose, to the point where he started to lose much of the man he used to be – the distant traveller from Gallifrey was becoming more and more human. And not always the best example of one. The consequences of this humanisation will follow him throughout his tenth incarnation, with devastating results...

Rose Tyler – Billie Piper (Rose to Doomsday and Partners in Crime, and Turn Left to Journey's End, plus The End of Time)

She was so sure she knew the Doctor, but as the new face is presented to her Rose realises she knows nothing. Despite witnessing the change of face she cannot believe it at first, and is convinced that an imposter has replaced the Doctor. That it is some kind of body swap, or maybe a teleport. She even thinks that somehow it is a Slitheen in disguise – despite the obvious lack of zip on the forehead. He insists it is him, but Rose really does not like it, and wants him to change back. In spite of her distress she still asks about Jack, and the Doctor simply says he has remained behind to rebuild Earth (an obvious lie, as we later learn in *Utopia* when the Doctor reveals he actively ran away from Jack – or, more accurately, what Bad Wolf-Rose did to him). She is quite clearly scared when the regeneration begins to fail, and the unstable Doctor sends the TARDIS crashing towards Christmas 2006.

The TARDIS alerts both Jackie and Mickey to its imminent arrival, they both hear the engines long before it materialises mid-air, so they are both on hand at the beginning of *The Christmas Invasion* to help Rose with the Doctor. Jackie is understandably confused, and intrigued by the notion of the Doctor having two hearts, but Rose is in no mood to humour her mother and responds with irritation. Although she is curious as to why there are a pair of men's pyjamas and dressing gown at her mother's flat – they belong to one of Jackie's many male 'friends' (when we consider how loose Jackie is with men it is not hard to understand why Rose herself is so fickle with her own affections). Rose sits vigil over the Doctor as he recovers in the spare room, finding it difficult to explain what has happened to Jackie. The more she looks at him the more her heart breaks – on some level she is convinced that she has lost the Doctor. Worse, that he has *left her*. As a distraction she goes Christmas shopping with Mickey, who offers his support once more, even though he is tired of hearing about the Doctor. Naturally it is not long before they are being attacked and have to rush back to the flat – Rose is very certain that the robot Santas are after the Doctor. When a Christmas tree attacks them in the flat, tearing through the door and wall into the spare room, it is only a whisper from Rose that wakes the Doctor and he instantly disposes of the tree and confronts the Santas, which he calls pilot fish, signalling the arrival of something much more dangerous. That something is the Sycorax, and when they appear on a news programme Rose realises just how much trouble they really are in – even she cannot understand what they are saying, as if somehow the Doctor's damaged the circuit in the link between her and the TARDIS. Things become even more desperate when the Sycorax ship hovers over London and they take control of a large percentage of the Earth's people. After hearing a plea from Prime Minister Harriet Jones, who begs for the Doctor's help, Rose breaks down. To her mind the Doctor really has gone. She knows she cannot cope without him and the only thing she can think of to do is hide him in the TARDIS. This she does and, along with Mickey, is transported to the Sycorax ship. She attempts to use knowledge gained from her travels against them, speaking for Earth, but she is mocked by the Sycorax who call her bravado 'borrowed words'. As soon as she starts to understand the language of the Sycorax she is the first to work out what it means and turns, with some nervous anticipation, to the TARDIS where the Doctor is standing in his dressing gown. Watching him face the Sycorax convinces her that he is still the Doctor, even though he is rude to her. Once they are defeated, Rose realises that she does still want to travel with him, even though she thinks it is weird that he can change his face and grow a new hand. Once again she does not consider how this will affect Mickey or her mum, only this time the Doctor is right there with her indifference.

They appear to remain on Earth for a while longer (the Doctor at least moves the TARDIS between stories, but it is heavily implied that they are only now setting off on their travels again – perhaps Jackie convinced them to stay for the New Year), but they soon head off and travel further than they have ever travelled before – to *New Earth*. While they rest on the cliff's edge looking out towards New New York, Rose shows how much she now totally accepts the new Doctor – indeed, she states that she loves travelling with him, and together they are much more tactile than before; holding hands and hugging on many occasions. She finds it difficult to get her head around the notion of the Cat People, and when she comes face-to-skin with Cassandra, who survived their previous encounter in *The End of the World*, she thinks that Cassandra deserved to die. This is a radical change of view – when Cassandra apparently died before, Rose was shaken up by it and did not think such an outcome was necessary. But she is very aggressive to Cassandra this time around and Cassandra gets her own back when she steals Rose's body, suppressing Rose in the process. Rose is aware of what is going on, but cannot affect anything. Cassandra draws much from Rose's mind, including her obvious attraction to the Doctor, and enjoys snogging him. She thinks Rose is a chav. It is not only Rose who has developed a new aggressive streak, but the Doctor too, as seen when he realises that Rose has been possessed by Cassandra. It seems that as a result of his regeneration he has become much closer to Rose, both emotionally and in attitude, almost as if her proximity to him when he regenerated imprinted some of her personality on him.

The most obvious example of this personality imprint can be seen when they arrive in the Scottish highlands in 1879. In *Tooth and Claw* they meet Queen Victoria, and go on to Torchwood House with her; the Doctor's psychic paper telling the queen that he is James McCrimmon, a doctor who has been assigned by the Lord Provost as her protector. The Doctor passes Rose off as a feral child he 'bought for sixpence in old London Town. It was either her or the Elephant Man'. Rose cannot believe she is meeting Queen Victoria, and makes a bet with the Doctor that she can get the queen to say, 'I am not amused'. Throughout this story we are shown the complete lack of respect Rose has for Queen Victoria – speaking to her like she is a regular woman, constantly trying to get her to say she is 'not amused'. Such questionable actions are only compounded by the Doctor actively taking part in the bet – although he at least has the decency to look embarrassed from time to time. This does not stop him from laughing and cheering with Rose, *in front* of Her Majesty, when Victoria finally says, 'and I am *not* amused' for which she gives them both a proper dressing down before banishing them both from the British Empire (after knighting them Sir Doctor of TARDIS and Dame Rose of the Powell Estate, for saving her life from a werewolf). She tells them both that she sees a bad end for them if they continue 'straying from all that is good'. Unfortunately, though, as demonstrated throughout the 2006 series, neither takes any heed of what she tells them.

They are called back to 2007 by Mickey, who has heard reports of possible alien activity at a local London school in *School*

Reunion (Rose thinks he has called her back just because he wants to see her, but he tells her no). Investigating the school proves to be quite an eye-opener for Rose when she meets the Doctor's old companion, Sarah Jane Smith, who has not seen the Doctor for some twenty-seven years (assuming he dropped her off in her own time of 1980 in *The Hand of Fear*). Rose is threatened by Sarah's presence, and is very jealous of the bond she shares with the Doctor. As Mickey points out it is almost like Rose is meeting the Doctor's ex. As a result Rose turns into an über bitch, constantly making snide comments relating to Sarah's age. She is confronted with what the Doctor calls the 'Curse of a Time Lord' – although she may live her entire life with him, he can never live his life with her. She will grow old and die, but he will simply regenerate and carry on. Rose does not like the idea that the Doctor may one day leave her, like he did Sarah, since once they were obviously as close as he and Rose now are. She remains competitive with Sarah throughout, until they end up arguing over the things they have seen and Sarah trumps with the announcement that she met the Loch Ness Monster! They burst out laughing and finally bond by mocking the Doctor over how he tends to explain things at such a high speed that they can never keep up, and how he strokes bits of the TARDIS. In the end Rose seeks Sarah's advice – should she continue travelling with the Doctor? Sarah says that yes, some things are worth getting your heart broken over. Rose is less impressed with the idea of Mickey joining them on their travels. The Doctor asks Sarah to go with them, but she refuses, feeling she is too old for it, but she suggests he take Mickey – the Doctor needs a Smith on board. Rose mouths a 'no' to the Doctor, but he appears not to notice and agrees to let Mickey join.

For some reason, Rose's view on Mickey's presence totally shifts in the time it takes them to reach the space station, *SS Madame de Pompadour*. From the beginning of *The Girl in the Fireplace* Rose enjoys having Mickey around, and teaching him the rules of travelling with the Doctor. In some ways the camaraderie between the three of them is reminiscent of that which existed between the Doctor, Rose and Jack at the beginning of *Boom Town*. This would normally suggest a lengthy passage of time between stories, except Mickey explicitly states that this is his first journey. As is to be expected, Rose is not impressed by the Doctor's preoccupation with Reinette (or Jeanne-Antoinette Poisson to use her given name, the infamous Madame de Pompadour) and Mickey takes great pleasure in this, quoting Sarah and Cleopatra as further examples of the Doctor having a 'girl in every fireplace'. Rose insists it is not like that, but her protests come across as quite hollow. Unusually, for Rose, she is impressed when she meets Reinette and shows the woman some respect – way more than she has ever shown anyone else who has shown interest in the Doctor. After the Doctor appears to be stranded in the past, Rose sheds a tear, realising he has no way back and she cannot pilot the TARDIS to him (any knowledge she had was removed when the Doctor took the vortex out of her in *The Parting of the Ways*). Naturally the Doctor finds a way back. After receiving a letter written for him by Reinette before her death, Rose does not know how to reach him through his pain, and it takes Mickey to lead her away, allowing the Doctor to grieve on his own.

The Doctor and Rose are back to their old selves again in the following story, *Rise of the Cybermen*, ganging up on Mickey as they share stories and leaving him with his finger pressed on a button for no reason at all. He is quite clearly the spare tyre and realises this. They arrive on an alternative version of Earth (Pete's World, as it becomes known), where Rose discovers her father is not only alive, but is rich and still married to Jackie. The Doctor tries to warn her that the Pete of this world is not her father, but she will not have any of it – she *has* to go and see him. She walks off, leaving the Doctor torn between her and Mickey, who heads off to explore London on his own; as Mickey points out, 'there is no real choice is there? It will always be Rose.' They soon learn that Rose does not exist in this reality, although Jackie does have a dog she calls Rose – a fact that amuses the Doctor endlessly.

Rose is less impressed. She explains to the Doctor about Mickey's past, and how he was raised by his Gran who died some years ago (she is alive on Pete's World), and begins to realise that she has always taken Mickey for granted. It is a realisation that comes somewhat too late, since Mickey has discovered his Gran (or rather Ricky's Gran – Ricky being the Pete's World version of Mickey, who dies at the hands of the Cybermen) and finds a place for himself on the alternative Earth.

Once again jealousy rears its head after the Doctor and Rose disguise themselves as waiting staff to gatecrash Jackie's birthday party. The Doctor tells her what he learned from Lucy, another waitress, and Rose responds with some typically scathing comments. It seems that she is threatened by any interaction between the Doctor and other females – not a character trait one expects from someone who the Doctor once referred to as 'the best'. She talks to Pete, who finds himself opening up to her, although he cannot understand why since he has only just met her. Later, when told who Rose is, he just cannot deal with the idea that she is his daughter, and walks away from her. He is not her father. This crushes her, as the Doctor warned her it would. Her conversation with Jackie is even worse. At first Jackie opens up, possibly feeling the connection between them, but when Rose starts to offer advice on Jackie's marriage, Jackie looks at Rose as though she is nothing. To her mind Rose is just staff. It is a particularly nasty exchange, but no worse than some of the attitude Rose dishes out to those who attract the Doctor's attention. Once again we see that, even in a parallel world, Rose is very much Jackie's daughter.

She finds it hard to believe that Mickey is going to remain behind, and tells him that she needs him – perhaps realising that her relationship with the Doctor is doomed ultimately and when that happens only Mickey will be there for her. Mickey does not agree, saying that she has the Doctor, but on Pete's World he has his Gran, and she *does* need him. Still upset, the Doctor returns her promptly to Earth Prime (the main Earth seen in *Doctor Who*) to her mother and she cries in Jackie's arms, perhaps realising finally just how bad she has been to Mickey.

As ever with Rose she soon bounces back and throws herself into the 1950s lifestyle of rock 'n' roll and preparations for the coronation of Queen Elizabeth II in *The Idiot's Lantern*. She surprises the Doctor with her knowledge of the contemporary dialect, a result of watching endless repeats of Cliff Richard movies when she was a child – the Doctor laments that he should have known Jackie would be a Cliff fan. When they invade Eddie Connolly's house, Rose takes him to task over the incorrectly positioned Union Flags (and points out to him that it is only the Union Jack when it is flown at sea). She heads off to investigate Magpie's Electricals on her own, again doing her Doctor impersonation, but she soon finds herself out of her depth when she is confronted by the Wire, who steals Rose's face. The Doctor's anger at this act propels him to defeat the Wire and restore not only Rose but all those who have lost their faces to the Wire. When Eddie is kicked out of the house by his wife (he was the one who snitched on his mother-in-law and their neighbours), his son Tommy is glad to see the back of him, because he is 'an idiot'. Rose points out that yes, he is an idiot, but he is still Tommy's dad. It is something that Rose can relate to and she sends Tommy after Eddie. It is a nice touch, and shows the softer, sympathetic side of Rose that has rarely been on display since the Doctor's regeneration.

This more sympathetic side of Rose is seen once more shortly after she and the Doctor arrive on Sanctuary Base Five, on the planet Krop Tor (a planet impossibly orbiting a black hole) in *The Impossible Planet*. She does not understand why the Ood are so willing to serve humanity, and wonders when humans needed slaves anyway. She shows a great politeness to the Ood, despite the way the personnel of the Sanctuary Base take them for granted. When they think they have lost the TARDIS, Rose starts to wonder what they will do in 432K1 (the forty-second century). She thinks they will settle down together, a prospect the Doctor does not seem as happy about as one would expect (could it be that having met Sarah recently was the wake-up call he needed? Note that later, in *Fear Her*, when Rose mentions she will always be with the Doctor, he quickly changes the subject). She builds up a good rapport with pretty much everybody on Sanctuary Base, and is as fearful as the rest of them at the notion that deep within the bowels of Krop Tor lives Satan. She wonders if the Devil is real, and the Doctor assures her that there is no such thing – although such a belief is shaken later when he meets the Beast, possibly the source of the myth.

The Beast tells her that she will soon die in battle, a revelation that shakes her up, but the Doctor explains that the Beast is merely playing on her fears – on *all* their fears, in fact. As it turns out, in *Doomsday*, Rose does die (after a fashion) as she is listed among the dead after the Battle of Canary Wharf ends.

When the Ood become possessed by the telepathic field emanating from the Beast, Rose's rapport with the crew comes in useful as she finds herself having to motivate them into taking a stand and finding a way to remove the threat. Before falling down the pit, and being on the verge of a 'leap of faith', the Doctor realises he could well die and expresses his absolute belief in Rose – but she does not hear any of this exchange – and he struggles to find the right goodbye message for her deciding that she will *know* how he feels about her. After learning from Ida that the Doctor has fallen down the pit, Rose refuses to accept that the Doctor is dead despite the Ida's that no-one could have survived such a fall. Such is her belief in the Doctor's survival, that Rose will not leave the base, even though the whole planet is about to fall into the black hole. She is rendered unconscious and dragged to the escape rocket, and when she comes to she freaks out. She has little choice but to accept her fate. Despite her grief, she is the first to notice that Toby Zed has been possessed by the Beast, and uses a bolt gun to break the screen in the rocket cockpit, sending the Beast into the black hole. She is, understandably, elated when the TARDIS latches on to the rocket and prevents it from following the Beast into the black hole. She subsequently shares a very happy reunion with the Doctor in the TARDIS.

In *Love and Monsters* we get a rare look at what it is like to be left behind, when we see life through Jackie's eyes for a short time. Her sadness and fear for Rose is palpable, never knowing where her daughter is, or if she is ever going to return home again. She sometimes gets a phone call, but it is never enough. Nonetheless, she is fiercely loyal to both Rose and the Doctor when she discovers that Elton has only befriended her to find out more about Rose. When Rose next rings her mum, Jackie tells her all about Elton. Rose then tracks him down to give him a piece of her mind. Despite her anger, Rose realises how upset Elton is over losing the woman he loves, and she sits and comforts him, once again showing her compassionate side, so often overshadowed by her obsessive attraction to the Doctor.

Once more Rose finds herself alone, having to solve an alien problem without the Doctor in *Fear Her* after he is turned into a drawing by a girl called Chloe Webber who has been imbued by the Isolus. She is not very good with children – indeed she calls them 'little terrors' at one point – and is shocked to learn that the Doctor was a dad once.

Once again Rose says she is going to stay with the Doctor forever at the beginning of *Army of Ghosts*, but she soon learns that it is not going to be that easy. Like so many teenagers who live away from home, she still brings her washing to her mother whenever she and the Doctor return to see Jackie. While Rose is operating the TARDIS console, helping the Doctor track the source of the 'ghost shifts' happening throughout London, Jackie expresses concern that Rose is becoming like the Doctor. She is convinced that one day she will not be 'Rose' anymore, but a stranger that Jackie does not recognise. Rose is not sure that is a bad thing at all.

On finding their way to Torchwood Tower (in truth One Canada Square, also known as Canary Wharf), the Doctor passes Jackie off as Rose after Yvonne Hartman, director of Torchwood

One, points out he is known for travelling with a companion. Rose remains inside the TARDIS as it is moved into the storage area of Torchwood Tower, and decides to investigate herself. She uses the psychic paper to enable this, showing some of the brazen-like qualities the Doctor often uses (or, as the Seventh Doctor once said, 'act as if you own the place'). She is a lot more confident this time around, having learned much from her moments without the Doctor since *The Christmas Invasion* when she failed so miserably to impress the Sycorax. Unknowingly, she is guided to the Sphere Room by Mickey, who has already infiltrated Torchwood under the name Samuel. When he reveals himself, just as the Sphere becomes active, Rose is very pleased to see him, noticing a change in him since *The Age of Steel* (for him it has been three years, since time on Pete's World moves faster than on Earth Prime).

While the Cybermen invade elsewhere, having passed through the void between realities following the Sphere (a Void Ship as the Doctor later calls it), Rose and Mickey find themselves facing four Daleks who are hiding in the Void Ship, safe from the Time War. These four, led by Dalek Sec, are the Cult of Skaro, a specially bred Dalek group tasked with thinking of new and unconventional ways to continue the Dalek Empire beyond the Emperor. Rose uses her knowledge of the Daleks to keep herself and Mickey alive, but when they continue to threaten her she takes great pleasure in pointing out she destroyed the Emperor. The Daleks have something called the Genesis Ark, later revealed to be a prison of Time Lord design, housing millions of Daleks. It can only be opened by the genetic imprint of someone who has travelled through the time vortex – which includes both Rose and Mickey. To save Mickey's life – who she calls the bravest human she knows – Rose agrees to open the Ark. As it turns out, Mickey accidentally provides the genetic imprint when he stumbles during a rescue by the Doctor and a combined army of Torchwood militia and Cybermen. Pete also returns, and Rose is there to witness the reunion between him and Jackie. It is a deeply emotional moment, although tinged with humour when Jackie discovers Pete is rich

('I don't care about that. How rich?' Jackie asks. 'Very,' is Pete's response. 'I don't care about that. How very?' Jackie then wants to know). The only way to defeat the Daleks and the Cybermen is to return them to the Void, but to do so will drag in anyone else who has crossed realities – this includes Rose. The Doctor realises that she has to return to Pete's world, but she refuses to go, even when Pete tricks her into travelling there. She immediately returns to Torchwood One, leaving Jackie and Mickey heartbroken in the knowledge that they will never see her again. But Rose seems not to care – all that is important to her is being with the Doctor. While the Daleks and Cybermen are sucked into the Void, Rose loses her grip on the lever controlling the breach in the Void, and almost falls into it but is rescued at the last second by Pete who takes her to his world. The breach is closed one final time, and Rose, realising she can never get back, falls apart while her parents and Mickey watch on, unable to do anything to comfort her.

After several months living on Pete's World, and now working for their version of Torchwood, Rose hears the Doctor's voice in her dreams. She easily convinces her parents (Jackie now three months pregnant) and Mickey to travel with her to find the source of the Doctor's voice, which is a beach in Norway called Dårlig Ulv Stranden (Bad Wolf Bay). The Doctor has found the final breach and is burning a star just to send Rose a final message. As they say goodbye, Rose's heart breaks and she asks if she will ever see him again. He says there is no chance; once the breach is sealed that is it. To cross the dimension again would destroy both worlds. She tells him, finally, that she loves him to which the Doctor replies 'quite right, too. And I suppose, if it's my last chance to say it... Rose Tyler...' He never gets a chance to finish his sentence, as the breach closes and he is left alone in the TARDIS with a tear falling.

It is unclear how much time passes before we see Rose again, but taking into account the faster-than-normal flow of time on Pete's World we can safely assume that more than two years have passed (two years being the time between *Doomsday* and *Turn Left* for Earth Prime). Certainly there is a confidence to Rose that was never seen before, and her voice has aged somewhat. Torchwood on Pete's World has created the Dimension Cannon, a device that is able to send people from one world to another. They have also discovered that something is wrong with the timelines – the stars are disappearing and the darkness is approaching. For reasons Rose cannot work out the timelines are converging on Donna Noble, and they meet briefly in early 2009 in *Partners in Crime* after Donna puts car keys in a bin for her mother to find later, before heading off with the Doctor. Neither knows each other at this point and Rose looks confused. She tries to contact the Doctor directly, first on the TARDIS scanner in *The Poison Sky* and later through a television in *Midnight*.

She eventually tracks the Doctor down on Christmas Day 2007. However she ends up in Donna's World (an alternative reality created by the Time Beetle which has latched on to Donna) in *Turn Left*. She arrives too late, and the Doctor is dead. Without Donna to stop him, he drowns when he empties the Thames to kill the Racnoss buried in the centre of the Earth. She continues to return at various points over the next couple of years, but always in Donna's World and she realises that somehow Donna is the nexus. By this point she has learned all about Donna, clearly having studied the timelines since she knows about the raffle ticket Donna will be buying the following Christmas (2008), and is aware that Jack and his Torchwood team manage to defeat the Sontarans in 2009. She spends some time working with UNIT in Donna's World, although she will not tell them her name, and shows them how to scrape off the surface technology of the TARDIS (found in London, left behind when the Doctor dies at Christmas 2007), enabling them to create a primitive time machine using mirrors. She convinces Donna that she has to return to Earth Prime and find a way to make her younger self turn right and head towards her ultimate destiny with the Doctor. This Donna does, and Rose is able to finally cross over to Earth Prime where she stands over the dying Donna. Rose gets Donna to pass on a message to the Doctor – two words: Bad Wolf. These words help convince the Doctor of the impending danger, and that Rose is soon to return to him.

Rose is finally reunited with the Doctor on Earth Prime, which has been shifted to the Medusa Cascade by the Daleks in *The Stolen Earth*, but not before saving Wilfred Mott and Sylvia Noble, Donna's grandfather and mother. She is not happy being excluded from the subspace network – which links the Doctor and Donna with Harriet Jones, Martha Jones, Jack, and Sarah – but she does seem to have got over her old hang-up about the Doctor having companions other than her. She uses the Dimension Cannon to deposit her near the TARDIS, and once the Doctor spots her, the two of them run towards each other, their smiles getting bigger with each step. Unfortunately before the Doctor can reach her, a Dalek appears and shoots him – exterminating half of his body. She is not surprised by the arrival of Jack, who destroys the Dalek, and together they rush the Doctor into the safety of the TARDIS. Any chance of a happy reunion is destroyed when the Doctor begins to regenerate – Rose cannot believe it, just as she has found him again he is about to become a new man. Luckily the Doctor has his spare hand (cut off by the Sycorax in *The Christmas Invasion* and returned to him by Jack in *Utopia*) nearby and is able to feed all his regeneration into that, thus healing himself. They joke around a little, the Doctor coyly enjoying the fact that Rose came all this way just to find him. Their reunion is short-lived however since the TARDIS, its defences ripped away, is transported to the Crucible, the hub of the Dalek fleet massed at the Medusa Cascade. They become captives of Davros, while Jack is apparently exterminated. From Rose's reaction it is clear that she does not know Jack is now immortal, but she does not comment or react with surprise when he reappears later alongside Sarah, Mickey and Jackie. She thinks Martha is 'good' when Martha attempts to hold the Daleks ransom with the Osterhagen key, while Martha is surprised that the Doctor finally managed to find Rose again, a comment that makes Rose smile – it is the first time she learns that the Doctor has told others about her. Once the Daleks are defeated by Donna and the Meta-Doctor (see page 292 for Donna's entry and details on the creation of the Clone Doctor) created from the Doctor's spare hand, the Doctor and his companions return Earth to its normal place in space. It is there that Mickey finally takes his leave of Rose – he is not stupid, he knows what's coming. Rose has her Doctor. But he is OK with that. Since his gran on Pete's World died peacefully he walks off and joins Martha and Jack. Rose and Jackie are returned to Dårlig Ulv Stranden on Pete's World, and she finds out the Meta-Doctor is half human, specifically the physical part. He can never regenerate, and can grow old with her. Rose is not sure, but when he tells her what the Doctor never could in *Doomsday*, Rose realises he is as much the Doctor as the real Doctor is. The Doctor and Donna leave in the TARDIS, and Rose turns to her Doctor – finally having the man of her dreams.

It is here that Rose's story appears to end. Although she is due to return to *Doctor Who* in the anniversary story in November 2013.

That Sarah would return seems, in hindsight, to have been inevitable. Her return had originally been planned for season eighteen, to help smooth the transition from Fourth to Fifth Doctor, but actress Elisabeth Sladen declined the offer. However, she did accept a pilot for a potential series, and so returned in 1981 for *K9 & Company: A Girl's Best Friend*. Although the series did not transpire, Sarah returned again for the twentieth anniversary adventure, *The Five Doctors* in 1983 and later in the *Children In Need* charity crossover with the cast of popular soap opera *EastEnders*, *Dimensions in Time* in 1993. The popularity of Sarah is beyond question, and she has appeared in many official and unofficial productions beyond the parent show, so when it came time to bring an old companion back for the twenty-first century continuation of *Doctor Who*, Sarah seemed the obvious option. So successful was her return, both on screen and behind the scenes, that when Children's BBC asked executive producer Russell T Davies to create a new spin-off show, the obvious choice was one based around Sarah. Thus *The Sarah Jane Adventures* was created, and proved to be the most successful show on CBBC. It ran for four and a half series, cancelled only by the untimely death of Elisabeth Sladen, and featured the Doctor on two separate occasions. Sarah, herself, returned to *Doctor Who* twice more, both times with her adopted son, Luke.

Sarah Jane Smith – Elisabeth Sladen, continued... (*School Reunion* and *The Sarah Jane Adventures*, plus *The Stolen Earth* to *Journey's End* and *The End of Time*)

It has been over twenty-five years since Sarah heard from the Doctor (Christmas 1981, in *K9 & Company: A Girl's Best Friend*), so she is in for quite a surprise when, in early 2007, she investigates the strange goings-on at Deffry Vale High School. Ostensibly she is there to do a piece on the new Headmaster, Mr Finch, and he introduces her to the faculty which includes the substitute science teacher, Mr John Smith. She is delighted to meet him, and confesses to him that there is no harm in doing a little investigating while she is there – John Smith agrees totally. She also tells him that she once had a friend who went by that name. She has no idea that it is the Doctor she is talking to, and once she walks away from him, he remains looking at her, his face beaming, 'Oh good for you, Sarah Jane Smith.'

Later that night Sarah breaks into the school, and finds herself looking in a utility room adjacent to the gym – there she finds the one thing she never expected to see. The TARDIS! She is beyond stunned, and staggers out, having dropped the crowbar. It is perfectly clear that a part of her wants to run, but as she turns around she comes face-to-face with 'John Smith'. 'Hello, Sarah Jane,' he says, probably reminding her of those few tender moments of past years, and she immediately knows who he is, greeting him with the same two words she uses upon meeting the

Third Doctor in *The Five Doctors* (not that she remembers such an event – more of that later); 'It's you,' she says, her voice breaking with the shock. 'Doctor. Oh my god, it's you, isn't it? You've regenerated.' The Doctor points out that he has regenerated 'half a dozen times' since they last met (thus in his fourth incarnation, ignoring the brief meeting between the Fifth Doctor and Sarah in *The Five Doctors*). She thinks he looks incredible, but she believes she looks old, although the Doctor disagrees UFO sightings and the unusual results the school was getting, before the emotion bursts forth from Sarah. Over twenty-five years of fear and hurt escape when she says; 'I thought you'd died. I waited for you and you didn't come back and I thought you must have died.' In a moment of absolute perfection, the Doctor finds himself about to open up entirely about the Time War; 'I lived. Everyone else died.' It is telling of the bond the Doctor and Sarah share that ever since the Time War, the Doctor has been very reticent about discussing it, and any information garnered has been eked out of him. But with Sarah it seems obvious that he is about to pour it all out, that is until they are interrupted by a scream from Mickey.

There is some initial friction between her and Rose, who does not take well to the fact that the Doctor once travelled with someone else, whereas Sarah is a little hurt to learn that the Doctor has never mentioned her. After showing him K9 (who has not functioned for a long time) they take a moment to regroup in a nearby cafe where the Doctor repairs the robot dog. In a quiet moment, Sarah asks the Doctor the questions she never got to ask before. She wants to know if she did something wrong because he just dumped her and never came back. She waited for him. The Doctor responds by saying he doesn't think that Sarah needed him, since she got on with her life. Sarah disagrees; 'You were my life.' She says it was difficult readjusting to life on Earth, after having seen so many wonders. She tells him, 'You could have come back', but he doesn't agree. She goes on to tell him that it was not South Croydon where he deposited her in *The Hand of Fear*, but was in fact Aberdeen. 'That's close to Croydon,' he responds jokingly.

Mickey realises that he is the 'tin dog'; the one who stays behind, is called on from time to time. This is what leads to Mickey joining the Doctor and Rose for a short while. Sarah also has a revelation or two for Rose. She helps her see that travelling with the Doctor does not last forever – there was a time when Sarah and the Doctor were as close as he and Rose, but it came to an end. When the Doctor is tempted by the idea of being able to stop the Time War by using the Skasis Paradigm, it is Sarah who convinces him that it is a bad idea: 'No. The universe has to move forward. Pain and loss, they define us as much as happiness or love. Whether it is a world or a relationship, everything has its time. And everything ends.'

One such ending falls to K9, who sacrifices himself to stop the Krillitanes. This upsets Sarah greatly even though he was only a 'stupid dog'.

She gets to see the interior of the TARDIS and, although she prefers how it was back in her time, she likes it. Finally she gets to say goodbye to the Doctor, to give her the closure she needs. 'Please, say it this time,' she tells him, not willing to leave without a goodbye again. 'Goodbye, *my* Sarah Jane,' the Doctor says, giving her a huge bear hug. Turning away from the TARDIS she fights to hold back the tears, probably convinced she will never see him again, but he has left her a gift – once again it is K9, a brand new Mark IV version, and a few helpful tools including two sonic lipsticks.

She does not see the Doctor again until sometime in 2009 in *The Stolen Earth* but in the meantime she is not idle. Indeed, having met the Doctor again, her entire life is re-energised and she sets herself up doing her best to protect Earth and help stranded aliens in *The Sarah Jane Adventures*. As seen in a flashback in *SJA: The Lost Boy,* she is sent a crystalline structure by geologists who cannot define it, and it communicates with her via her laptop, telling her that it is a Xylok and can help her to defend Earth. Together they rebuild her attic in Bannerman Road, Ealing, creating the super computer Mr Smith (possibly a nod to the Doctor) which houses the Xylok. It is just as well she has Mr Smith to aid her, since K9 ends up secreted in a safe in the attic, where he is occupied in a long-term attempt to stabilise a black hole – he does return on occasion, however, when the need arises (including in *Journey's End* when he is required to upload the TARDIS base code to Mr Smith). She survives on her late aunt Lavinia Smith's inheritance, as well as using the income she gets from being one of the most prestigious journalists in the United Kingdom (*SJA: The Man Who Never Was*). She has a reputation for being an odd woman among the residents of Bannerman Road, and actively keeps herself to herself, not willing to risk anyone else's life, until a girl called Maria Jackson moves into a house across the road, and becomes curious about Sarah, in *SJA: Invasion of the Bane*. Maria helps Sarah defeat Mrs Wormwood and the Banemother, who are trying to create the perfect human – the Archetype – to assist in their invasion attempt. They rescue the Archetype, a human boy who appears to be about fourteen-years old, but is 'born' on the day he is rescued by Maria and Sarah. Sarah adopts him, with the help of her contacts at UNIT (most likely the Brigadier – *SJA: Enemy of the Bane* makes it clear that Sarah's only real contact with UNIT is either directly with him, or with people he trusts), and calls him Luke. Joined by another teenager, Clyde Langer, the four of them defend the Earth, while Sarah learns what it is to be a mother. In some ways she finds fighting against attempted alien invasions easier than being a mother to Luke – an experience she is unprepared for. During 2008 she comes up against a rogue group of Slitheen, twice, as well as meeting Bea Nelson-Stanley, whose late husband once met the Sontarans, and has her first encounter with the Trickster, what is left of the Pantheon of Discord, who seems particularly interested in altering Sarah's timeline, using her to feast on the Doctor's timeline.

After an apparent Earthquake in *The Stolen Earth*, Sarah is horrified when Mr Smith plays her the transmission coming from a fleet of ships entering the Earth's atmosphere. The sound of the Daleks' voices terrify her to the core – a sound she never expected to hear again. She clings to Luke, the tears falling, saying, 'but he was so young', pretty convinced that their days are numbered. She is later a little surprised, but flattered, when Jack tells her she is looking good during the subspace network conference with the Doctor, and displays Luke proudly, although she never gets the chance to explain the circumstances of Luke's arrival in her life (when the Doctor next sees Sarah in *SJA: The Wedding of Sarah Jane Smith*, he seems to know a lot about Luke, and the other teenagers who work with Sarah – clearly having done his homework at some point after *Journey's End*). Her joy, though, turns to horror again when Davros breaks through the subspace network, and during a confrontation thinks it fitting that Sarah should be there to witness the ultimate triumph of his Daleks, having been there at the very beginning (*Genesis of the Daleks*). Sarah agrees, but she tells him that she has learned to fight since then, before she and Jack hold him to ransom with a warp star given to her by a Verron soothsayer (probably the same soothsayer who gave her the puzzle box used in *SJA: Whatever Happened to Sarah Jane Smith*). She says a quick goodbye to the Doctor this time, wanting to make haste and return to Luke, but before going she does make a point of telling the Doctor that, although he acts lonely, he has got the biggest family of them all (his companions all over the planet) – reiterating a point she made about herself in *SJA: The Lost Boy*.

During the next year, Sarah and her team continue to defend the Earth, taking on Kaagh, the only survivor of the attempted Sontaran invasion in *The Sontaran Stratagem*, who wishes to take Sarah back to Sontar in order that she stand trial in the Doctor's stead. We also discover that she comes up against the Trickster a further two times. First, in *SJA: The Temptation of Sarah Jane Smith*, he tempts her with a trip into the past, where she meets her parents in the small village of Foxgrove in 1951. Luke follows her there and tries to convince her to let her parents go, even though to do so will mean their deaths, but Sarah cannot do it. The emotional pull of saving her parents is too much. She also meets herself as a baby, and when she realises the mistake she has made, she is delighted to spot a Police Box and is certain the Doctor has arrived to help her. It is, however, just a Police Box and not the TARDIS. She eventually restores the timeline, at great personal cost. The second encounter with the Trickster is at her wedding to Peter Dalton, a man who has died and made an agreement to live only if he can marry Sarah. Peter is the first person she has had a proper romance with since leaving the TARDIS in 1980, no man could live up to the memory of the Doctor. By marrying him, Sarah is willing to give up her life as a defender of Earth, but the Doctor arrives to stop the wedding. It is only her faith in the Doctor that convinces her to do the right thing, and she shows Peter the truth of his 'angel', the Trickster. Peter alters his deal and the Trickster is defeated, once more at a cost to Sarah's emotional wellbeing. After showing Luke, Clyde and Rani (who has moved into Maria's old house) around the TARDIS, the Doctor and Sarah say goodbye again, in a manner that echoes their first parting in *The Hand of Fear*, and the Doctor tells Sarah not to forget him. She does not think anyone will ever forget him.

She encounters further Raxacoricofallapatrians on two occasions and a return match with Mrs Wormwood, who wishes to claim Luke as her son, having been the one who created him. Luke ultimately chooses Sarah. She is reunited with Brigadier Sir Alistair Lethbridge-Stewart (not seen on television since *Battlefield* in 1989), who helps her against Mrs Wormwood and Kaagh the Sontaran. They have not seen each other in some time, and have a very sweet and respectful relationship.

Following the fiasco with the 'Master race', she has Mr Smith send out a cover story, and very briefly sees the Doctor, who saves Luke from being run over by a car. No words are passed between them in *The End of Time*, but tears glisten in Sarah's eyes for she is certain it will be the last time she will see this incarnation. The following year she discovers how right she was when she is informed by UNIT that the Doctor is dead, in *SJA: Death of the Doctor*.

She refuses to accept his death, but agrees to go to the memorial service, taking Luke, Clyde and Rani with her for emotional support. On seeing the casket and hearing how badly wounded he was, Sarah almost crumbles, the doubt setting in. It is only when she meets Jo Jones (nee Grant) that she realises that she is not alone in her belief in the Doctor's continued survival – both are certain that if the Doctor had died they would both *know*. Shortly after, they meet the Doctor – now in his eleventh incarnation. Sarah recognises him instantly, and helps convince Jo. She seems to feel a little sorry for Jo, especially when explaining to Jo how many times she has seen the Doctor since they stopped travelling together. 'Oh, he must have *really* liked you,' Jo says sadly, having never seen the Doctor since she left to get married. Despite this, there appears to be a look of jealousy on her face when the Doctor and Jo are making their peace, Sarah watching from a distance. Not entirely unlike Rose, Sarah does not really like the idea of sharing the Doctor – not after all this time. Sarah shares a look with the Doctor, later in the TARDIS, when Jo mentions him getting into trouble with the Time Lords – she understands about the Time War now, and the pain the Doctor carries within. She shares an amused goodbye with Jo, who tells Sarah to find a good man, then reminisces with her team about how she sometimes does a search for the Doctor's other companions; like her, there are others out there protecting the Earth in their own way.

The last time we see Sarah is in *SJA: The Man Who Never Was*, by which time she has adopted a young girl called Sky, K9 has finally come out of his safe, and she continues to have the assistance of Luke, Clyde and Rani.

For forty years Sarah has been out there, travelling, defending the Earth, but now she has found much more. As she says; 'I've seen amazing things out there in space. But strange things can happen wherever you are. I've learned that life on Earth can be an adventure, too. But, in all the universe, I never expected to find a family.'

And Sarah's story goes on... forever.

At the end of *Doomsday* we are introduced, very briefly, to 'the Bride', who has mysteriously appeared in the TARDIS console room mere moments after the Doctor's heartfelt goodbye with Rose. It is an unexpected cliffhanger – a surprise ending kept from everyone beyond those involved. Donna Noble was not created to be an ongoing companion, but rather the complete opposite of Rose, someone who would help the Doctor get over his loss, and pave the way for the new ongoing companion, Martha Jones. Indeed, many other characters were considered for the next ongoing companion, including Elton Pope (previously seen in *Love & Monsters*) and a new companion, Penny (as producer Russell T Davies relates in *The Writer's Tale*, published in 2008). It was only after actress Catherine Tate mentioned to producer Jane Tranter that she would be interested in returning that plans were made for the inclusion of Donna in series four...

Donna Noble – Catherine Tate (The Runaway Bride and Partners in Crime to Journey's End, plus The End of Time)

Donna makes quite an entry. She appears in the TARDIS barely seconds after the Doctor's tearful farewell to Rose at the end of *Doomsday*. She is as surprised as the Doctor and immediately throws him off balance, not even giving him a chance to work through his grief. The Doctor is so shocked in fact that he can barely answer her torrent of questions... 'Where am I? What is this place?' She doesn't accept that 'TARDIS' is a real word and even thinks he has kidnapped her. She runs to the doors and flings them open into space. She pauses for a moment, long enough for the Doctor to try and explain things a little. She spies Rose's coat and assumes the Doctor kidnaps people – but the Doctor snatches the coat off her and point blank refuses to discuss Rose.

Throughout *The Runaway Bride* she proves herself to be volatile, constantly shouting her way through everything, taking none of the Doctor's nonsense. All she wants to do is get back to the church – from which she was removed abruptly while walking down the aisle to marry her fiancé, Lance. The Doctor is not sure why she would want to get married on Christmas Eve, but Donna points out she hates Christmas and is looking forward to her honeymoon in Morocco. She is highly skilled at sarcasm, as can be seen when she is being heckled by drivers who think she is a man in drag. Even more so when the Doctor asks if she has money for a taxi and she points out that when choosing a wedding dress the last thing on her mind was pockets.

Such is her rush that she ends up in a taxi driven by a Robot Santa (of the type last seen in *The Christmas Invasion*), but the Doctor chases her in the TARDIS. While racing down the motorway she is faced with the simple option – either jump from the taxi into the waiting arms of the Doctor, or continue in the taxi with the Robot Santa. Even then she is not convinced, but the Doctor tells her to trust him, she asks if Rose did. The Doctor tells her that Rose not only trusted him, but she is safe and well, which is all Donna needs to know to jump.

When they get to her wedding reception, which her guests are enjoying without her, she puts on a show of her own, playing the upset bride until everyone gathers around her offering sympathy. She then throws herself into the party, until it is crashed by Robot Santas. The Doctor is surprised that Donna seems to keep on missing the bigger picture – she somehow missed the big ship hanging over London the previous Christmas, and all the Cybermen in peoples' houses earlier that year (she had a hangover on Christmas Day 2006, and was scuba diving when the Daleks and Cybermen battled it out in 2007). We see the first signs of her acceptance of the Doctor when he points out that he could not get rid of her if he tried – her response? A smirk of agreement.

She is initially upset at Lance's betrayal when she discovers he has been filling her with huon particles for the Racnoss (which is what pulled her to the TARDIS in the first place), but is still upset when he dies later. To help her gain some perspective, the Doctor shows her the creation of Earth.

Despite the volatility of Donna's personality, she is smart enough to realise that the Doctor is going too far when he floods the Racnoss's lair (indeed it is because she is *not* there to stop him that he dies in the parallel world created in *Turn Left*), and she realises that is why he travels with people. He needs someone to ground him, to stop him from going too far. The Doctor asks her to join him, but she will not – his life scares her, but she does decide that she is going to travel, see more of the world. Before he leaves, she makes the Doctor promise to find someone, because he *does* need to. In return the Doctor tells Donna to be magnificent, and she responds with a smile; 'I think I will, yeah.'

For Martha Jones the producers wanted something a little different from Rose. Someone less emotional and instinctive, someone a bit more educated, and slightly older. The rebound girl, in many ways, a 'new soul mate'. She would be, as Russell T Davies says in *The Inside Story*, 'a true twenty-first century girl. She'll have a family, but they're very different from Rose's because there are lots of different ways of approaching it.'

Martha Jones – Freema Agyeman (*Smith and Jones* to *The Last of the Time Lords*, and *The Sontaran Stratagem* to *The Doctor's Daughter*, and *The Stolen Earth* to *Journey's End*, plus *The End of Time*)

It is quite clear from the moment we meet her that Martha is a far cry from Rose. She is the family mediator, sorting through the arrangements for her brother, Leo's party to ensure that her mother, Francine, doesn't have to share the same room as her father's (Clive Jones) girlfriend, Annalise, whom Clive left Francine for. As well as juggling her semi-dysfunctional family, she is studying to be a doctor at the Royal Hope Hospital, and paying the rent for her London flat. She briefly meets the Doctor while she is on the way to work; he steps out before her, takes his tie off, and wanders off again. She is not too sure what to make of the encounter. When she comes across him in the hospital later, having signed himself in as John Smith, she asks him about their earlier meeting. The Doctor has no idea what she is talking about, but her curiosity catches his interest, and his double heartbeat catches hers. After the entire hospital is transported to the moon by an H2O Scoop, she is the only one not to panic, and even attempts to calm people. The Doctor observes this, and overhears her remark about how the windows are not airtight, so even if she doesn't open them it wouldn't matter, the air would have been sucked out by now. The Doctor is impressed, and offers to take her out on a veranda to observe the moon; she is up for it even when he points out that they might die, to which she responds, 'We might not'. Such a positive attitude attracts the Doctor to her, and over the next few hours they work together to hold back the Judoon while unmasking the Plasmavore who intends to destroy half of the Earth's population to make her escape. Once Leo's party falls apart – because Annalise refuses to accept Martha's story about the moon – Martha sees the Doctor standing on the corner of an alley. He invites her to go with him for one trip, as a thank you. She is initially resistant, until he proves the TARDIS is a time machine by going back to the morning and removing his tie in front of the day-younger Martha. After learning about Rose, Martha points out that she is not even remotely interested in him, although despite her teasing it is perfectly obvious that she is totally taken in by him.

For a while the Doctor remains oblivious to her attraction, even when she makes snide comments about Rose while visiting 1599 London in *The Shakespeare Code*. She is initially a bit wary about stepping into the past, frightened she might alter her own future and wonders if her dark skin might cause a problem. She soon finds out otherwise, indeed William Shakespeare finds her quite attractive and attempts to woo her calling her 'a queen of Africa' and a 'Blackamoor lady', which only succeeds in causing

Martha some mild offence. Her knowledge of *Harry Potter* helps Shakespeare repel the Carrionites, and he tells her that the Doctor will never be interested in her, although we know that Shakespeare is. Martha is less than impressed with Shakespeare's bad breath.

After the trip into the past the Doctor suggests another journey into the future. He asks Martha where she would like to go. She suggests the planet of the Time Lords, but he refuses and instead takes her to New Earth (*Gridlock*). She can tell that he is hiding something but doesn't push the issue. However when she realises he is taking her to places he once took Rose, she realises she is now the 'rebound' girl. She is kidnapped by Milo and Cheen and threatens them with a gun she finds in their car. She is disgusted to learn that Cheen is using drugs while pregnant. She gets caught up in the pure emotion of the moment and joins the multitude of drivers trapped beneath New New York, singing *The Old Rugged Cross*, which brings her to tears. She comes to the realisation that she has followed the Doctor blindly. She could die a long way from home and her family would never know. She is with the Doctor when the Face of Boe dies. When it is time to leave New Earth, she refuses to go. She asks the Doctor what the Face of Boe told him? He doesn't want to talk about it. Martha makes him tell her about the Time War and all that he has lost.

Perhaps as a thank you for understanding, the Doctor extends their time together with another trip, this time to the New York of 1930 in *Daleks in Manhattan*. There she meets a showgirl, Tallulah, who spots Martha's attraction to the Doctor immediately and says it is obvious, to which Martha responds 'not to him'. She is repulsed by the pig slaves at first, until she realises they were once human before the Daleks altered them. She is horrified by the Daleks' callous killing of Solomon, especially after his speech about them all being outcast and working together. She wants to go with the Doctor when he offers himself up in place of the inhabitants of Hooverville, but he doesn't want her to get injured. However when he slips her his psychic paper she realises he wants her to do something else; she can use it to enter the

Empire State Building, and find a way to interfere with the Daleks' plans. While the Doctor tries to remove the dalekanium from the mast at the top of the building, Martha works out a way to channel the lightning to defend them against the pig slaves. She is saddened by their death. After reuniting Tallulah with Laszlo, Martha comments there is someone for everyone, and when the Doctor says 'maybe' she knows that he may be looking at her, but he is seeing Rose.

He finally returns Martha home in *The Lazarus Experiment*, and this time (unlike *Aliens of London*) it really has only been twelve hours, much to her disappointment. She truly believes he is simply going to leave her and when the TARDIS dematerialises from her flat she is clearly crushed. However, the TARDIS reappears seconds later and the Doctor pops his head out, his attention having been caught by something he heard. She beams!

Martha is not known for having a social life, as fits a medical student and her sister, Tish, is surprised to learn Martha has had two nights out in a row. Despite it only being twelve hours since they last saw her – for Martha it has been somewhat longer – and she hugs her family in a way that confuses them. Martha is surprised by her mother's frosty meeting with the Doctor. Her mother is not impressed by this man, especially since Martha has never mentioned him before. Leo and Tish take to the Doctor well, and are both rather chuffed to see that Martha has a man in her life.

When confronted with Tish's interest in Lazarus – an old man who has managed to rejuvenate his body – Martha warns her of the danger. Tish is annoyed with Martha, saying that she always finds fault with her boyfriends. In this instance Martha is right, since Lazarus' DNA is breaking down and turning him into a nightmarish creature. Martha's family do not understand why she would rush into a dangerous situation to help the Doctor. Francine, in particular, fears for her daughter (a weakness that Mr Saxon's people are keen to exploit). This fear is so strong that when Francine confronts the Doctor, she slaps him, making

Martha angry and confused. Nevertheless, this does not stop Martha from following the Doctor to Southwark Cathedral for a final confrontation with the Lazarus creature. Inspired by Martha's loyalty, Tish also comes along.

The Doctor asks Martha to travel with him again, but she refuses, telling him that it is unfair for him to take her on 'one more trip'. She won't be a passenger. The Doctor tells her 'If that's what you want', and she takes it to mean that he is going to leave on his own, until he says she is welcome to join him on her terms. As they leave together he goes on further, 'You were never really just a passenger'.

It comes as no surprise to learn in *The Infinite Quest* that Martha's heart's desire is the Doctor. When the Infinite grants her this, she is somewhat embarrassed when the Doctor appears.

While trapped in an escape pod with Riley Vashtee and crashing into a living sun (*42*) Martha holds on to the belief that the Doctor will save her. The Doctor risks his life to do so and dons a spacesuit.'I'm not going to lose her,' he says, having lost more than enough already. As hope slips away Martha phones her mother, trying to keep things light and to let Francine know that she loves her, but this only serves to worry Francine more. Unable to deal with the pain and her mother bad-mouthing the Doctor again, Martha hangs up, unaware that the call is being recorded by Mr Saxon's people. When the Doctor is consumed by a fragment of the living sun, Martha doesn't trust anyone else to work on him. He wants to tell her something important, but doesn't get the chance. Martha has no idea how close she is to learning about regeneration.

Having discovered that the only way to save them is to dump the *SS Pentallian's* fuel, Martha takes command and demands they dump it. As things unfold Martha works out that Riley has fallen for her, but all she can say is 'It was nice. Not dying with you'.

The Doctor gives her a TARDIS key. Martha calls her mother again, and agrees to come for tea on Election Day. Naturally they do not get there straight away, but instead, after a dangerous encounter with the Family of Blood, the Doctor realises he needs to hide for three months – the remainder of the Family's lifespan – until they die. To do this he puts his life in Martha's hands by transferring his essence into a fob watch via something called a Chameleon Arch, which can turn a Time Lord into a human. Together they hide out in a small village called Farringham in 1913 (*Human Nature*). Under the guise of a maid, working for school teacher John Smith, Martha protects and watches over the Doctor, and also finds herself having to deal with the prejudices of the time. She finds it hard to remember her 'place', often speaking out when she should neither be seen nor heard. She builds up a good friendship with another maid, Jenny, who thinks that Martha says the strangest things at times. She watches John Smith's budding romance with Joan Redfern, the school nurse, and feels slightly rejected that there is 'always someone else'. She goes to the TARDIS, which is hidden away and powered down, and finds herself saying hello to it like it is an old friend, then bemoans that she is 'talking to a machine'. She runs through the list of instructions the Doctor left her, but typically the Doctor had not considered that John Smith might fall in love. It is a situation Martha doesn't know how to handle.

When she discovers that the Family have managed to track them down, she knows it is time to bring the Doctor back, but the fob watch has gone missing. To get John Smith's attention she slaps him, and he dismisses her instantly, leaving her feeling like she alone has to somehow keep the Family at bay. She thinks the Doctor is 'rubbish' as a human and finds herself having to push him into action. He uses the children of the school as soldiers in its defence which horrifies her – the Doctor would never condone such an action. Although she feels sorry for Joan, and the effect it will have on her, Martha has no choice but to explain things to her – and uses her medical training to try and convince Joan that she is telling the truth.

John Smith refuses to accept the truth despite both Martha and Joan telling him he needs to. Smith wonders what the Doctor needs Martha for, and she tells him it is because the Doctor is lonely, and that she 'loves him to bits'. Eventually the Doctor returns, and after a very sad farewell to Joan, who cannot even look at the Doctor, he returns to Martha who tries to palm off her revelation of love as an attempt to shake him up. The Doctor accepts this, much to Martha's relief, and he thanks her for looking after him.

After an attack by the Weeping Angels in *Blink*, the Doctor and Martha find themselves stranded in 1969, where she has to get a job in a shop to support the Doctor.

The TARDIS returns to Cardiff 2008, in *Utopia*, to refuel at the Rift, and Martha mentions that she remembers hearing about the earthquake in 2006. She is oblivious to the reason behind their sudden departure from Cardiff, and can only hold tight to the console as the TARDIS is propelled through the time vortex to the end of the universe. She is a little spooked by the idea that the Doctor doesn't know what is out there – even the Time Lords have a limit to their knowledge – and excitedly follows him onto the surface of Malcassairo. There she spots a body lying in the dust – a man in a World War II uniform.

The Doctor tells her not to worry about him. She is surprised to learn that the Doctor knows him, and sad to announce that the man is dead, that is until he miraculously comes to life before her. She is receptive to the flirtatious ways of Jack and watches the slightly off-key reunion between him and the Doctor. She is bitter when Jack celebrates the fact that Rose survived the Battle of Canary Wharf, and is unsurprised to learn that Rose is a blonde. After learning what happened to Jack, Martha wonders if the Doctor dumps them all eventually. She is surprised that Jack is carrying a hand in a jar, and learning that it is the Doctor's does not help. She builds a quick friendship with Chantho, the assistant of Professor Yana, and is fascinated by the way Chantho speaks, having to play 'chan' and 'tho' at the start and end of every sentence. To do otherwise would be akin to swearing, which Martha gently bullies Chantho into doing. She also relates to

Chantho's unrequited love for Yana – going unnoticed by the object of one's affection is not a new thing for Martha. Indeed, she discovers that it is not only her that the Doctor fails to see, but Jack too, in *The Sound of Drums*. She sees Jack killed by electrocution, and is shocked once more by his revival – the man who cannot die. She listens as Jack and the Doctor talk about how Rose resurrected Jack, and she is somewhat sad by the affectionate way both men talk about Rose. She is the first to espy Yana's fob watch, and to work out what it means. The possibility scares her, although she is not sure why, but she rushes off to tell the Doctor that Yana is another Time Lord made human by a Chameleon Arch. She does not understand the Doctor's refusal to believe it – the Doctor is not alone – just as the Face of Boe said. After Yana is revealed to be the Master, who regenerates inside the TARDIS, having locked the Doctor, Martha and Jack out, she finds she recognises his voice but cannot quite place it.

They return to Earth via Jack's vortex manipulator only to discover that they missed the general election and the Master, calling himself Harold Saxon, has become Prime Minister. The Master sets a trap in Martha's flat, and blows it up. She contacts her mother, fearing for their safety, and is surprised to learn that Francine and Clive are getting back together – this alerts Martha to another trap; her parents wouldn't get back together 'in a million years'. Nonetheless she insists on going to see them, against both Jack and the Doctor's warnings. After seeing her parents carted away in a police van, and her car being shot at, she blames the Doctor and will not listen to a word he says – it is only Jack who can reach her and commands her to dump the car. Fearing for her siblings' safety, she rings back Tish and Leo – Tish is taken into custody while on the phone, and Leo is holidaying. At least one of them is safe.

She is made public enemy #3 by the Master, and goes on the run. She cannot believe she is hiding out. When the Doctor explains the story of the Master, and their centuries-long conflict, she expects the Doctor to say that the Master is his brother. Seeing the Master humiliate her family, she expresses that she wants to kill him. Unable to do anything but watch the Master age the Doctor, she accepts Jack's vortex manipulator and agrees to go on a mission for the Doctor, escaping *Valiant* (a UNIT aircraft carrier designed by the Master), and leaving them behind. But she promises to return.

She circumnavigates the world for a year, crossing the Atlantic on her own, and travels from the ruins of New York to the Fusion Mills of China, witnessing the devastation caused by the Master's domination of Earth. While she does so, she spreads two stories; a rumour that she is collecting a weapon capable of destroying the Master (built by UNIT and Torchwood), and the truth of the Doctor – the story of the man who will save the Earth when everything is in place. Upon returning to Britain, she meets Tom Milligan, a medic who is allowed free travel across the UK, and is immediately attracted to him. She comments wistfully that once again she is travelling with a doctor. When the Master learns that Martha has returned he tracks her down, and Tom sacrifices himself for Martha. The Master takes Martha to *Valiant* where he intends to kill her before the Doctor and her family. But she laughs at him, and confesses the truth of her mission. The year is reversed, and Martha and her family, caught in the eye of the temporal storm are among the very few who remember the Year That Never Was – the emotional fallout is incredible. Martha can only watch as her mother threatens to shoot the Master, the death she has seen is too much for her. They watched millions burn. This convinces Martha that she needs to remain on Earth, to help her family heal. She also realises that she cannot be second place in the Doctor's affections anymore, and so gets 'out' while she can. But she leaves her phone with the Doctor, promising that she will be in touch and when she does he better come running. The Doctor is sad to see her go, but he understands her reasons.

Sometime after leaving the Doctor, and having qualified as a doctor herself, she is offered a job with UNIT. When she tells Jack this in *Torchwood: Reset*, they both believe it was the Doctor's doing, later confirmed in *The Sontaran Stratagem*. In 2009 she is called in to help Torchwood. She tells Jack that her family is getting better and that she sometimes misses the Doctor. There is an obvious fondness between Jack and her which intrigues the Torchwood team – even though Jack has been closer to them since his reunion with the Doctor (*Utopia - The Last of the Time Lords*) he is still something of a mystery and they enjoy having someone there who knows him personally. Martha is careful to not reveal much about Jack, seemingly enjoying the mystery, and she particularly bonds well with Gwen Cooper and Owen Harper. When Torchwood need someone to go undercover and infiltrate the Pharm, Martha offers. The team are not so sure, but Jack is confident. As Martha says, she has been in worse situations. She takes on the alias Sam Jones (a clever in-joke and nod to an Expanded Universe companion of the Eighth Doctor). She is somewhat curious about Jack's private life, and his interpersonal relations with the Torchwood team, in particular Ianto Jones. When questioned, Ianto plays it coy, and offers up very little information but just enough to make Martha even more curious than before.

Due to her journeys through time, she has undergone several positive mutations, and is thus a perfect incubator for the alien Mayfly. She is saved by Owen – twice. Once, when he removes the Mayfly from her and later when Pharm Director, Aaron Copley, attempts to shoot her and Owen takes the bullet. Owen is resurrected by Jack, and he begins to flirt with Martha, but she tells him that she is already dating someone. Difference is, Owen says, he saved Martha's life, but then Martha points out that the man she is dating also saved her life (an oblique reference to Tom Milligan who laid his life down for her during the Year That Never Was – confirmed later in *The Sontaran Stratagem*). Despite her best efforts, while serving as Torchwood's temporary medic (*Torchwood: Reset - A Day in the Death*), she fails to find a way to restore Owen's life, but signs him off as fit for duty again. She goes to great lengths to point out that she doesn't want Owen's job – she is just staying on as a favour to Jack. She is aged by the Duroc (Death itself), but is restored when Owen beats it (a third save for Owen!). Before leaving Torchwood, she gives Jack a snog, explaining that 'everyone else has had a go'. Jack tells her she can come back at any time, and she responds with a 'maybe I will'.

Martha makes good on her promise to call the Doctor back. She summons him to help with a UNIT investigation into ATMOS (*The Sontaran Stratagem*). They have a very warm reunion, and Martha takes well to Donna, who is now travelling with the Doctor. Donna explains that the Doctor talks about Martha all the time, that he says 'really good things' and Martha realises that the Doctor has told Donna everything. Noticing Martha's engagement ring Donna says, 'Didn't take you long to get over it, though. Who's the lucky man?' Martha tells them about her and Tom. Both the Doctor and Donna are a little alarmed at how involved she is with UNIT, even though the Doctor recommended her, and Donna queries if he has turned Martha into a soldier (a good point, and not far from the mark as later revealed in both *Journey's End* and *The End of Time*). Martha points out that she doesn't wear a gun, and that it is OK for the Doctor, he can just come and go: 'I've got to work from the inside. And by staying inside maybe I stand a chance of making them better.' The Doctor is pleased, thinking that sounds more like the Martha he remembers. Martha tells Donna about the damage done to her family – that if you stand too close to the Doctor you end up getting burned. 'It wasn't the Doctor's fault, but you need to be careful. Cause you know the Doctor – he's wonderful, he's brilliant, but he's like fire.' She has Security Level One clearance in UNIT, which shows how high up she actually is. She is cloned by the Sontarans, which the Doctor notices almost immediately. He questions the clone's lack of concern for Martha's family when the ATMOS gas spreads out – a pointer to his suspicions. When Martha is revived, she sits comforting the clone, watching it die. She wears the Doctor's coat for a short time, and Donna tells her it 'sort of works', but Martha points out that she feels like she is walking around in her dad's clothes. 'Oh well, if you're calling him "dad" you're definitely over him.' Both Donna and the Doctor want Martha to come with them, but Martha is happy to stay behind. She has got her job, and she has got Tom, and when the TARDIS takes off unexpectedly with Martha still on board, she screams out for the Doctor to take her back. But it isn't his doing!

Despite this, when the TARDIS lands on Messaline in *The Doctor's Daughter*, Martha finds herself excited about stepping onto an alien world again. She is there when Jenny is created from the Doctor's DNA, but shortly after is separated from the Doctor, Donna and Jenny, finding herself a prisoner of the Hath. She wins their trust immediately by using her medical knowledge to tend to a wounded Hath, who quickly bonds with her. Despite the fact that the Hath do not use words to communicate, Martha seems able to understand them – presumably via the TARDIS' telepathic circuits. When she starts sinking into a bog, the Hath jumps in to save her, even though he then dies as a result. The grief overpowers her for a while, but she still manages to make her way across the surface of Messaline and finds the Doctor once more. When Jenny is shot, Martha is the first to realise she is dead, that even though she is made from the Doctor, she is not going to regenerate. She knows that she can't carry on in the Doctor's world anymore, and Donna wonders how Martha can go back to a normal life after seeing all this. She is sure she'll carry on with the Doctor forever. Nonetheless, Martha leaves the TARDIS once more and walks towards her house, fingering her engagement ring.

Months later we see she is now working in New York for UNIT's secret Project: Indigo as medical director. She seems to be on first name terms with all the staff, and when the Earth is transported to the Medusa Cascade in *The Stolen Earth*, she receives a call from Jack, who is fully aware of the project. The Daleks attack the UNIT base and Martha is forced to use the teleporter even though Jack strongly warns her against it – and she is given the Osterhagen Key by General Sanchez, the ultimate defence of Earth placed in her hands.

Once she is convinced there is little hope for Earth against the Daleks, she travels to Germany and uses the key as ransom . If she uses the key, it will destroy the planet. She offers them a chance to surrender, believing she is doing as the Doctor would want, but the Daleks lock onto her and transport her to the Crucible. There she is amazed to see that the Doctor has managed to find Rose again. She helps pilot the TARDIS in towing the Earth back to its proper spatial location, and says her goodbyes to the Doctor once again. She walks off with Jack, who tells her that he is not so sure about UNIT anymore, implying that he wants her to join him at Torchwood (since Owen died a final time they need a new medic). They are joined seconds later by Mickey.

During the 456 crisis, a suggestion is made for Torchwood to contact Martha (*Torchwood: Children of Earth*), but Jack won't have it, as Martha is on her honeymoon and she deserves to be happy. It is implied that Martha and Tom have finally married. However when we next see Martha in *The End of Time* she is working freelance and is married to Mickey. It is an odd development that makes very little narrative sense, since everything points towards her marrying Tom. This is odd considering Martha and Mickey never shared a single word during *The Stolen Earth/Journey's End* two-parter. Clearly more happened off-screen after Mickey caught up with Jack and Martha than has ever been mentioned on television.

Jack Harkness – John Barrowman continued... (*Torchwood* and *Utopia* to *The Last of the Time Lords*, and *The Stolen Earth* to *Journey's End*, plus *The End of Time*)

Jack's return occurs in 2008 in *Utopia*, seemingly two years after the Doctor leaves him on Satellite 5 at the end of *The Parting of the Ways*. He appears, running across Roald Dahl Plas, Cardiff Bay, towards the TARDIS which has stopped to refuel. The Doctor spots Jack, and with a look of distaste, he sets the TARDIS in motion again. With a yell of 'Doctor!' Jack jumps onto the TARDIS, clinging to it as it travels through the time vortex to the year one trillion, a journey which kills him.

But what is he doing in Cardiff in the twenty-first century and how did he get back there? Jack uses his vortex manipulator to travel back to Earth, getting the dates wrong, and ends up on Earth in 1869. It isn't until 1892 though, when he is shot on Ellis Island and survives that he begins to question his mortality. A few more deaths show him an unmistakable truth – he is 'the man who cannot die'. He realises that only the Doctor can explain to him what has happened, so he makes his way to Cardiff to situate himself near the Rift, knowing that eventually the Doctor will return to refuel the TARDIS. After waiting six months he comes to the attention of Torchwood Three (*Torchwood: Fragments*) in 1899. They enlist him for one job and offer him more work, but he isn't interested, until a fortune teller tells him that the Doctor will not return until the centuries turn twice. Realising he needs something to do in the meantime, he agrees to work for Torchwood.

In 1944 he meets and falls in love with a woman called Estelle Cole, but eventually has to leave. He contacts her again at some point before 2007, posing as his own son (*Torchwood: Small Worlds*). In 1975 he dates another Torchwood agent, Lucia Moretti, and has a daughter, Melissa. At some point, Melissa enters a Witness Protection programme under the name of Alice Sangster. He keeps in semi-regular contact with her, and is known to her son (Jack's grandson) as 'Uncle Jack' (*Torchwood: The Children of Earth*).

After a hundred years serving as a field agent for Torchwood, Jack returns on New Year's Eve 1999 to discover that the head of Torchwood Three, Alex Hopkins, killed the rest of the team before committing suicide. As the new head of Torchwood Three, Jack realises he will need to assemble a new team, and change Torchwood from within; rebuilding it in the Doctor's honour.

By the time of *Torchwood* series one, Jack has taken to wearing a uniform similar to one he sported in *The Empty Child*. It could be suggested that Jack's mode of dress is a constant reminder of why he is on Earth and who he is waiting for.

Not long before the Doctor returns, Jack travels back to 1941 (*Torchwood: Captain Jack Harkness*) where he meets the real Captain Jack Harkness, whose identity he borrowed shortly before first meeting the Doctor in *The Empty Child*. The two Jacks fall in love, but Jack is very aware that Captain Harkness is due to die the next day – they enjoy a romantic dance before Jack returns back to 2008. Shortly after, Jack dies for several days, his life force having fed Abaddon, the son of the Beast (*Torchwood: End of Days*).

At some point Jack obtains the Doctor's severed hand, cut off by the Sycorax leader on Christmas Day 2006 (*The Christmas Invasion*), and keeps it in a jar in the Torchwood Hub – he later calls it his 'Doctor detector', which makes perfect sense since it reacts to the presence of the Doctor, as seen in *Torchwood: End of Days*. It is this reaction, and the sound of the TARDIS materialising above the Hub, that sends Jack running towards it.

At this point in his long life, Jack has become a much harder character, bitter almost for having to live over a hundred years on Earth just to find answers. He has no idea what happened to him on Satellite 5, or why he can no longer die. During his time in the twentieth century he even pays occasional visits to the Powell Estate to watch Rose grow up, but he is careful to not let her see him. After the Battle of Canary Wharf (*Doomsday*) Jack notices that Rose's name is on the list of the dead, and he finds himself carrying this loss with him for almost two years until the Doctor tells him about Rose's life on Pete's World, which is a joyous moment for Jack. In *Torchwood: Everything Changes* Jack enlists police constable Gwen Cooper into Torchwood service, and throughout the first series she serves a very similar function to Rose during the 2005 series of *Doctor Who*. In much the same way as Rose helps the Ninth Doctor rediscover himself, through her enthusiasm and passion for life, Gwen's own passion for life and people, reminds Jack of the man he used to be before he became hardened by a century of service with Torchwood. He recognises this early on (in *Torchwood: Day One*), and tells her to hold on to her life outside Torchwood – it keeps her grounded, and that's something they all need.

In *Utopia*, when Martha steps out of the TARDIS on Malcassairo, she is certain that Jack is dead, but the Doctor tells her not to bother with him. He is very aware of Jack's state, and when Jack comes-to, he scares the pants off Martha. And then, as is his way, flirts with her while saying hello. Some things don't change, regardless of time. His reunion with the Doctor is not a very happy one, 'You abandoned me,' Jack points out and receives a very blasé response from the Doctor. Jack does not understand the Doctor's attitude towards him, but as the three of them race to rescue a man being chased by an angry mob of Futurekind, Jack remembers the joy of being with the Doctor, 'Oh, I've missed this!' he says, beaming. When Jack attempts to shoot some of the mob, the Doctor stops him, but he doesn't stop the guards of the Silo – they're not the Doctor's responsibility, Jack is. 'That makes a change,' says a very bitter Jack.

Later the Doctor almost falls into the Silo, but Jack pulls him back and wonders how the Doctor survived without him. Eventually the Doctor and Jack talk, and the Doctor explains that he had to run away from Jack because Rose not only brought him back to life, but she brought him back to life forever. Jack is, to the Doctor's mind, wrong – a fixed point in time; he is impossible. Jack admits to being called that before. Even the TARDIS tried to shake him off. Jack finds the Tenth Doctor kind of cheeky, and rather enjoys his flirtatious nature, quite a change from the Doctor he previously knew.

After the Master steals the Doctor's TARDIS, the Doctor uses Jack's vortex manipulator to return them back to 2008, just in time to discover that the Master has become prime minister of Great Britain in *The Sound of Drums*. He tries to contact Torchwood but there is no response (he later discovers that the

Master has sent them on a fool's errand to the Himalayas). After Martha's home is blown up he takes command of the situation, calming Martha down after she witnesses her parents being taken into custody. The Master makes him Public Enemy #3 (the Doctor and Martha are #1 and #2), so the three of them go into hiding. Jack, rather reluctantly, reveals to the Doctor his association with Torchwood and the Doctor does not approve, until Jack convinces him that Torchwood has been rebuilt in the Doctor's honour. Once again Jack demonstrates his knowledge of the Time Lords and cannot comprehend how such a society could produce a psychopath like the Master. He learns the truth about the Tempered Schism, a rip in reality, and how young Gallifreyans are brought to look into it at a very young age. Most run away, some go mad.

Jack still has his TARDIS key. The Doctor uses it to create two further perception filter keys to enable them to wander the streets unnoticed. He is amused by the filters' effects on Martha, and the Doctor explains that it is like fancying someone and them never noticing you. At this point Jack realises Martha's attraction to the Doctor, and how the Doctor never really notices her because his head is still full of Rose, 'You, too, huh?' Jack asks, understanding how she feels. Difference is, although Jack loves the Doctor, he is used to not being the most important person in the Doctor's world.

Once aboard *Valiant*, Jack is killed by the Master's laser screwdriver. He recovers in time to realise that the Master has unleashed death upon Earth in the form of six billion Toclafane, ordered to decimate one tenth of the Earth's population. Knowing he cannot leave the Doctor alone, Jack gives his vortex manipulator to Martha, insisting she escapes while she can.

He spends the next year bound in the bowels of *Valiant*, constantly tortured and killed, but he still keeps up his humour. He is prepared, knowing the Doctor has a plan – he frees himself and faces several Toclafane to destroy the Paradox Machine the Master has built out of the Doctor's TARDIS. He makes it to the bridge of *Valiant* just in time to prevent the Master from running, and is the one who removes the gun from Lucy Saxon (the Master's abused wife) after she shoots the Master. The Paradox Machine destroyed, time rolls back a year, leaving Jack one of the very few to remember the Year That Never Was. The Doctor returns Jack to Cardiff Bay, and once again disables the time travel capabilities of the vortex manipulator. The Doctor asks Jack to join him and Martha, but Jack admits he had a lot of time to think in the last year and realises he is responsible for the Torchwood team he built and has to return to them. But before he goes he asks the Doctor how long will he live, and whether he will age (having spotted the odd grey hair), but the Doctor doesn't know. Jack tells the Doctor how he was the first person from the Boeshane Peninsula to enter the Time Agency, and was a poster boy – the Face of Boe they called him.

Going from the evidence on screen there is every reason to believe that the Face of Boe is indeed the ultimate evolution of Jack, having lived for billions of years. In *Gridlock* the Face of Boe tells the Doctor, 'You are not alone', preparing him for the revelation that Professor Yana (YANA = You Are Not Alone) is the Master (in *Utopia*), and of course the Face of Boe would know because he was there, billions of years younger, as Jack. What causes him to evolve into a giant head in a jar, however, is yet to be revealed. There is a heavy implication in the episode *The Pandorica Opens*: River Song purchases a vortex manipulator from Dorium Maldovar, who took it 'fresh from the wrist of a handsome Time Agent'. It is known that Dorium often works with the Headless Monks, who decapitate people. Could it be that River ends up with Jack's manipulator (as well as his squareness gun) and that the Headless Monks are responsible for Jack losing his body in the fifty-first century? Is this the first step towards Jack becoming the Face of Boe?

Jack makes a triumphant return to *Torchwood*, and builds a deeper connection with each member of his team – no longer stand-offish as he has found *his* Doctor and got the answers he needs. Much happens during the second series of *Torchwood*, and Jack learns as much about himself as he does about others. Owen Harper, Torchwood's resident doctor, dies at one point, and Jack brings him back to life – ostensibly to get codes only Owen knows, but Jack later reveals in a quiet moment between the two of them that he just wasn't ready to give up on Owen. It is also clear that Jack is deeply in love with Gwen Cooper, the *facto* leader. It is a mutual love but they both realise she needs someone more reliable so Gwen marries her long-term fiancé, Rhys. He also engages in a more open romance with Ianto Jones, and develops a much deeper respect for Toshiko Sato, the technical buff on the team.

Along the way Jack enlists the help of Martha, who takes over as Torchwood's doctor during Owen's enforced leave after his death. They reminisce over their experiences in the Year That Never Was, and Jack tells his team that he would trust Martha to the end of the world. Jack is also reunited with another former Time Agent, and ex-lover, Captain John Hart (almost certainly an assumed alias, since they exchange dialogue which heavily implies John is wearing someone else's identity, much like Jack is). We meet Jack's brother, Gray and see flashbacks to Jack's childhood on the Boeshane Peninsula, wherein we discover that his real name is indeed Jack. Blaming Jack for abandoning him Gray buries him alive in 27AD, in the grounds of what will become Bute Park, next to Cardiff Castle, and Jack spends 1,874 years constantly suffocating, dying, being brought back to life, suffocating, dying, etc... until he is found in 1901 by Torchwood and is, at his own request, for fear of crossing his own timeline, suspended in Torchwood's cryogenic facility until he is revived again in 2009, where he forgives Gray and chloroforms him – storing his brother in the deep freeze. By this point, however, both Owen and Tosh are dead as a result of Gray's revenge scheme.

Jack returns to *Doctor Who* once more in the two-part story *The Stolen Earth/Journey's End*, this time with the remainder of his Torchwood team. It takes place shortly after the events of *Torchwood* series two, with Jack, Gwen and Ianto still dealing with the deaths of Owen and Toshiko. When the Earth is shifted across space to the Medusa Cascade by the Daleks, Jack's first port of call is Martha, now working in New York on Project: Indigo for UNIT. Neither has heard from the Doctor. Martha is surprised to learn that Jack knows of Project: Indigo, a mobile matter transmitter, cannibalised from Sontaran technology. Jack doesn't think it will work, and believes Martha dead when she uses it to escape the Daleks' attack on the UNIT building. Once Harriet Jones enables the subspace network, and Jack discovers that Martha is alive, he is very relieved and finds out the base code that fixes his vortex manipulator, which he uses to take him to the Doctor. Before he goes, though, he promises Gwen and Ianto that he will be back – he will not leave them wondering again, as he did in *Torchwood: End of Days / Doctor Who: Utopia*. Upon seeing the Doctor on the subspace network his first remark is an angry, 'what kept you', before he compliments Sarah Jane Smith on her work with the Slitheen (*The Sarah Jane Adventures: The Lost Boy*), and even flirts a little with her. He destroys a Dalek, which almost kills the Doctor, and helps Rose to get the Doctor into the safety of the TARDIS. Despite being the first time he has seen Rose in over two thousand years, Jack doesn't get to share a happy reunion with her, since the Doctor half-regenerates before the TARDIS is transported to the Dalek Crucible. Jack has a very blasé attitude to regeneration, once again revealing his knowledge of the Time Lords, and when confronted with the Daleks and Davros, he intentionally gets himself shot knowing his 'dead' body will be removed, freeing him to work against the Daleks while the Doctor keeps them distracted. Nothing is made of the fact that Jack is now at least twice the Doctor's age, although clearly with little of the wisdom or experience.

After making his way through the Crucible, tracking human signals on his vortex manipulator (which appears to have almost sonic screwdriver-like abilities), he finds Mickey, Jackie and Sarah. Mickey calls him 'Captain Cheesecake' while he calls Mickey 'Mickey Mouse' – still, they share a hug, obviously having missed each other. It is a bit odd that more is made of their reunion than that of Jack and Rose. He teams up with Sarah, using her warp star, an explosion waiting to happen. Alas, before the device can be used, the four of them are transmatted to the vault and a final showdown with Davros and Dalek Caan.

In his time Jack has flirted with every companion he has met, from Rose through to Sarah, including Mickey, but the only companion to really show an interest in Jack is Donna. As soon as she sees him on the subspace network he catches her eye, and when the Doctor survives his almost-regeneration, hugs abound and Donna tells Jack, 'You can hug me', but he just laughs it off. Later, when all the companions are helping the Doctor pilot the TARDIS and tow Earth back to its correct place in space, Donna tells Jack that she thinks he is the best. Once Earth's spatial location is successfully restored and everyone is celebrating, Donna pulls Sarah away from Jack so she can get a hug in.

Jack leaves with Martha, telling her that he is not 'sure about UNIT these days', suggesting she should join Torchwood – who does, of course, need a medic. Mickey catches them up and the three of them walk off into the distance, possibly to more adventures together.

Whether or not Mickey and Martha worked with Torchwood is never revealed, since by the time we return to Jack in *Torchwood: Children of Earth* he is in the process of looking for a new medic. Martha is off on her honeymoon and Jack refuses to interrupt that. In this five-part story we discover that in 1965 Jack, under direct order from the government, gave up twelve children as a 'gift' for the 456. These aliens return in late 2009, wanting 10% of the Earth's children – who are a drug for the 456. During this story Jack finds himself having to confront his own mistakes, and along the way a bomb is planted inside him, which not only blows him up but destroys the Torchwood Hub. He survives, but is buried in concrete. He is eventually rescued by Gwen and Rhys, and together they seek to find a way to defeat the 456, but the only way to do so is to use the children of Earth against them. Jack is forced to use the only child available to him – his grandson, Steven. As a result Steven is killed, causing Jack much pain in the process. So much so, in fact, that he cuts himself off from everyone, including Gwen. Alice, his daughter, walks away from Jack, never able to forgive him for killing her son – there should have been another way. He spends six months travelling the Earth, trying to run away from his pain, but it is not enough, and so he catches a lift on a cold fusion freighter which is at the edge of the Solar System. Gwen tries to tell him that he cannot just run away, but a distraught Jack says, 'Yes I can. Watch me,' and does. Jack is thus declared dead under the 456 Regulations.

His last, brief encounter with the Doctor (so far) occurs some time later in *The End of Time*, at which point he is in some alien bar still drowning his sorrows. The Doctor gets the bartender to pass on a note to Jack, which offers him an introduction to Alonso Frame (whom the Doctor met during *The Voyage of the Damned*). It is not clear, but there is a suggestion in this scene that the Doctor is aware of Jack's actions on Earth, and as his tenth incarnation nears its end, the Doctor is offering Jack some kind of forgiveness for the sacrifice he made to save Earth.

Jack returns to Earth in *Torchwood: Miracle Day*, seemingly having been monitoring it since he discovers that the word 'Torchwood' is being emailed all across the world. He uses malware to expunge all references of Torchwood, before heading back to Wales to save Gwen from assassins, and along the way discovers he has lost his immortality just as, across the globe, humanity discovers that it has become immortal. This turns out to be a result of the Three Families introducing Jack's immortal blood to the Blessing (which runs through the centre of the Earth). Jack and Rex Matheson are able to reverse the effect by introducing more of Jack's blood (which, through transfusion, now runs through Rex) to the Blessing. The result is as hoped; except Rex joins Jack in the immortal stakes (perhaps Rex is one of Boekind, mentioned in *The End of the World*?). Although he is still plagued by the guilt of his grandson's death, saving Earth once more seems to have helped Jack rediscover himself and he decides it is time to resurrect Torchwood...

Donna Noble – Catherine Tate, continued... (*The Runaway Bride* and *Partners in Crime* to *Journey's End*, plus *The End of Time*)

By the time the Doctor appears in Donna's life again, over a year has passed, during which time Donna has been seeking out the Doctor by exploring strange events. In early 2008 she visits Egypt in the hope of finding some excitement, but upon returning she realises that her same old boring life will always be there. She wants to see more, *feel* more. She often sits with her gramps, Wilfred Mott (who, unbeknown to either of them, met the Doctor briefly on Christmas Day 2008 in *Voyage of the Damned*), looking up at the stars. Wilf is concerned about Donna – he believes she is waiting for something, and so she tells him about the Doctor, adding that she is not waiting for the Doctor to romance her, it's not like that, but rather to show her the true wonders of the universe. Wilf hopes she finds him. Sylvia, Donna's mother, is constantly on her back to get a proper job, which always riles Donna. In early 2009 Donna investigates Adipose Industries, unknowingly at the same time as the Doctor (*Partners in Crime*). They almost bump into each other on several occasions until one fateful day when they eventually see each other across an open office. Donna is looking through the glass in a door, while the Doctor is outside the building in a window-cleaning cage. Donna cannot believe her luck, and she explains to him, in mime, how she has been looking for him. Once spotted by Miss Foster, they both run and meet up on a staircase. They barely have time for more than a quick reunion before they are on the run again and Donna remarks that she was right, 'It's always like this with you'.

She tells him that she believes everything now – including crop circles. Although she doesn't believe the story about the replica of the Titanic almost crashing into Buckingham Palace on Christmas Day (an event the Doctor was involved in). Despite all the danger, she is excited by the chase and helps the Doctor stop Miss Foster from breeding more Adipose from the fat of people. As they stand on the roof of Adipose Industries, she finds herself waving as the baby Adipose are transported to the nursery ship, and can't help but laugh. She tells the Doctor that she must have been dumb to turn down that offer, and when the Doctor enquires what offer, she says the one he made about joining him.

'Come with me?' he asks, as if he has forgotten, to which she quickly replies, 'Oh, yes please!' The Doctor isn't entirely sure it is a good idea, concerned that things may get complicated again like they did with Rose and Martha. This time he just wants a mate and tells her so. After a little confusion, during which Donna thinks the Doctor wants *to mate*, she realises what he is in fact offering. She unpacks her car, amazed that they should park in the same place, showing the Doctor she has been ready for ages. Before leaving she places the car key in a bin and rings her mother to tell her where she is leaving it. She then talks to a blonde girl, completely unaware that it is Rose. She gets the Doctor to fly the TARDIS past Wilf, who looks through his telescope and sees Donna and the Doctor waving. He is overjoyed that Donna's found the man she has been waiting for.

Her first journey takes her into the past in *The Fires of Pompeii*, and she is not initially convinced, thinking that the Doctor has just taken her to Epcot. He explains about the TARDIS' telepathic circuits and how it translate language for her. Donna is amused that she 'just said "seriously" in Latin'. She decides to try some actual Latin, and the stallholder she speaks to tells her that he does not speak 'Celtic'. The Doctor explains that she sounds Welsh to the natives of Pompeii. Realising that they are mere hours away from the eruption of Mount Vesuvius, and thus the death of everyone in Pompeii, Donna wants to warn them, to clear the town, but the Doctor tries to tell her that they cannot – that this is a fixed moment in time. She won't have it, and tells him straight, 'I don't know what sort of kids you've been flying around with in outer space, but you're not telling me to shut up. That boy – how old is he? Sixteen? And tomorrow he burns to death.'

When introduced to Caecilius, the Doctor and Donna are mistaken for a married couple, and not for the last time (a reoccurring motif throughout their time together; they are confused for a married couple on four separate occasions). Meeting with the soothsayer, Lucius, is confusing for Donna. He tells her that there is something on her back (foreseeing, in part, the events of *Turn Left*). When attacked by a Pyroville, a creature made of fire, lava and rock, the Doctor defends himself and Donna with a water-pistol – Donna is gobsmacked.

For some reason she thinks she comes from 2008, even though her native time is clearly 2009 (since Wilf met the Doctor the previous Christmas, which was 2008, a year after Donna met the Doctor on Christmas Eve 2007). Faced with the dilemma of either dying or erupting Vesuvius themselves, Donna is crushed by the weight of the decision, but learns a valuable lesson: some things just cannot be changed. She cries as she makes the decision to erupt the volcano, and continues to cry in the streets of Pompeii as she tells everyone to run to the hills and not the beach. They escape in the TARDIS but Donna demands that the Doctor must go back, 'You can't just leave them!' She uses the destruction of Gallifrey against him, reminding him why he travels and why he needs someone like her. 'Just someone. Please. Not the whole town. Just save someone.' The Doctor relents and saves Caecilius' family, admitting that Donna is right. He does need someone.

Donna gets her first taste of an alien world when they arrive on the Oodsphere in the year 4126 (*Planet of the Ood*). She is a little stunned by the idea of it, until she steps out into the snow. While the Doctor is showing off his knowledge, she pops back into the TARDIS to get a warm coat and totally misses what he was saying. She is deeply affected by the death of Ood Delta-50 – another example of the depth of emotion Donna feels. She may be a woman with opinions, and is not afraid to express them, but she is also a woman who feels everything deeply. She is disgusted by the idea of the Ood being treated as slaves, even though the

Doctor tries to tell her that it is not so different from her time. After discovering the truth about the Ood, who are born with their brains in their hands, Donna realises that they weren't a threat to anyone and humanity has lobotomised them. She wants to hear the Ood song, the song of captivity, so the Doctor shares his telepathic awareness with her. However she finds the song difficult to bare, and is brought to tears. The Ood refer to them as DoctorDonna – another portent of things to come.

In *The Sontaran Stratagem* we see Donna piloting the TARDIS, and she is doing much better than she should, even the Doctor cannot believe it. When Martha's phone rings, Donna is shocked to find the Doctor has one too. What could have been an awkward first meeting with her predecessor is quickly disarmed when Donna notices Martha's engagement ring. She does not take kindly to being virtually ignored by Colonel Mace of UNIT, who almost bows before the Doctor, and tells him that she will have a salute. The Doctor nods in approval and Mace reluctantly salutes Donna. She is surprised to discover that the Doctor used to work for UNIT, and that he is technically still on staff since he never actually resigned. Her temping experience comes in useful when she routes through the personnel files at the ATMOS factory and learns that not a single member of the workforce has ever been ill. This alerts the Doctor and UNIT to the conditioning of the workforce. Martha advises Donna to look in on her family, and Donna takes the advice, although the Doctor believes she is leaving him for good. He tells her of the wonders he wanted to show her, like the fifteenth broken moon of the Medusa Cascade, before he realises she is just popping home for a visit. Returning home Donna learns she has only be gone a few days, although to her it seems a whole lot longer and she shares a tearful reunion with Wilf. She tells him everything, and he is extremely happy for her – excited by the adventures she is having. Her mother, Sylvia, is her usual miserable self, but Donna does not bite back this time and merely shares a knowing smile with her gramps. The Doctor is powerless to save Wilf, who becomes trapped in Donna's car, choking on the fumes coming from the ATMOS device. It is Sylvia who saves him with a pickaxe. Donna knows she has to go with the Doctor, but Sylvia does not want her to. Wilf, however, tells Donna to leave. 'Don't listen to her. You go with the Doctor. That's my girl!'

The Doctor hands Donna a TARDIS key, which he calls a big moment, but she reminds him that they can get all sentimental after the world's finished choking to death. Donna is accidentally transported to the Sontaran ship high above the Earth. She is full of doubt when the Doctor tells her that she can figure out how to transmat back to Earth. While stranded on the ship, she rings home from the Doctor's phone, and once again refuses to bite at Sylvia's words. She shares a tearful moment with Wilf, certain the Doctor will fix things. Once the Sontaran invasion is stopped, Donna suggests Martha join them.

As the TARDIS heads off to Messaline, seemingly of its own accord, Donna is shocked to discover that the hand in the jar, which sits nears the console, is the Doctor's. Martha points out the hand got cut off and he grew a new one, to which Donna tells the Doctor, 'You are completely impossible'. She is not overly impressed upon meeting Jenny, *The Doctor's Daughter*, who considers the loss of Martha as collateral damage, and calls her 'GI Jane'. She watches the Doctor's reaction to Jenny, and decides he is not a natural father. She is later surprised to learn that he was once, but he lost every member of his family. She works out why the Doctor is so resistant to Jenny; he cannot bear the thought of losing anyone else. Donna helps the Doctor accept Jenny by pointing out that she has two hearts – that he is no longer the last. She is certain with Jenny around, the Doctor will improve. When Jenny dies, Donna is within earshot when Martha mentions regeneration, but clearly does not pay much attention to it (as her shock at the end of *The Stolen Earth* proves). Once they return Martha to Earth, Donna explains that she is going to be with the Doctor forever.

When they arrive in the 1920s in *The Unicorn and the Wasp*,

Donna is not easily fobbed off by the Doctor's apparent ability to tell the date just by smelling the air, since she has already espied a car nearby. She is dumbstruck at meeting Agatha Christie, who spots that the Doctor and Donna are *not* a couple. Donna gives Christie the idea of Miss Marple and asks to retain the copyright. She is not too impressed with being called 'the plucky young girl' who helps the Doctor out. To save the Doctor from cyanide poisoning, Donna kisses him to produce the shock he needs to stimulate the inhibited enzymes into reversal. Donna's quick thinking helps save Christie, by luring the Vespiform (a giant wasp) into a lake. The Doctor bemoans this loss of life, saying that the Vespiform could not help itself. 'Neither could I,' Donna replies.

The Doctor takes Donna to the Library, a fifty-first century repository of every book ever printed (*Silence in the Library*), only to discover the entire planet is empty. He shows her the message he received on his psychic paper. The Doctor has been summoned by Professor River Song, who calls the Doctor 'pretty boy', which amuses Donna. She is disturbed by the idea of nodes, which wear the donated faces of dead people. When Miss Evangelista 'ghosts', an echo of her conscious is stored for a few moments after her death. Donna is distraught and talks to her, attempting to ease her pain. She thinks it is the most horrible thing she has ever seen. River knows Donna's fate, coming from the Doctor's future, but she will not reveal it to Donna. For the first time Donna has to face the very real possibility that she will not be with the Doctor forever. To save her from the Vashta Nerada, the Doctor attempts to teleport Donna back to the TARDIS but instead she is uploaded to the moon-sized hard drive in orbit around the Library. She finds herself living in a false reality, one in which she gets married and has kids, living the dream she had always wanted before meeting the Doctor. It is only the appearance of Miss Evangelista that convinces her that it is all fake. The park she is in, for instance, is populated by many copies of the same two children – her own. When she is restored to reality, she wonders if her husband 'Lee' was real too, and she tries to find him. He is real, and he sees her a second before he is transported from the Library, unable to call out to her because of his stutter. The Doctor and Donna share a quiet moment, both pretending to be alright, when in truth they have both lost so much – her: a husband and children, and him: River, the only person who know his name.

While the Doctor explores the planet Midnight, Donna stays behind to relax in luxury, enjoying the break from their hectic life (*Midnight*). He returns sometime later to tell her about the horror he faced, of the creature that stole his voice, and Donna tries to make light of the situation by telling him how she cannot imagine him without a voice.

Donna's greatest challenge arrives in the most unlikely way in *Turn Left*. She visits a fortune teller on Shan Shen, who merely distracts her while a Time Beetle, one of the Trickster's brigade, leaps onto her back and changes reality around her. All she has to do is turn right and head to an interview to become Mr Chowdry's personal assistant, instead of the temp job with HC Clements. Her mother bullies her into doing so, and Donna's World is created, a world in which she doesn't meet the Doctor on Christmas Eve 2007 and is not there to stop him going too far against the Racnoss, which results in his death. The extensive fallout is felt throughout the following year and a half. Throughout this horrible ordeal, Donna is visited by a blonde girl who will not say her name, but she insists that Donna is at the heart of everything, that the timelines converge on her. Eventually, Donna agrees to go with the girl from UNIT, and she learns about her real life. She is convinced to go back in time, to prevent herself from turning right, so she can meet the Doctor and fix the timeline. This Donna does, but only by allowing herself to be run over by a truck. As she is dying, the blonde girl tells Donna to give the Doctor a message, and whispers two words. Back on Shan Shen, Donna snaps out of the trance and the Time Beetle falls off her back. The fortune teller cannot believe that Donna was able to resist. The Doctor is puzzled by the coincidences, as if there is something binding them together. All Donna can remember is the blonde girl. The Doctor wants to know what the girl's name was, but Donna doesn't know, recalling only the message: 'Bad Wolf.'

Donna realises the truth. Rose is coming back – and that has to be good. It is the Doctor's happiness that concerns Donna the most, and even when the Earth is taken from beneath them, Donna continues to focus on the good. However, she is concerned about her family. The Doctor does not have the answers, but decides it is time to visit the Shadow Proclamation. While there, Donna hears a heartbeat echoing around her. She is told by one of the women at the Shadow Proclamation that she is 'something new', that she is sorry for Donna's losses yet to come. She helps the Doctor when she mentions that the bees keep on disappearing, and learns that some of them are aliens from the planet Melissa Majoria. They track the Earth to the Medusa Cascade, but none of the lost twenty-seven planets are there. For the first time ever the Doctor seems to give up, and Donna gets almost hysterical, unable to accept it. 'Don't do this to me. Not now. Tell me, what are we going to do? You never give up. Please!'

She calls the subspace network an 'Outer Space Facebook', and is happy to see Martha again, particularly liking the look of Jack. When they arrive on Earth, Donna is the first to notice Rose, and encourages the Doctor towards her. She stands, beaming with fondness as the Doctor and Rose run towards each other, then watches in horror as a Dalek appears and shoots the Doctor. She freaks out when she thinks the Doctor is going to die, and is almost hysterical when no-one will explain what is happening. Once again Rose explains that the timelines all converge on Donna, but Donna doesn't get it. She is just a temp from Chiswick, nothing special. Once the TARDIS has been transported to the Dalek Crucible, the TARDIS locks Donna inside, knowing what is to come. As the time ship appears to burn up at the centre of the Crucible, Donna feels compelled to reach out to the Doctor's spare hand, and a Doctor clone is grown as a result. He explains that he is the result of an emergency meta-crisis, a half-human Doctor, grown from both Donna and the Doctor's hand. Donna is out of her depth, and somewhat insulted when the Meta-Doctor throws her own mannerisms back at her. Again Donna points out that she is nothing special, but the Meta-Doctor tells her, 'No, but you are. Oh... You really don't believe that, do you? I can see, Donna, what you're thinking. All that attitude, all that lip. Cause all this time you think you're not worth it.'

He explains that something had been binding them together for a long time. The truth is revealed when they meet the insane Dalek Caan. It is revealed that Dalek Caan broke the timelock and delved into the heart of the Time War, manipulating events so the Doctor and Donna would be in the right place, at the right time. After receiving a shot of energy from Davros, the meta-crisis becomes complete and Donna's mind opens up. Donna receives a copy of the Doctor's mind, becoming the DoctorDonna, as the Ood foresaw. Along with the other two Doctors she manages to disable the Daleks, and return all the planets to the correct spatial locations. She then helps pilot the TARDIS and Earth back home. While she encourages the collected companions, she pays particular attention to Jack who she calls 'the best' and later pulls Sarah away so she can hug him herself. Even now she is still Donna, regardless of the Doctor side of her.

In a tragic turn of events, she realises that her head is crammed full of too much information – the reason there has never been a Time Lord-human meta-crisis before is because there cannot be one. Donna will die if she goes on, and the only way to save her is for the Doctor to put a block in her mind. She knows this means she will forget everything about him, every single thing she has experienced since Christmas 2007.

'I can't go back. Don't make me go back. Doctor, please! Please don't make me go back.' Wiping her memory, the Doctor takes the unconscious Donna home, to the heartbroken Wilf.

'She was better with you,' he tells the Doctor. Sylvia wants to refute this, but even she knows it is true. The Doctor tells them that she saved the universe, and that 'for one moment, one shining moment, she was the most important woman in the whole wide universe.' In a rare moment of pride Sylvia tells the Doctor that Donna is still the most important woman, 'She's my daughter.' At this point Donna awakens, and she is back to shouty-Donna, the personality she had before she met the Doctor, who she no longer remembers at all. While leaving, Wilf tells the Doctor; 'Every night, Doctor, when it gets dark, and the stars come out, I'll look up on her behalf. I'll look up to the sky and think of you.'

During the Christmas of 2009, Wilf tracks down the Doctor and brings him into close proximity of Donna in *The End of Time*, who is now engaged to Shawn Temple. Wilf tells the Doctor that, 'Sometimes I see this look on her face... she's so sad... and she can't remember why.' He urges the Doctor to go over to Donna, to make her better. 'You need her, Doctor. I mean, look, wouldn't she make you laugh again?' The Doctor wants to, but he knows it would mean Donna's death. If she remembers, her brain will burn and she will die.

When the Master transplants himself across the planet and turns humanity into the Master-race, only Donna is unaffected, and the surrounding chaos makes her start to remember. But the Doctor leaves a defence mechanism, which saves her. She wakes up once the Master is defeated, none the wiser. She gets married in the spring of 2010, and once again she is oblivious to the Doctor's presence, who has arrived to give her a wedding present; a winning-lottery ticket. He gives the ticket to Wilf and Sylvia, and tells them he borrowed the pound off Jeffrey Noble, Donna's late-father, to pay for the ticket. Donna thinks it is a bit cheap, as presents go, but then remembers there's a triple roll-over prize draw coming up. Wilf and Sylvia look away smiling at the departing TARDIS.

A tragic, but nonetheless bitter-sweet happy ending for Donna...

The Eleventh Doctor
Matt Smith

> *'One day your life may depend on it. I am definitely a*
> *mad man in a box.'*
> The Doctor – *The Eleventh Hour*

After travelling for months, possibly longer, on his own, the Doctor regenerated after saving Wilfred Mott's life – but he managed to hold off his regeneration long enough to see not only those who had travelled with him throughout his tenth incarnation, but every companion he ever had. Such was the extent of his self control that the regeneration energies finally unleashed were enough to explode the TARDIS console and set the TARDIS crashing towards Earth and the life of young orphan, Amelia Pond...

Amelia 'Amy' Pond & Rory Williams – Karen Gillan & Arthur Darvill
(*The Eleventh Hour* to *The Angels Take Manhattan*)

It is Easter 1996 when seven-year-old Amelia Pond – who has spent her whole life in Leadworth but never lost her Scottish accent – is praying to Santa, worrying about a crack in her bedroom wall. She asks Santa to send a policeman and is interrupted by the sound of the TARDIS materialising in her garden – breaking the shed in the process. Her home is mysteriously void of anyone else. This is quite strange. Why would anyone leave a seven-year-old home alone at night?

Despite this, Amy is amused by the strange Doctor and proves to be reasonably self-sufficient at such a young age. She cooks him a variety of food stuffs before they settle on fish fingers and custard. The crack in the wall scares her more than the Doctor. She tells him her parents are dead and she wants to go with him. The Doctor agrees, sort of – but would he really have taken a seven-year-old with him had the TARDIS been working properly?

Amy rushes off to pack a suitcase and sits to wait for him, but doesn't see him for another twelve years, by which time she has become a kiss-o-gram. She pretends not to know him at first; certain he is nothing more than her imaginary friend. She is angry at the Doctor for not returning. The Doctor wonders why she calls herself 'Amy' now – he liked 'Amelia', but she considers that name too 'fairytale'. She introduces her fiancé, Rory, as a friend; a fact he is clearly not happy about. Rory is surprised to see the Doctor, and reveals that Amy used to make him dress up as the Doctor. Amy reveals that she always dreamed the Doctor would return to save her. Rory's only real love is Amy; he doesn't care about anything more than her.

Once the mystery of Prisoner Zero is solved, and the Doctor warns the Atraxi off Earth, he rushes off into the newly restored TARDIS, and returns two years later, 2010. Amy is not impressed, but he soon wins her over again: 'Amy Pond, the girl who waited. You've waited long enough.' Just as they are about to head off, Amy tells him that she has to return by the next day, but she will not tell him why. However, she doesn't tell him is that it is the night before her wedding to Rory.

During her early moments in the TARDIS (*Meanwhile in the TARDIS*), she cannot stop babbling, and constantly asks the Doctor questions. She doesn't know what a Police Box is, or how the control room can fit inside a wooden box. She wonders if the Doctor is a 'little slug in a human suit'. To keep her quiet, and show her the splendour, the Doctor casts her outside the TARDIS, to float in an atmospheric pocket. By the time they arrive on Starship UK (*The Beast Below*) she has calmed down. Amy explores the starship and comes across an ugly truth, but she votes to forget this truth; it is too much for her, much like it is for everyone else on the starship. When the Doctor discovers the starship is propelled by a huge space whale, held captive and tortured by the humans, he is ready to put an end to it, but Amy prevents him from killing the whale.

Amy is worried about returning to Leadworth and her wedding, and she obliquely asks for the Doctor's advice: 'Have you ever run away from something because you were scared? Or not ready? Or just… just because you could?' The Doctor tells her that yes, he did, a long time ago (referring to his leaving Gallifrey).

Amy is surprised when Winston Churchill calls the TARDIS to speak to the Doctor, and is very impressed to meet him when they visit London, 1941, in *Victory of the Daleks*. She doesn't recognise the Daleks, something that worries the Doctor greatly. She has somehow forgotten all the planets in the sky, too (*Journey's End*). It is the second concern about Amy's life – which, to the Doctor, doesn't make sense. Amy is worried about the Doctor's reaction to the Daleks, convinced that they are what they claim to be – Ironsides, created by Doctor Bracewell, whom Amy takes to, being a 'Paisley boy'. When Bracewell is revealed to be a Dalek-created human replicant, which houses a bomb, Amy helps him hold onto his humanity by talking about the idea of 'fancying someone you know you shouldn't'.

Saving Earth means letting the new Daleks get away to rebuild their empire, something that leaves a bad taste in the Doctor's mouth, but as Amy points out; 'You saved the Earth. Not too shabby, is it?'

The most important moment of Amy's life happens when they visit the Delirium Archive in *The Time of Angels*, although she will have no idea of this for at least another year. It is the final resting place of the Headless Monks, and the biggest museum ever. Amy is less than impressed with visiting a museum, after all the Doctor has a time machine. Why would he need to visit a museum? Then she works it out; he visits to keep score. She is not sure of the significance of the 'black box' they find, or the words carved in it, not even when the Doctor points out that 'there were many days – these words could burn stars', but still Amy fails to learn that the words are Old High Gallifreyan, the ancient language of the Time Lords. But she does learn that they say 'hello sweetie'. Amy is carried along by the Doctor's excitement, and when Doctor River Song arrives, Amy finds herself highly intrigued by this woman, who seems to know the Doctor so well. River shows an amazing knack for piloting the TARDIS, more so than the Doctor in fact. Amy wants to know how River can do it, and she explains that she had lessons from the very best, a compliment the Doctor takes but River goes on to hint that it wasn't him who taught her (it is later revealed she learned from the TARDIS itself). Amy watches River and the Doctor compare notes via River's blue book, and the Doctor warns Amy away from it. It is River's diary, '*our* diary' River corrects him, and the Doctor explains that he and River keep meeting out of order and that she is from his future. Watching them more, Amy is certain that River is the Doctor's wife from the future, but he actively avoids confirming or denying this point. Even River will not confirm who she is. 'You're so his wife,' Amy says, but River simply responds with, 'Oh Amy... This is the Doctor we're talking about. Do you really think it could be anything that simple?'

River shows a great affection for Amy. This makes perfect sense following later revelations. Amy becomes infected by a Weeping Angel; an image of one becomes stuck in her eye. She tries to keep her spirits up, but finds it difficult. The Doctor reminds her to remember what he told her when she was seven, but she doesn't understand (as is later revealed in *The Big Bang*, this is a Doctor from some months in their future). Once River is returned to the Stormcage Containment Facility and the Angels are defeated, Amy decides that it is time to return home. Arriving in Leadworth, Amy attempts to seduce the Doctor. He rejects her advances, not keen on repeating the mistakes he made with Rose and Martha. She forces him into unlocking visual records of all his past companions, and she is amused by how many women there have been (*Meanwhile in the TARDIS, part 2*).

Rory is enjoying his stag-do when the Doctor jumps out of

the giant cake. 'Now then, Rory, we need to talk about your fiancé. She tried to kiss me. Tell you what though, you're a lucky man. She's a great kisser.' Unsurprisingly this doesn't go down well, leaving Rory both angry and embarrassed. Amy is not too happy about having Rory join her in the TARDIS – invading her little fantasy world. Rory takes the interior of the TARDIS in his stride, and when the Doctor starts to explain about transcendental dimensions, Rory shows his understanding of such things. 'I've been reading up on all the latest scientific theories. FTL travel, parallel universes...'

The Doctor is determined Amy & Rory remain together and decides to take them on a date, to Venice in 1580 (*The Vampires of Venice*). Rory is not happy that Amy's been travelling with the Doctor for a while, but he is secure enough in their relationship that he doesn't feel the need to fight over it. However, he does feel a little threatened by Amy and the Doctor's close friendship. When they need to go undercover into Rosanna Calvierri's private school, Amy suggests the Doctor pretend to be her fiancé, which annoys Rory as *he* is her *actual* fiancé. Amy doesn't help the situation when she suggests that Rory pretend to be her brother instead. Rory fights Francesco to save Amy, but she ends up saving him instead, which leads to a kiss. The Doctor wants to give Amy away at her wedding, but she is reluctant to get married. Rory realises that Amy wishes to remain with the Doctor, and asks to be returned to Leadworth, but Amy suggests Rory join her and the Doctor; 'My boys,' as she calls them.

Amy & Rory find themselves living in a false reality in *Amy's Choice*, a life five-years hence, where she and Rory are married, living in Leadworth still, and she is pregnant. The Doctor visits them now and then. When they awake in the TARDIS, Amy reveals that a life with Rory and a baby is not her ideal, but it is Rory's. She doesn't wish to give up her life with the Doctor, and wants to postpone the wedding. Rory isn't happy about this at all. In the false reality, Rory is a bit of a bumbling man who thinks growing a ponytail makes him interesting. Amy is torn, unsure who to choose; the Doctor or Rory? When Rory dies before her in the false reality, she is angry at the Doctor for not saving him. 'What is the point of you?' she cries, realising she just wants Rory, and would rather die than not have him.

In *The Hungry Earth* they arrive in a small mining town in South Wales in 2020, and from a distance spot their older selves who have passed by to wave at them. Amy is surprised to learn that they are still together ten years later. Once again it seems Rory has much more faith in them than she does. He is also worried about her engagement ring, certain she will lose it. She returns it to him and he takes it into the TARDIS to keep it safe. Upon stepping out he is mistaken for a policeman by Ambrose Northover, and her son, Elliot. Rory plays along and pretends to investigate the local graves. He is impressed by Elliot, who quotes Sherlock Holmes saying the improbable is true. Rory agrees – he has seen enough improbable things since Venice.

Trying to rescue Tony Mack, Ambrose's father, from being eaten by the Earth, Amy herself is sucked beneath the ground. She shows her usual bolshiness when she comes to, a prisoner of a Silurian scientist, but it gets her nowhere. She manages to free herself, and with Mo Northover, she explores the Silurian city, picking up a weapon along the way. After the Doctor talks the Silurians down, he appoints Amy and Nasreen as representatives of humanity in the initial peace-talks (he failed to broker peace three times before, but is determined not to make the same mistake a fourth time). As they flee the Silurian city for the TARDIS, Rory is shot by one of the Silurian warriors, Restac. Amy is distraught, but as a temporal crack appears, the Doctor pulls Amy away but Rory is consumed by it. The Doctor drags Amy into the TARDIS, telling her she needs to hold onto the memory of Rory, but he knows she is going to forget him (just like she forgot her parents and the Daleks). It is a vain attempt since the memory of Rory soon fades completely. Amy spots her future self again, and waves, and the Doctor is disheartened to see that it is only Amy – Rory has been erased from history.

Following this, the Doctor starts being extra nice to Amy, taking her to Arcadia, the Trojan Gardens, and in *Vincent and the Doctor* the *Musée d'Orsay*. She jokes about him being so nice to her, and he responds that he is always nice to her. 'There's nothing to be suspicious about,' he points out. 'OK,' Amy says, 'I was joking. Why aren't you?' He won't say. Upon meeting Vincent van Gogh, Amy starts flirting with him, and Vincent especially loves her hair colour, thinking that they would have really amazing babies together ('the ultimate ginger'). She is surprised he doesn't like sunflowers (and is later stunned when she sees 'for Amy' inscripted on the infamous Sunflower painting). Vincent can see Amy's sadness, although she has no idea why she is so sad, or why she is crying. She really believes that they managed to save Vincent from his depression, but he still kills himself after they depart. At one point Amy remarks that she is not the marrying kind.

While the Doctor deals with a mysterious flat that should not exist in *The Lodger*, Amy is trapped inside the TARDIS. From there she advises the Doctor on how to be a normal, everyday kind of guy; going to the pub, playing football, watching TV, etc… She also reveals a sound understanding of the console, even though we have yet to see her learn how to use it. Once the Doctor has returned, Amy searches his jacket for a pen and finds instead a box containing her engagement ring. She looks at it curiously, having no recollection of it at all.

The Doctor and Amy are once more summoned by River Song in *The Pandorica Opens*, where she is camped with a legion of Romans near Stonehenge, pretending to be Cleopatra. Amy is confused by River's timeline, certain this is River from after their last meeting, but River points out that the crash of the *Byzantium* (*The Time of Angels*) has yet to happen for her. The Doctor draws attention to the fact that both Pandora's Box and Romans are among Amy's favourite things, and tells her that they should never ignore coincidences. He tells her that her life doesn't make sense – her house with too many empty rooms, her lack of parents, and her lack of knowledge of the Daleks – which is why he took her with him. When River returns to the Roman camp to secure an army to defend Stonehenge and the Pandorica which sits beneath it, she meets a very special centurion – Rory! Possibly due to Rory having been erased from history River does not recognise him, even though she really *should* (later revelations about her origins leave no room for such a lack of recognition), and this is compounded when she is later in Amy's bedroom and sees a picture of Amy & Rory together.

After rebooting the universe, and losing the Doctor, Amy wakes up on her wedding day in 2010, to find that her parents are there and Rory back in existence. She is sure there is something missing though, and rings Rory to see if he feels the same; he does, but only because he 'loves and fears' her. At the wedding reception, she sees River walk past the hall and begins to cry – sad about a huge loss. River's TARDIS-blue diary reminds her of something, and upon seeing a bowtie and a pair of braces Amy remembers the Doctor. 'When I was a kid I had an imaginary friend. The Raggedy Doctor. My Raggedy Doctor… I remember! I brought the others back and I can bring you home, too.' Rory cannot believe that he forgot the Doctor, or that he was once a plastic replica.

The Doctor's first attempt to give Amy & Rory a wonderful honeymoon fails because the spaceship they are travelling on is crashing into the planet Ember in *A Christmas Carol*. They are stuck on the ship, and call the Doctor for assistance. He eventually finds a solution, and they join him on the planet. He wants to know why they are dressed in their kiss-o-gram and centurion outfits, but Amy shushes him. Rory asks if the Doctor has any more honeymoon ideas, and in *The Sarah Jane Adventures: Death of the Doctor* he tells Sarah and Jo that he left Amy & Rory on a honeymoon planet.

After their honeymoon, the Doctor returns them to Earth 2011 where they spend at least two months. At the start of *The Impossible Astronaut* they think the Doctor is being intentionally ridiculous, appearing in the most obscure historical stories (even in a *Laurel & Hardy* film), as if he is trying to attract their attention. Although no one knows it, Amy is replaced during this time by a Ganger, while the now-pregnant real Amy is being held at Demon's Run (*The Almost People* and *A Good Man Goes to War*). Amy, Rory and River witness the Doctor's death but agree not to tell the Time Lord.

Amy feels queasy as a result of her encounter with the Silence – a strange reaction of the Ganger's connection to the real, pregnant Amy. When the Doctor is threatened again by an astronaut, revealed to be a little girl inside the huge suit, Amy shoots to protect the Doctor.

Amy, Rory and River go on the run for three months at the start of *Day of the Moon*, to see how far the Silence is spread out. Amy confesses to the Doctor that she is not pregnant after all, but thought she was. While investigating Graystark Hall, Amy finds a nursery containing photographs of herself and a baby. She soon works out that the baby is the girl in the astronaut suit.

By accident Rory overhears Amy talk about the man who is coming for her, who 'dropped out of the sky', and mentions his 'stupid face'. Rory is convinced she is talking about the Doctor again. He admits to the Doctor that he remembers the 2000 years he spent waiting for Amy to be released from the Pandorica, and the Doctor tries to reassure Rory that Amy loves him. While River and the Doctor deal with the Silence, Rory frees Amy and she tells him that he needs to get his 'stupid face' to safety. It is then that he realises she was talking about him all the time, not the Doctor, and that she was waiting for him to come and rescue her. After River shoots down the remaining Silence she wonders if her 'old fella' has seen her, and looks back at Rory who is watching. When the Doctor asks Amy why she told him that she thought she was pregnant rather than Rory, she tells him that it is because 'you're my best friend'. Rory is listening in through the nanorecorder, but Amy knows he is listening and intentionally winds him up over it. As the two of them leave the console room, the Doctor turns back to the scanner, and finds out that the TARDIS cannot decide if Amy is pregnant of not.

In *The Curse of the Black Spot,* when Rory is close to death, he insists that only she can save him, because he knows she won't give up on him. Later, in the TARDIS, the Doctor calls her 'Amelia', and Amy points out he only does this when he is worried about her. In response the Doctor agrees that he is always worried about her. A feeling Amy cannot help but share – worried as she is about the Doctor's impending death. Rory reminds her that they agreed she cannot tell him.

After receiving a message from an old Time Lord friend, the Corsair, the Doctor pushes his TARDIS into another universe (*The Doctor's Wife*). The TARDIS' soul is forced into the body of a woman called Idris and the ship is possessed by an entity called House. Together Rory and Amy flee deeper into the TARDIS. House plays mind games with them, separating them. Amy comes across an older Rory, who is angry at her for not waiting. 'Two thousand years I waited for you and you did it to me again!' Fortunately she is soon reunited with the real Rory, but the emotional damage has been done. It becomes obvious that Amy feels extremely guilty about Rory's sacrifice for her. When Idris attempts to contact Amy & Rory, the Doctor suggests she get a message to Amy. 'Which one's Amy? The pretty one?' She sends a message to Rory. The Doctor is incredulous; 'the pretty one?' They find their way to the previous console room – destroyed when the Doctor last regenerated, although the TARDIS reveals she stores all the console rooms. Amy demonstrates that she is able to operate the console even though she has never seen this particular console before. Rory and Amy can do little but sympathise as the Doctor breaks down when the TARDIS/Idris dies. Amy particularly doesn't know what to do, since she has never seen the Doctor so distraught before. Later, while the Doctor is distracting himself by working on the TARDIS, Rory tells him something that Idris whispered before she returned her matrix to the TARDIS-proper; 'the only water in the forest is the river,' which makes no sense to either of them. For now...

At the beginning of *The Rebel Flesh* we see a much more domesticated side to life in the TARDIS, with Amy & Rory playing darts while listening to music. For the first time, we can see that they are really living there, not just travelling from one adventure to another. The Doctor wishes to go off and do 'things', dropping off Amy & Rory to have chips, but Amy refuses to leave his side, saying she wants to be involved in whatever he is doing. In the event the TARDIS is pulled to a factory on a small Earth island – the destination the Doctor has in mind, although he wishes to explore it alone for reasons that become clear later. On this island they are introduced to the Flesh, fully programmable matter which can replicate any living beings.

Rory and Amy have a hard time getting their heads around things, especially Amy when later confronted by a Ganger-Doctor who she does not consider real at all. Rory befriends Jennifer, who is revealed to be a rogue Ganger, and shows sympathy for her despite her increasingly unstable mental state. The Doctor seems unusually concerned about Amy and tells her, 'I never thought I'd have to say this again. Amy. Breathe.' Amy is confused by this. 'Yeah, I mean, thanks. I'll try.' Once again Amy sees Madame Kovarian through a non-existent hatch, and she tells the Doctor about it. He calls it a mirage, a time memory, and then dismisses it. When apologising to the Ganger-Doctor for how she treats him, she confesses that she saw the Doctor die, and thinks it might have actually been the Ganger who dies on Lake Silenco.

She is so certain she knows which Doctor is which, and is surprised to learn how mistaken she is. When the Ganger-Doctor is about to give his life to save them, he whispers into Amy's ear, 'push... But only when she tells you to,' leaving Amy none-the-wiser. As they escape into the TARDIS, Amy convulses in pain, much to Rory's surprise. The Doctor explains that she is feeling the contractions and insists that Rory stand away from her. Such is the power of his voice Rory complies, although he clearly fears for Amy at this point. Amy is beyond confused, and the Doctor explains that he has to learn more about the Flesh to block the signal. Amy is frightened, *properly* frightened, but the Doctor promises he will find her. 'However hard, however far, we will find you.' He disrupts the signal and Ganger-Amy dissolves in front of a horrified Rory. Amy snaps awake, inside a medical capsule on Demon's Run, and Madame Kovarian opens a hatch and tells her that the little one is almost ready to 'pop'. Amy is shocked by her own pregnant body and promptly goes into labour.

We see more of Amy's faith in Rory at the start of *A Good Man Goes to War* when she tells the newly born Melody Pond that she knows Rory will come for them – not even an army can stand in his way. Proving her faith, Rory attacks the Twelfth Cyber Legion just to get Amy's location.

During the final battle of Demon's Run, Rory heads off to the front line, but Amy makes him promise to let all the others die first. 'You're so Scottish,' he tells her. Madame Kovarian escapes with Melody while the baby in Amy's hands is revealed to be a Ganger and dissolves as pre-programmed to do so. Amy is furious and seeks solace in Rory.

When the Doctor tries to comfort her, Amy backs away – the first time there has ever been a distance between them. The Doctor is hurt, but when River arrives she reveals her secret. The Doctor rushes off to find Melody, and orders River to get Amy & Rory home. Beyond tired and emotionally exhausted, Amy draws a gun on River and demands answers. River points to the cot. Amy & Rory realise the shocking truth. 'The Doctor will find your daughter. And he will care for her, whatever it takes. And I know that. It's me. I'm Melody. I'm your daughter.'

In *Let's Kill Hitler* we are introduced to Mels, Amy's best friend from childhood. She has never been seen, or mentioned, before, but apparently Amy and Mels have been friends forever – Mels is the first person to notice that Rory and Amy have a thing for each other and points it out. Prior to this Amy has always thought of Rory as being gay.

When Amy & Rory track down the Doctor, Mels gatecrashes

the reunion. She pulls out a gun, deciding they should all go and kill Hitler. Confronted, Rory punches Hitler and stores him in a cupboard, and they all stand back in shock as Mels starts to regenerate. Amy & Rory didn't need to look for Melody after all; she found them when they were seven years old. She last regenerated in 1969 (at the end of *Day of the Moon*), into a baby, and lived throughout the twentieth century, growing (very, very) slowly, until she found her parents. Paradoxically, Amy reveals that she named Melody after Mels. Now looking like River, although she has yet to *become* River Song, Melody attempts to kill the Doctor with a kiss, her lips layered with poison from the Judas tree. In the TARDIS the Doctor activates a hologram interface, which initially appears as Rose, Martha and then Donna. He feels guilty seeing them, and when he asks for someone who he has not screwed up, the hologram takes the form of young Amelia – a telling moment for the Doctor.

After recent events, the Doctor decides it is time for a holiday and takes Amy & Rory to Apalapucia (*The Girl Who Waited*). Amy finds herself trapped in a faster time-stream. She has to outrun the Hand-bots, who wish to cure her of Chen-7, a disease she does not have – any such cure will kill. The Doctor sends Rory in after her, since he is susceptible to Chen-7 and will die should he enter Amy's time-stream. Rory finds Amy, only it has been thirty-six years for her. She tells him, coldly, that she has been waiting for him. She had given up hope of them coming for her, and blames the Doctor totally. In the time she waited she reprogrammed one of the Hand-bots and called it Rory. She finds the glasses that Rory is wearing ridiculous (he has to wear them so that the Doctor can communicate with him), and Rory states that anything is better than a fez. This makes Amy laugh – the first time she has done so in many, many years. She considers that she has lived through hell, and berates the Doctor again, telling him it is his fault. The Doctor finds a way to restore the timeline, to save younger Amy so she never has to become the twisted older version. Old Amy doesn't like this idea, and she refuses to help. She tells them that when she was Young Amy she remembers that her old self refused to help, and so by doing so she is ensuring her timeline remains unchanged. Rory stands aside as the two Amys discuss how Rory has always loved them, and how Young Amy needs to be saved *for* Rory. This moves Old Amy and she resolves to pull time apart for Rory, but only if the Doctor allows her to travel with them. The Doctor has no choice but to agree, but he is lying. He knows it cannot happen. Nonetheless they find a way to merge the two timelines, and Rory finds himself having to choose between his wives. It tears him apart, and he tells the Doctor that he doesn't want to travel with him anymore – like Old Amy, Rory blames the Doctor for everything. This highlights, once more, that he has never been totally OK with the Doctor's influence on Amy's life. Rory is a little awkward around Old Amy once he has his wife back – he thinks it is like being with her mum. Young Amy doesn't want Old Amy to come with them. He makes his choice, by carrying Young Amy while Old Amy fights the Hand-bots, and the Doctor supports this decision by closing the TARDIS doors on Old Amy. Rory is not happy with this situation, and stands by the TARDIS door while Old Amy stands outside; he snaps at the Doctor, 'this isn't fair – you're turning me into you!' Rory is about to let Old Amy in, regardless of the consequences, but Old Amy won't let him. She has forgotten how much she loved being Young Amy. While waiting for her to wake up, Rory wants to know if the Doctor ever thought they could save both Amys, but the Doctor doesn't answer directly.

Rory's disenchantment with travelling continues in the next story, *The God Complex*, illustrating how worried he gets when the Doctor becomes friendly with someone – he feels as though he should notify their next of kin. In a moment of clarity he says, 'after all the time I've spent with you in the TARDIS, what was left to be scared of?' The use of past tense is noted by the Doctor; it is clear that Rory is pretty much done with it now. When seeing a Weeping Angel in one of the rooms of the Ersatz Hotel, Amy thinks it is for her – somewhat ironic considering later events in

The Angels Take Manhattan. Much like he did in *The Curse of Fenric* with Ace, the Doctor forces Amy to lose faith in him to stop the Minotaur's food supply. He tells her to stop waiting for him and to start seeing people as they really are. The final straw for Amy is when the Doctor calls her 'Amy Williams'.

The Doctor takes Amy & Rory back to Earth, 2011, and presents them with their new house. Rory accepts the keys straight away and goes to get champagne – for him the journey is over, and it is welcome. But not so for Amy! She wants to know why the Doctor is leaving them, and he tells her it is because they are still breathing. Amy doesn't want him to go, but he tells her, somewhat prophetically, 'what's the alternative? Me standing over your grave?' Tears are shed and the Doctor leaves. Rory wants to know where he has gone, and Amy tells Rory that the Doctor is 'saving them'.

Some two hundred years later for the Doctor, he visits Craig, a man he befriended the previous series in *The Lodger*, and spends the weekend with him, helping look after Craig's son, Alfie, and defeat an attempted Cybermen takeover in *Closing Time*. While shopping, Amy & Rory almost bump into the Doctor, but he stays out of sight and watches them from afar. Amy is now a model for a perfume called Pertrichor, for the 'Girl Who Waited'. He watches her sign an autograph for a little girl, and leaves them to it, smiling sadly.

During the confused events of *The Wedding of River Song* we discover that it is River herself in the astronaut suit at Lake Silenco, and it is she who killed the Doctor – as part of her conditioning by the Silence, overseen by Madame Kovarian. But River cheats, and creates a parallel world that is stuck at 17:02 always. In this One Minute World, Amy works alongside River to rescue the Doctor. Even though Amy knows she has never met him, she still knows the Doctor and remembers everything. But she doesn't remember Rory, although one of her key officers is Captain Williams, who is always close at hand. Amy doesn't know why she keeps him so close, but Rory does and is, as ever, waiting. As the Silence break out of their water-cages, Rory stands his ground, even though his eye-drive – an eye patch that enables him to remember – malfunctions and causes him great pain. Amy rescues him; even in this reality their bond is as strong as ever. And she allows Madame Kovarian to die after Kovarian points out that everything River has become is because of her. Amy says, however, that 'she didn't get it all from you, sweetie.' Amy & Rory watch while the Doctor marries River in a handfasting ceremony, which requires him to tell her his name (he doesn't, but pretends to). Upon contact, the real world is restored and River kills the Doctor at Lake Silenco.

Back in the real world Amy is visited by River, and they check their diaries – by this point they often see each other – and they work out that this River is from just after Amy first met her (*The Time of Angels*). Amy still mourns the Doctor, believing him to be dead, but River mentions that she still has adventures with him and she tells Amy the secret; he never died at all. Rory returns to find his wife and daughter dancing in joy, but then something occurs to Amy; now that River and the Doctor are married; she has become the Doctor's mother-in-law.

Two years pass until they see the Doctor again, and he abruptly turns up at their house on Christmas Day 2013 in *The Doctor, the Widow and the Wardrobe*. Amy is happy to see him, but she is also a little bitter that he has taken so long to visit them. Eventually Amy asks him if he wants to join them for Christmas dinner, and she tells him she has a place set for him. 'But you didn't know I was coming.' Amy smiles; they always set a place for him.

When we next see Amy & Rory in *Asylum of the Daleks*, it is unclear how much time has passed, although enough for them to drift apart and begin divorce proceedings. Rory seems the most hurt by this. He clearly doesn't want a divorce, while Amy is bitter and extremely furious with him. Amy, who is still modelling, is actively pushing him away. Both are pulled out of time by the Daleks and taken to the Parliament of the Daleks, where they are reunited with the Doctor. The Doctor suspects something is not right, but he doesn't query it for a while, too busy dealing with the Daleks, who want his help. Amy is, of course, delighted to see the Doctor, but Rory a little less so. After they are cast down to the Daleks' asylum planet, the first person Amy calls out for is Rory – a notable reaction. Despite having the Doctor back, it is Rory who she calls for when distressed. Rory finds himself alone in the heart of the asylum, surrounded by insane Daleks. He accidentally wakes up the Daleks, but receives help in the shape of a young woman called Oswin Oswald, who is trapped inside her ship, which crashed into the asylum planet some time ago.

Amy finds that she has missed the danger (which makes sense, since it has been over two years, at least, since the Doctor left her on Earth at the end of *The God Complex*), and the Doctor asks her what has happened to her and Rory – 'Don't give me those big wet eyes, Raggedy Man. It's life. Just life, that thing that goes on when you're not there.' Amy becomes infected by the Dalek nanogenes, designed to turn people into Dalek puppets, and her memories and feelings start to get overwritten. The Doctor tells her to hold on to 'scared', as 'scared' is very un-Dalek. Rory responds favourably to Oswin's flirting; it is a feeling he has not had for some time. Amy seems convinced that fixing their marriage is a lost cause, and when she expresses this to Rory he is clearly unimpressed. Her aggression hurts him. They finally have it out, while Amy is apparently holding on for her life, and Rory tells her that he believes he loves her more than she ever loved him – it is a fact as far as he is concerned. This angers Amy, who tells him not to dare say that again, but then he reminds her how he waited for her for over two thousand years, and it was she who kicked him out. Amy responds by saying she did that because Rory wanted children, and after what happened on Demon's Run she couldn't have any more. She didn't kick him out – she gave him up. After getting all this out, they realise that the Doctor placed his nanocloud bracelet (which prevents the transformation into Dalek) on Amy's wrist, and they realise that the Doctor didn't tell them because he wanted them to fix things. Fear of death is a good motivator. The Doctor returns them home, where Amy invites Rory back into the house. He celebrates when he thinks she isn't watching, but she tells him, 'I can see you.' Rory smiles and pretends to be ashamed.

It is another ten months before we come across them again in *Dinosaurs on a Spaceship*, and we meet Brian Williams, Rory's father, who thinks Rory is lucky to have Amy. Once they are transported to the Silurian Ark, Brian finds himself rambling at the Doctor, who initially thinks he is a spy until Rory points out the Doctor materialised the TARDIS around them. Rory, who is known for his own ability to ramble, clearly gets this from his father. Rory is now thirty-one (it is never made quite clear if he is older than, or the same age as, Amy, despite the stories of their school life together). Amy reveals she is a fan of Queen Nefertiti, but considers Nefertiti and John Riddell (a twentieth century game hunter) her companions while they explore the Silurian Ark, and she will not have them flirting. This is kind of ironic considering how much she flirts with both the Doctor and Rory. To save the ship from being destroyed by missiles, two pilots are needed with the same DNA – it is fortunate Brian was there changing a light bulb when the Doctor materialised the TARDIS around them. Sharing a quiet moment amongst the chaos, Amy reveals that she cannot settle, always waiting for the Doctor to arrive to spirit her away on another adventure. But she worries that the gaps between visits are getting longer, almost as if he is weaning her off him. The presence of Nefertiti and Riddell concern her – when first seeing them she wonders if they are the Doctor's new companions. The Doctor tells her; 'the others; they're not you. But you and Rory, you have lives, each other. It was what we agreed.' Amy is not entirely convinced, certain there will be a time when he will never return and she will just be left there… waiting. Despite these concerns, both she and Rory want to go back home, but not forever, just for a couple of months.

Aiming for the Day of the Dead festival in Mexico, they

instead end up in *A Town Called Mercy* in 1870, and find the townsfolk protecting an alien doctor called Kahler-Jex from a cyborg gunslinger. When the Doctor discovers that Kahler-Jex is a mass murderer, he wants to hand him over to the gunslinger to save the townsfolk. Rory sides with him, leaving Amy to wonder what has happened to them. She doesn't believe Rory will let the Doctor take Kahler-Jex's life; 'Save us all? Yeah, I am,' Rory tells her. Amy will not have it and challenges the Doctor directly, drawing a gun on him to make him listen. This is what happens, she says, when the Doctor travels alone for too long. 'We can't be like him. We have to be better than him.' Her words strike home and the Doctor acquiesces with a simple 'Amelia Pond'.

In *The Power of Three*, Amy & Rory are concerned they have two lives: Doctor life and real life. Rory believes they need to make a choice, and Amy agrees. Amy is now writing magazine articles, while Rory continues to be a nurse. The Doctor is surprised to learn they both have jobs, until they point out that they don't just sit around waiting for him in between visits. Amy explains that for them, her and Rory, it has been ten years since they first travelled with the Doctor. Not for him, or even for Earth, but for *them*, further muddying the dating of their current life. They are introduced to Kate Stewart, daughter of the Doctor's old friend Brigadier Lethbridge-Stewart (see page 330 for his story), head of scientific research at UNIT – the Doctor is surprised that science now runs the military, and delighted to learn it is Kate's doing. Amy especially likes Kate, relating to her irreverent humour – the Doctor believes the Brigadier would be proud of Kate. Amy & Rory realise that they are almost at the end of their time with the Doctor as they are both making commitments months ahead – for the first time ever. Amy agrees to be a bridesmaid and Rory agrees to go full-time at the hospital. Nine months later the Doctor arrives for their wedding anniversary and whisks them off to the Savoy Hotel in 1890 as a gift, only to find themselves embroiled in an attempted Zygon takeover. Amy even, accidentally, marries Henry VIII. Amy tells the Doctor that she isn't sure if she can have both lives anymore, because they pull at each other. There was a time – years – when she couldn't live without him, but now she and Rory are settled, they have built a life. The Doctor has been expecting this, and that is why he keeps on running back to Amy, because she was the first person he saw in his eleventh incarnation (a big change, since he has never run back to other companions who first saw any of his previous incarnations). He tells her that she is seared onto his hearts, and always will be. 'I'm running to you, and Rory, before you fade from me.' Brian helps them decide, telling them that they have to go with the Doctor and save every planet they can. Who else gets a chance to do that? Life will still be waiting for them, and so will he. Amy realises what 'the power of three' is – them. Her, Rory and the Doctor. Unbeatable.

A picnic in 2012 New York (*The Angels Take Manhattan*) goes wrong when Rory finds himself transported to the 1930s by a Weeping Angel and meets his daughter, River. Amy and the Doctor manage to track them down with the TARDIS, fixing onto River's vortex manipulator. In 2012 Amy and the Doctor find an old Rory whose timeline has been eaten by the Angels. Amy watches him die, a fact Rory finds very hard to handle. She thinks they can run, but the Doctor tells them they are not after her, just Rory. By escaping they can create a paradox, and thus poison the Angel's food source.

Rory realises the only way to do it is to kill himself. Amy will not let him, but he tells her that he would rather die than not have Amy in his life. As ever he will do anything to save her. This time, though, she is not willing to just let him do it, so she says they either jump together or not at all. The Doctor and River reach the rooftop just as Amy & Rory jump, unable to stop them. They return to the graveyard where the TARDIS stands, happy to have beaten the Angels, but a lone Angel survives. Before they can do anything, the Angel takes Rory.

Beside herself, Amy insists they can take the TARDIS and get him from the past, but the Doctor tells her he cannot – one more paradox would rip New York apart. Amy refuses to believe this until River tells her it is true. Unwilling to be without him, Amy realises that there is space on his gravestone for one more name, and she willingly gives herself to the Angel. The Doctor tries to stop her, but River tells Amy to do it. 'You look after him,' Amy tells River, whom she calls Melody once more. The Doctor tells her if she does this she will be creating a fixed point in time, and he will never be able to see her again. Amy knows she will be fine, because she will be with Rory.

'Raggedy Man, goodbye!'

The Doctor is understandably devastated, but takes a little comfort in knowing that River, at least, will pop in to see Amy & Rory from time to time.

As revealed in *The Bells of Saint John* Amy goes on to write children's books as Amelia Williams, and both she and Rory live to an old age in New York's past. Rory dies aged 82, and Amy aged 87.

Amy leaves a message for the Doctor in Melody Malone's book, 'Don't be alone, Doctor.'

Over the past few years many old companions have left us, actors so well regarded by the fans. Tributes are always made, usually with an onscreen caption, or in the case of Nicholas Courtney an acknowledgement of his death via his character in *The Wedding of River Song*, but the only companion to transcend the classic and new series of *Doctor Who* is Sarah Jane Smith, and her death is marked with a very fitting tribute. A new companion for the fiftieth anniversary, named after her; Elisabeth *Clara* Miller (or Sladen, as she is commonly known by the world at large).

Clara Oswald – Jenna-Louise Coleman (*Asylum of the Daleks* and *The Snowmen* plus *The Bells of Saint John* to *The Name of the Doctor…*)

We have, so far, met three versions of her; Oswin Oswald in *Asylum of the Daleks*, Clara Oswin Oswald in *The Snowmen*, and the version who becomes the Doctor's companion, Clara Oswald in *The Bells of Saint John*. She is a mystery, a companion splintered through time and space, with potentially billions of her existing to help the Doctor wherever he materialises – only she doesn't know it, until he turns up and she finds herself drawn into helping him.

In *Asylum of the Daleks* the Doctor, Rory and Amy find themselves being helped through the asylum by Oswin, the Junior Entertainment Manager of the starliner *Alaska* which crashed onto the Dalek Asylum planet. Throughout the story Oswin believes she is still trapped in the *Alaska*, passing the time by making soufflés, while keeping the insane Daleks at bay. But when the Doctor finally makes his way to her, he discovers the worst possible truth – she is a Dalek! Due to her exceptional intelligence, she has been fully converted, unlike the rest of the *Alaska* crew who are converted into a variation of the Daleks' robomen, but as a result Oswin creates a dream world in which she is holding the Daleks at bay. She is horrified to discover the truth, and has to fight the Dalek instinct to exterminate the Doctor, this she does and lowers the defences of the asylum so the Doctor can destroy the planet. Before he departs, Oswin tells the Doctor 'run, you clever boy, and remember'.

The second time the Doctor meets her is in Victorian London in *The Snowmen*, where she is living two lives; as Clara Oswin Oswald she is a barmaid at The Rose & Crown, while maintaining a secret life as 'Miss Montague' the governess. This version was born on 23rd November 1866, and helps the Doctor solve the mystery of the Ice Governess. She falls to her death, and before she dies, she again tells the Doctor 'run, you clever boy, and remember'. It is enough to convince the Doctor that she and Oswin are the same woman. This is enough to keep him on the lookout for her next appearance.

He first meets twenty-first century Clara Oswald when she is a young child, swinging in a park. He spends some time watching her life, trying to uncover the mystery, and is surprised to learn she has a normal life, with parents. Her mother dies in March 2005. She is not terribly computer literate, and comes to the Doctor's attention when she calls tech support, having been given the number from a 'woman in a shop' – the number is a direct line to the TARDIS. She uses the phrase 'run, you clever boy, and remember' to assist her in remembering the password for her Wi-Fi. Almost uploaded to the Great Intelligence's datacloud, her mind is returned with the technical knowledge that she receives while in the cloud. Her favourite book is *Summer Falls* by Amelia Williams, and she likes chapter *eleven* better than *ten*. She is a bit confused and weary of the Doctor initially, since he is so certain they have met before, but she gradually warms to him and finds herself gladly helping him. She is fascinated by the idea of time travel, but refuses to go away with him at first. Instead she tells him to come back the next day and ask again. Which he promptly does in *The Rings of Akhaten*, and promises to take her 'somewhere awesome'.

While on Akhaten she is annoyed that the TARDIS will not let her back in, and is convinced that it does not like her. She takes the plethora of aliens in her stride, and helps Merry Gajelh, the young Queen of Years, find the strength to sing the Long Song at the Festival of Offerings. She gives up her mother's ring, which is of great sentimental value, but it is returned to her by the people of Akhaten after she helps save them by sacrificing the leaf that brought her parents together. She later encounters a Martian Ice Warrior in 1983 on the Soviet submarine, *Firebird*. She acquits herself well when it is down to her to question the warrior, Grand Marshall Skaldak, and doesn't shy from the danger presented when Skaldak emerges from his armour to hunt them down. She is out to impress the Doctor at first, and asks how she did when questioning Skaldak. He tells her it is not a test, however she did great. When the Doctor tells her to remain where she is, safe with Professor Grisenko, she agrees and the Doctor is slightly shocked by compliance – so many companions before her would always wander off regardless. They go to Caliburn House in *Hide*, ostensibly to uncover the mystery of the 'Witch of the Well', but really the Doctor wants to consult with Emma Grayling, an empathic psychic, to find out what Clara is. He is disappointed to learn that Clara is just a normal young woman. Her continued belief that the TARDIS doesn't like her is compounded when the voice interface appears as a holographic copy of her, and they argue about trying to save the Doctor. Having seen the entire life cycle of Earth, she confronts the Doctor, thinking that she is nothing more than a 'ghost' to him. When she is trapped inside the TARDIS, in *Journey to the Centre of the TARDIS*, she discovers the Doctor's name after finding *The History of the Time War* book in the TARDIS library. Her mistrust in the time ship seems validated by the constant reconfiguring of the internal dimensions when she is lost, constantly finding herself back in the console room. The Doctor confronts her, convinced she is a trap for him, but she maintains she has no idea why he keeps meeting her. Time is snapped back to the point before the TARDIS is snatched up by the scavenger vessel run by the Baalen Brothers, and Clara no longer remembers anything of her time trapped in the TARDIS, neither does she remember knowing the Doctor's name.

In 1893 Clara finds herself a victim of The Crimson Horror, but is saved by the Doctor. Once again he teams up with Madame Vastra, Jenny Flint and the Sontaran nurse, Strax. Jenny, in particular is confused by the appearance of Clara, having seen her die in The Snowmen; all the Doctor can say is 'it's complicated'. Clara returns home to her job as nanny to discover that Angie and Artie have found pictures of her travels with the Doctor, including a picture of Clara Oswin Oswald – who is definitely not her. Suddenly the Doctor's confusion about her makes sense to Clara. She convinces the Doctor to take her wards on a quick trip to the holiday planet, Hedgewick's World of Wonders. There she hints at a possible love-interest in the Doctor, but dismisses it. She is, however, intrigued that the Doctor thinks she is the 'most important' person. But she is Clara Oswald and she was ' born to save the Doctor.' The stage is set for the revelations at Trenzalore!

Ninth, Tenth & Eleventh Doctors
Expanded Universe

With the regeneration of Doctor Who into the more marketing savvy and 'brand' conscious world of 2005 and its reintroduction back into mainstream popular culture, the Expanded Universe expands like, well, a Big Bang. There are the additions of spin-off shows such as *Torchwood* and *The Sarah Jane Adventures* and the appearance on magazine shelves of titles such as *Battles in Time*; collectable trading cards that were reinforced by a magazine containing a comic strip of the Tenth Doctor's adventures. Pitched at a much younger audience, *Battles in Time* has a colourful, stylistically simple and easily accessible look, as does another magazine, *Doctor Who Adventures*. Then there is the *Doctor Who Storybook*, a role playing series called *Decide Your Destiny* and, keeping in mind this is also a post-Internet world, the expansion continues into online projects such as *BBC Online* comics; an online series of comic strips posted on the BBC website by professional *Doctor Who* writers.

Travelling with the Ninth Doctor, Rose's first visit to an alien planet, Justicia (mentioned in passing during the episode *Boom Town*), a penal colony sprawled across seven planets, is the subject of the 2005 *Doctor Who New Series Adventures* novel, *The Monsters Inside*. Prior to this, Rose's travels have either been Earthbound or to space stations. She appears in all of the first twelve *New Series Adventures* novels, the next of which, *Winner Takes All*, sees her back on Earth and more specifically back on the Powell Estate, where her mum, Jackie, is mugged and Mickey reveals himself to be quite the obsessive gamer, talking about *Grand Theft Auto*, Sonic the Hedgehog, X-boxes and Playstations.

Rose's relationships with both her mum and Mickey are

touched upon in the *New Series Adventures* series, and none more so than in *The Feast of the Drowned*, where she travels with the Tenth Doctor. The story examines how the dynamics of not only these relationships are altered by Rose's increasing absences but also her friendship with an old school friend, Kiesha. When Rose returns to find that Mickey and Kiesha have got together she is unimpressed.

Her jealousy surfaces again in the 2007 *Doctor Who Magazine* comic strip, *The Green-Eyed Monster*, when the Tenth Doctor has a group of actors play Mickey's stunning girlfriends in a bid to flood the psyche of a creature possessing Rose, one that feeds on jealousy. Rose's attraction to the Doctor is directly addressed in the story and in order to further ensure the creature's defeat the Doctor even fakes a romance with Jackie.

Clayton Hickman comments on *The Green-Eyed Monster* (reprinted in the graphic novel *The Bethrothal of Sontar*. The comic strip was to begin with Rose, in the TARDIS, waking up in bed. However, this was quashed by Russell T Davies who said that in the new series, nobody sleeps in the TARDIS. (Though, in the TV episode *The Doctor's Wife*, it is disclosed that the TARDIS has bunk beds. Also, in the 2006 novel, *The Stone Rose* – in which Mickey discovers a statue of Rose in a museum – it is revealed that the Doctor has a set of *Winnie the Pooh* bed linens.)

In *The Stone Rose* the Doctor asks Rose if she has ever come close to marrying anyone that she shouldn't have. This could be a reference to Jimmy Stone, an ex-boyfriend of Rose's to whom she was engaged.

However, all this occurred prior to her meeting the Doctor and we'll return to that in a moment. More probable though is that it is a reference to one of Rose's stranger episodes in the Expanded Universe, namely the 2005 novel, *Only Human*, in which she marries a Neanderthal man named Tillun. Marriage sees her dispensing with Tyler and becoming Rose Glathicgacymcilliach. Technically though she ends up a widow as Tillun remains in his own time where he lives out his life.

Probably the best source of biographical information about Rose can be found in an article called *Meet Rose*, included in the 2006 *Doctor Who Annual* and written by Russell T Davies. Here we learn that Rose's middle name is Marion and that she has always dreamed of travelling. However, a school trip to France at the age of thirteen was the furthest she had ever got and this didn't end well; although it did reveal an early taste for adventure; Rose, and Shareen Costello, her best friend, gave their teachers the slip and rode a train to a completely different destination from the scheduled one. They were eventually found by the police and subsequently sent home.

Rose started dating Mickey Smith, who lived on the same estate, when she was fourteen years old, claiming that it really wasn't anything special. At school further trouble occurred when she managed to talk the school choir into going on strike, resulting in a three day suspension for her. Rose, despite her ongoing tendency for mischief, did reasonably well in her exams, getting an A, a couple of Bs, four Cs and finally a D in science. Encouraged by this she made plans to study English, Art and French at A-Level. Sadly though, this wasn't to be the case.

Jimmy Stone was twenty, had the title of fittest boy on the estate and played bass in a local band, No Hot Ashes. Rose fell very deeply for Jimmy and, after dumping Mickey and leaving home, she moved into a bedsit with him. Only five months later she was back at home, heartbroken and £800 in debt whilst Jimmy was in Amsterdam with a woman named Noosh. Mickey forgave Rose and they got back together. She then got a temporary job to try and pay off her debt before getting, with Jackie's help, a more permanent position in Henriks, which of course, was destined to go up in flames.

In addition to this Rose is a fan of the Vengaboys, according to the 2006 short story *Voice from the Vortex!* in *Doctor Who Magazine* (written in the style of 1960s comics), as well as the Erasure song *Sometimes* which she sings during *Opera of Doom*, included in the 2007 *Doctor Who Storybook*.

What kind of an individual would get stranded in the Ataline System with only a traffic cone? Welcome to Captain Jack Harkness. The Ataline incident is referred to in *The Stealers of Dreams*, a 2005 Ninth Doctor novel which is set in a world where fiction is against the law. Here Jack references his connection with the Time Agency. Jack tells the enemy that he is a Time Agent and will summon a Time Agency warfleet should he be forced to. This is a highly significant threat to most alien races as the Time Agency is much feared.

The Stealers of Dreams is also notable in that Jack mentions knowing the Face of Boe, touching on a contentious subject since the television episode *The Last of the Time Lords*; is Jack Harkness the Face of Boe? *The Stealers of Dreams* was released almost two and half years before *The Last of the Time Lords* was aired, and the idea of a connection hadn't yet been fully conceptualised. In this novel Jack recalls the Face of Boe as being a local figure of some fame in his own time, which doesn't negate the Face being Jack, living through Jack's own pre-Doctor life.

Rather than looking to the *Doctor Who* novels, audio stories and magazines as a source of information about the development of Jack's character, it is more fruitful to delve into *Torchwood*'s Expanded Universe. Although in *The Forgotten*, a 2008-2009 *Doctor Who* comic strip from IDW, during the Ninth Doctor part of the story Jack is mentioned by a soldier who talks about him surviving a bullet in the head. This is in keeping with Jack's TV timeline which suggests on a few occasions that he left Torchwood Three in order to enlist in both World Wars.

In the 2008 *Torchwood* novel, *The Twilight Streets*, the 1940s Jack is seen as being critical and disapproving of Torchwood's approach and methods and is persuaded by Greg, a former boyfriend, to become a freelance agent. Also in the novel is an explanation that during the events of *Boom Town* – in which a younger Jack arrives with the Doctor and Rose to refuel the TARDIS at Cardiff Bay – to avoid a paradox involving his past self Jack puts a lockdown on all Torchwood activity. *Trace Memory* also sees Jack still working as a freelance agent for Torchwood in the 1960s.

Much like *Doctor Who Magazine*, but with less frequency, the monthly *Torchwood Magazine* featured comic strips in which Jack made regular appearances. Perhaps most noteworthy here is the 2009 story *Captain Jack and the Selkie*, written by John Barrowman and his sister Carole E Barrowman. This writing duo return for the 2012 novel, *Exodus Code*, which is set after the events of *Torchwood: Miracle Day*, and sees Jack dealing with more consequences of his immortal life, brought down somewhat by becoming mortal in *Miracle Day*. He is no longer convinced he will remain immortal.

Martha makes her debut in the Expanded Universe a month before her first appearance on television.

In Terrance Dick's novella *Made of Steel* she mentions that she is the cousin of Torchwood Institute employee, Adeola Oshodi, which is later confirmed in *Smith and Jones*. (Her identical cousin?)

One of the traits to emerge regarding her character on reading the novels is that Martha is quite a dedicated blogger. In *The Last Dodo* she refers to the creatures as 'giant mental birds' in her blog, showing a flair for vivid description, while in *Wetworld* her entry reads 'the time the Doctor left me stuck in the TARDIS – in a swamp!'.

When she steps into the TARDIS, Martha is also entering the life of a Doctor who is still very much haunted by the memory of Rose, and, it appears, is still very much in a state of grief. Martha finds Rose's jacket in the TARDIS in *Peacemaker and the Doctor* doesn't cope very well with the discovery at all. Incidentally, in the same novel Martha mentions that she purchased her own jacket from Henriks. When the Doctor tells Martha not to be upset if the TARDIS refers to her as Rose in the 2008 novel, *The Many Hands*, there is a sense of how intimidating it possibly is for her living in a post-Rose TARDIS.

Focusing on the year between *The Sound of Drums* and the *Last of the Time Lords*, *The Story of Martha*, a 2008 novel, sees the character getting a story all to herself. It traces Martha's journey from the Toclafane attack, as she arrived on Earth, to her eventual return to the United Kingdom, where a showdown with the Master awaits. This, probably more than any other work, provides the reader with a real insight into Martha's courage, determination and resilience as she tries to survive in a hostile environment in order to spread the Doctor's story to as many people as possible.

Martha's medical expertise, her employment with UNIT and her personal life are all touched upon in the Expanded Universe. Her medical training is utilised occasionally, but in *The Last Soldier*, a comic strip in *Doctor Who Magazine*, she talks of returning to a planet in her professional capacity only. It tells of a world on which only the very last male and female survivors of a war, each from opposing sides, are able to reproduce. Martha talks about returning to deliver the new arrival. Referring to the war, she states that she sees quite enough fighting at the hospital on a typical Saturday night.

Tesseract, an IDW 2010 comic strip, sees Martha filling in as UNIT's Scientific Director while in another 2010 IDW strip, *Don't Step on the Grass*, the reason for Martha's departure from UNIT is established as being the incident involving the Osterhagen key. In this story she is working with UNIT on a strictly temporary basis as a freelancer, and even this is done only as a favour to Malcolm Taylor (UNIT's scientific advisor last seen on television in *Planet of the Dead*), who is a friend of hers. In both stories Martha's marital status is alluded to; *Tesseract* mentions her recent wedding but Martha doesn't specify the identity of the man she has married. *Don't Step on the Grass* however has Captain Erisa Magambo (featured on television in both *Turn Left* and *Planet of the Dead*) referring to her as Mrs Smith, which may indicate that she is now married to Mickey Smith. Fueling this allusion is Martha's observation that Matthew is suffering from 'tin-dog syndrome' – a depressed state of mind where the sufferer feels like the least valuable companion. Mickey Smith is, of course, the original victim of tin-dog syndrome in *School Reunion* but Martha isn't present and wouldn't have known about it unless she found out some other way...

Donna definitely tops Tegan in terms of referencing popular culture. Making her first Expanded Universe audio appearance in 2008's *Pest Control*, Donna makes repeated *Star Trek* references and joins the Doctor in briefly assuming the aliases of Captain Kirk (Donna) and Dr McCoy (the Doctor). You have to wonder if Donna is a bit of a Trekker as in *The Nemonite Invasion*, a 2009 audio adventure, she says the Doctor's mind-reading skills are very much like Spock's mind-meld. To this the Doctor comments that he thinks she watches far too much television. You can see his point as she goes on to refer to him as Joe 90 in the same story and even claims that she and the Doctor are in the employ of *The X-Files* when asked for identification at one point. Returning to *Pest Control*, Donna calls one of the centaurs, Firenze, which is also the name of a centaur in the *Harry Potter* series. She also appears to be a *He Man and the Masters of the Universe* fan as she twice refers to a villain as Skeletor; once to Meng in *The Immortal Emperor*, a comic strip in the 2009 *Doctor Who Storybook*, then again to one of the Sycorax in *The Widow's Curse*.

As for biographical details there's really very little to be gleaned from the Expanded Universe in terms of Donna. In the 2008 novel, *The Ghosts of India*, Donna mentions a cousin called Janice who must be a cousin on her father's side as Wilfred Mott, her maternal grandfather, informs the Doctor that Donna is his only grandchild in the TV episode *The Sontaran Stratagem*. While in *The Lonely Computer*, a short story published on the BBC website in 2008, Donna talks about working in telemarketing, and more specifically about the 'primitives' she was forced to work with, one of whom was a staunch Manchester United fan. You can understand this not getting a warm reception from Donna, who is a staunch West Ham United fan.

Amy does a great Dalek impression. In *The Silent Stars Go By*, a longer than usual 2011 *Doctor Who* publication featuring the Ice Warriors, Amy tries to describe the Daleks, saying, 'Ras-py voiced a-liens who talk like this and yell ex-ter-mi-nate.' She makes her debut in the 2010 novel, Apollo 23, and is joined by Rory in *Nuclear Time*, a 2010 novel, that has Rory comparing a quiet town to the one in *Texas Chainsaw Massacre*.

Like Tegan and Donna before them, Amy & Rory aren't slow in coming up with a reference to popular culture. Perhaps the most memorable moment though is when Rory notices that the Cemar, in the 2011 novel *The Good, The Bad and The Alien*, look just like meerkats. He turns to Amy and says 'simples' referencing the comparison website character, Aleksandr the Meerkat. Another worthy inclusion is Amy's reference to *Doctor Who* in the 2011 *Doctor Who Magazine* comic story, *The Professor, the Queen and the Bookshop*, where she is seen to be reading a copy of *Shada*, the 2012 *Doctor Who* novel.

The dynamics of the relationship between the Doctor, Amy & Rory, and all its tensions, bickering, affection and teasing are played out in the Expanded Universe, often following up the repercussions of events in the TV series. In *The King's Dragon*, a 2010 novel, Rory confronts the Doctor about having kissed Amy in the TV episode, *Flesh and Stone*. Rory actually slaps the Doctor in *The Cornucopia Caper*, a 2012 comic strip in *Doctor Who Magazine,* after which the Doctor states that he has been slapped by angry brides, angry mothers and angry archaeologists. When trying to impress Amy by telling her that the Doctor has taken him to the moon, Rory gets the response 'been there, done that' in the novel 2011 *Heart of Stone*, a two-in-one book also featuring the story, *Death Riders*. The Doctor's approach is criticised somewhat in *Death Riders* when Rory observes that without his sonic screwdriver the Doctor would simply resort to smashing controls with his shoe. In the same story Amy steals the Doctor's catchphrase of 'Geronimo!' leaving him feeling quite indignant at having missed out on an opportunity to use it; the catchphrase actually gets far more usage in the Expanded Universe than it does in the television series.

In regard to any new biographical details to be found in the Expanded Universe there are a few to be gleaned. The 2010 novel *The Forgotten Army*, tells us that before she moved to Leadworth, Amy grew up in Inverness, Scotland, which is also the home city of Karen Gillan who plays the character. According to the 2011 audio drama, *The Gemini Contagion*, Amy didn't see the point of learning French at school as she never believed she was ever going to go anywhere other than Leadworth (how wrong could she be!). The 2010 novel *The King's Dragon* includes the first reference in any *Doctor Who* media to Rory's family. Both Amy and Rory mention his grandmother and the especially impressive gravy she used to make.

Perhaps the most poignant piece of biographical information though is given in the 2012 *Doctor Who Magazine* comic strip, *Imaginary Enemies*, which is the final story to feature Amy and Rory. At the story's close the reader is presented with a series of images representing the later years of Amy and Rory's life after *The Angels Take Manhattan*, where they were trapped back in time by the Weeping Angels. Rory is pictured as a doctor, suggesting that he took his medical career further.

Other moments worth mentioning here are Amy slipping in a huge pile of dung in *The Forgotten Army*, a 2010 novel, which is packed with humour in a similar vein. In the 2012 novella, *Magic of the Angels*, Amy dons a sparkly catsuit once worn by Zoe Heriot, the Second Doctor's companion, while the Doctor wears the Third Doctor's outfit. Confusing!

So far Clara has only appeared in a handful of comic strips in *Doctor Who Adventures*, and one original novel, *Shroud of Sorrow*, which takes place on 23rd November 1963, the day of the very first episode of *Doctor Who*. This book also features Totter's Lane with much reference to *An Unearthly Child*. Understandably, due to the ongoing mystery of Clara, little of interest is revealed about her.

The Tenth Doctor has a whole host of Expanded Universe companions. Heather McCrimmon is probably the most distinctive companion created for the comics; created by Joanne Hall, the ten-year-old winner of a competition to create a companion for the *Doctor Who Adventures* comic strip. In terms of pure story count, Heather became one of the longest-serving companions, but her most interesting attribute is that she is a direct descendent of Second Doctor companion, Jamie, and his Expanded Universe wife, Kirsty. Such is her importance to the Doctor, that just before his tenth regeneration (*The End of Time*), he visits her briefly to save her life, much like he does with the television companions he travels with.

Other companions include Gisella who appears in several novels. An apparent twelve-year-old girl in charge of the underwater research base at Flydon Maxima, she is revealed to be an android in *The Pictures of Emptiness*. Space Major Jon Bowman, a one-off companion for *Prisoner of the Daleks* is notable for the similarity between his name and Captain Jack actor, John Barrowman. Majenta Pryce is another of those rare companions, in that she's not native to Earth. From the planet Vessica, she travels with the Doctor in the comic pages of *Doctor Who Magazine* issues *#394 - #420*. Heather is joined by Wolfgang Ryster, created by Hamish Cough, the twelve-year-old winner of a competition for *Doctor Who Adventures*. A sixteen-year-old exchange student from Austria, Wolfie leaves at the same time as Heather and is there when the Doctor drops by to save his and Heather's life prior to the Doctor's tenth regeneration. Matthew Finnegan and Emily Winter also join the Doctor for a series of adventures in IDW's *Doctor Who* comics.

Not to be outdone by his past selves and their predilection for strange comic companions, the Eleventh Doctor travels for a time with a robotic Tyrannosaurus Rex called Kevin Grimlock in the pages of IDW's *Doctor Who* comic, first appearing in *When Worlds Collide*. He leaves the Doctor to become the security chief of a space station in *Space Squid*. The Doctor is also joined by another shapeshifter (following on from the successful Kamelion and Frobisher) by the name of Decky Flamboon in *Doctor Who Adventures* – another result of a create-a-companion competition, this time created by Mitchell Collett.

No mention of the Eleventh Doctor's Expanded Universe companions is complete without acknowledging his very special companions, the entire crew of *USS Enterprise NCC-1701-D*, including Captain Jean-Luc Picard, Commander William Riker, Lieutenant Commander Data, Counsellor Deanna Troi, Lieutenant Commander Geordi LaForge, Lieutenant Worf, Doctor Beverly Crusher and Guinan. They all appear to help the Doctor, Amy & Rory combat a combined army of Cybermen and Borg in the pages of IDW's *Doctor Who/Star Trek: The Next Generation* crossover extravaganza. It's just a pity Donna isn't about at the time, being a Trekker she would have had a field day on *Enterprise*.

The Brigadier

Nicholas Courtney

'I just do the best I can.'
The Brigadier – *Battlefield*

Brigadier Sir Alistair Lethbridge-Stewart. No book about the Doctor's companions would be complete without an entry for the Brigadier – even though he was not technically a companion, he is the one character who transcends the entire series, and almost every Doctor, in one media or another. The Doctor's oldest friend...

Alistair Gordon Lethbridge-Stewart – Nicholas Courtney (The Web of Fear to Terror of the Zygons and Mawdryn Undead, The Five Doctors and Battlefield plus Enemy of the Bane)

When we first meet the Brigadier he isn't even a *brigadier*, but rather a colonel in the Scott's Guard. While the Great Intelligence is planning an assault on London with its robotic Yeti in the 1968 story *The Web of Fear*, Colonel Lethbridge-Stewart takes control of the armed forces there and bumps into the Doctor while searching the London Underground. They do not have the most auspicious of starts, with Lethbridge-Stewart being initially suspicious of this impish little man. The Doctor proves his worth, and the seeds of their friendship are planted when Lethbridge-Stewart places his trust, not to mention the safety of his men, in the Doctor's hands. After defeating the Great Intelligence, Lethbridge-Stewart considers the Doctor a hero, but the Doctor disappears after he learns that a reporter wants to make him a household name. It is some four years before they meet again, by which time UNIT (the United Nations Intelligence Taskforce) has been formed to counter alien threats, and Lethbridge-Stewart has been promoted to brigadier and commander of the United Kingdom branch of UNIT.

UNIT is investigating the strange goings-on at International Electromatics, run by industrialist Tobias Vaughn. The Doctor and Jamie stumble into things there and are spotted by UNIT surveillance, and brought immediately to a reunion with the Brigadier. It is a happy meeting, and the Brigadier immediately enlists the Doctor's help to prevent *The Invasion* of the Cybermen. Sometime later the Brigadier is trying to draft Liz Shaw into being UNIT's scientific advisor (*Spearhead from Space*). He talks about the Doctor as an expert on alien life, unaware that the Doctor is about to fall into his life in a rather permanent way. Freshly regenerated by the Time Lords and exiled to Earth, the Third Doctor is not initially accepted by the Brigadier, who doesn't believe it is the same man, even though the Doctor clearly knows him. He gradually warms to this new Doctor, who is somewhat brusque towards the Brigadier, dismissing him with a wave at one point. Once the first Nestene invasion is defeated the Brigadier asks the Doctor to stick around in case they should try again. The Doctor becomes UNIT's unofficial, although unpaid, scientific advisor, with Liz now serving as his assistant.

The Doctor remains for several years, even after his exile is rescinded, and over time an extremely strong friendship is developed between the two men. It takes some time, however, since the easy companionship the Brigadier and the Second Doctor enjoyed is gone, replaced by a Doctor who is less forgiving of the Brigadier's military mindset. One of the most notable early examples of them clashing was at Wenley Moor in *Doctor Who and the Silurians*. Once the Doctor has successfully beaten the Silurian plague, he wishes to broker a peace between humanity and the Silurians (the original owners of the Earth), and as soon as his back is turned, the Brigadier sets off charges and destroys the Silurian hibernation settlement beneath the moor; to the

Doctor this approaches genocide, or at the very least murder. Their relationship remains strained for a short while afterwards, but still stranded on Earth the Doctor continues in his role as scientific advisor.

Things come to a head once more at the end of *Inferno* when the Doctor decides he is leaving Earth, having seemingly got the TARDIS console working again. He makes a point of saying he will not miss the Brigadier, but when the console sends him to a nearby rubbish tip, he returns with his tail between his legs. The Brigadier takes great pleasure in reminding the Doctor of his harsh words before agreeing to help. This pretty much encapsulates their relationship for the next couple of years – two men who have a grudging respect for each other, but are not quite friends yet. One can almost suspect that the Brigadier's assigning of Jo Grant to the Doctor is an act of spite – faced with an agent he doesn't know what to do with; he simply palms her off onto the Doctor. When the Doctor wants rid of her, the Brigadier refuses to accept the responsibility of telling her, and says if he wishes to 'sack' Miss Grant he will have to tell her himself. One might argue the arrival of Jo mellows the Doctor and smoothes relations between him and the Brigadier.

In *Day of the Daleks* the Brigadier makes it quite clear that he doesn't believe in ghosts, a fact the Doctor enjoys mocking before explaining his scientific rationale behind such things. This kind of insight slowly changes the Brigadier's ideals about science versus military might, as reflected in the 2012 episode *The Power of Three* when his daughter, Kate, tells the Eleventh Doctor that her father drove into her that 'science leads'. By the time Jo makes known her intentions to leave UNIT (and the Doctor) to get married, the Doctor and Brigadier's friendship is strong enough to keep the Doctor attached to UNIT, even though he has no reason to remain behind any more.

The two men have a smilar sense of humour which is made obvious when, in *Planet of the Spiders*, the Doctor discovers, via the latent telepathic abilities of Professor Clegg that sometime ago the Brigadier had a tryst with a woman called Doris in Brighton, where she bought him a much-loved watch. The Brigadier takes the Doctor's ribbing well, but is clearly embarrassed by such private information being revealed by a stranger. He grows used to the Doctor's sporadic trips in the TARDIS, especially once Sarah joins him. The Brigadier is there when the Doctor undergoes his third regeneration; his reaction is a far cry from his protracted acceptance of the Third Doctor. He merely raises an eyebrow and says, 'Well, here we go again'.

He is more amused than annoyed when the newly regenerated Fourth Doctor departs abruptly rather than give an address at Buckingham Palace.

It is in *Terror of the Zygons* that we discover that the Brigadier is of Scottish descent, of the Clan Stewart, and proudly wears a kilt while in Scotland. Shortly after the Brigadier seems to become heavily involved in the bureaucracy of UNIT business, spending an increasing amount of time away from direct command of UNIT UK. When the Doctor returns in both *The Android Invasion* and *The Seeds of Doom*, UNIT is being commanded by two replacements while the Brigadier is away in Geneva.

The Brigadier leaves UNIT in 1976, and is replaced by Colonel Crichton (as seen in *The Five Doctors*). He moves on to teaching A-level maths at Brendon Public School in 1977. He meets Tegan in *Mawdryn Undead*, during the Queen's Silver Jubilee and becomes involved in an adventure which sees him losing much of his memory – particularly in connection with the Doctor. When the Fifth Doctor arrives at Brendon in 1983, the Brigadier totally fails to recognise him, despite the Doctor reminding him of their time at UNIT and his ability to regenerate. Eventually the Doctor jogs the Brigadier's memory, and he accompanies the Doctor on a ship stuck in a warp ellipse. There he meets his younger self from 1977 and as they touch hands the Blinovitch Limitation Effect shorts out the time differential, causing the 1977-Brigadier to lose all memory of the Doctor.

While attending a reunion at UNIT HQ, the Brigadier is visited by the Second Doctor, who is 'bending' the Laws of Time, in *The Five Doctors*. They are both time-scooped to the Death Zone on Gallifrey where they have to find their way to the Dark Tower and Rassilon, the single greatest figure in Time Lord history. There the Brigadier is reunited with other incarnations of the Doctor, the Fifth, Third and First and is reacquainted with both Sarah and Tegan. He strangely ignores Turlough, however, whom he taught at Brendon previously. He also takes great pleasure in flooring the Master with a single punch, 'how nice to see you again,' no doubt taking out years of frustration at being beaten by the Master so many times during his UNIT days.

It is many years before the Brigadier meets the Doctor again, in a piece of flam called *Dimensions in Time*. Giving the Doctor a helicopter ride to the Greenwich Meridian, he fails to spot that he has picked up the Third Doctor but is dropping off the Sixth. The Brigadier does say, however, that he is having trouble keeping up with all the Doctors. At some point before the 1990s, he gives up teaching and leaves UNIT permanently, and marries Doris. He is called out of retirement by Geneva, being told that the Doctor is back. Doris doesn't want him to go, but the presence of the Doctor is the deciding factor. He has to go.

In *Battlefield*, the Brigadier throws himself into the events at Carbury and rather enjoys the adventure. After reading the report of Brigadier Bambera, he assumes his replacement is a man and is a little surprised to discover that *Winifred* Bambera is a woman, although he doesn't let any respect for the fairer sex get in the way. His awkwardness around women is emphasised in his initial bad handling of Ace, but they soon bond over her love of explosives, and work together to blow up King Arthur's spaceship. The Brigadier, an old hand at regeneration by now, is not slightly fazed by the Doctor's new appearance, recognising him immediately; 'who else would it be?' he asks with a smile. He single-handedly stands down the Destroyer, armed with only his faithful revolver and silver bullets. The Destroyer asks if the world can do no better than the Brigadier, to which he replies, 'Probably. I just do the best I can,' and pumps bullets into the creature. The Doctor thinks the Brigadier has been killed as a result, and states how the Brigadier was supposed to die in bed, but the Brigadier waves this away. 'Have a little faith,' he tells the Doctor.

Over the following years the Brigadier is made a Commander of the British Empire and becomes Sir Alistair. Shortly after this he takes on a position as UNIT's special envoy, and is often sent overseas, especially to Peru, where he tends to get stuck quite a lot. This is evident in *The Sontaran Stratagem* when the Sontarans attempt to turn Earth into a cloning planet in 2009. The Tenth Doctor bemoans the lack of his presence. Shortly after returning from Peru he is debriefed by Major Kilburne and visited by a very old friend, Sarah Jane Smith (*The Sarah Jane Adventures: Enemy of the Bane*). Although they haven't seen each other in a long time, they have kept in contact and the Brigadier often pulls strings at UNIT whenever Sarah needs help (in such stories as *SJA: Invasion of the Bane* and *SJA: Revenge of the Slitheen*). By the time of Sarah's wedding and later when a faux funeral for the Doctor is arranged, the Brigadier is back in Peru and thus unable to attend.

Tragedy finally strikes at some point around 2012 when the Eleventh Doctor makes a phone call to speak to the Brigadier, only to discover the old soldier died peacefully in his bed, as the Seventh Doctor had previously anticipated. The nurse to whom the Doctor speaks informs him that the Brigadier always talked of the Doctor, and kept a small glass of brandy ready for him. The news hits the Doctor hard, and is enough to convince him to face his own death in *The Wedding of River Song*.

Their long-standing friendship inspires the Brigadier's daughter, who goes on to be a lead scientist in UNIT (now renamed the UNified Intelligence Taskforce), and she forces the old organisation to reform with scientists taking the lead and not the military. Kate Stewart (having dropped the 'Lethbridge' so as not to curry favour), finally meets the Doctor sometime after her father's death in *The Power of Three*. (In the apocryphal video/novel *Downtime* she previously meets Sarah in 1996, and we learn Kate also has a son, Gordy, named after her father. But it is important to note that none of this is referenced in the parent show). She explains why she changed UNIT, what her father taught her, and how he had 'learned that from an old friend'. When they part she tells the Doctor that he really is as remarkable as her father said, and kisses him. 'A kiss from a Lethbridge-Stewart – that's new!' the Doctor says, beaming.

Although Brigadier Sir Alistair Gordon Lethbridge-Stewart has passed, his name lives on with his daughter, and she makes an appearance in the anniversary special in November 2013, honouring her dad along the way...

Afterword

Back in 1995 when Mark Stammers and I wrote the book Doctor Who: Companions, we had just twenty-six years of *Doctor Who* on telly to contend with. So thirty-two television companions, a handful from films, stage plays, and other media, and that was it. It was a great book to write and research, talking to many of the actors and actresses, and scouring photo libraries for unseen pictures of the cast as they were in the series, and as they appeared outside of the show.

Since then we have met many more friends of the Doctor: Grace, Rose, Mickey, Martha, Donna and so, so many more. Not to mention a plethora in novels, novellas, comic strips and elsewhere! The television series has also changed focus with the times, putting the companion centre-stage and throwing the Doctor into mysterious shadow. So the subject was ripe for re-exploration.

In a way, we are all companions of the Doctor. Observing and participating vicariously in his adventures. Expressing opinions and asking important questions, journeying to far flung places and times, and feeling the excitement and terror that those visits bring. And with writers like Andy to guide us, we are in good hands.

Hopefully, in another eighteen years, there will be even more Companions to discuss and explore, and more adventures with the Doctor in time and space.

David J Howe, May 2013

With thanks

It's always said that no book is written by one person. This is doubly true of this book. I had the help and support of some great people, and they deserve thanks for their help, because without them this book would not be half the book it is.

For help with research and answering my barrage of questions, I thank *Doctor Who* experts (in no particular order), David Howe, Gary Russell, Paul Scoones, Paul Simpson, John Dorney, Joe Lidster, David McIntee, Justin Richards, Keith Topping, Martin Day, Mark Michalowski, and Steve Lyons.

Special thanks go to the team at Candy Jar Books for going beyond the call of duty in putting this all together: Shaun Russell, Hayley Cox, Richard Kelly, Jake Rudge, Rose Wildlake, Terry Cooper, Rebecca Lloyd James, Charles Lax, and Justin Chaloner.

Personal thanks for general support and interest goes to my family, as ever, and Phillip Archer, Jay Hartman, Katie Riggs, Jolene Ferries, Jack Adams, Lukus Therneau, Tom Webster, Luke Spillane, Owen and Damien (our very own Russell Howard) Moran, Rebecca Flower, Elizabeth Medeiros, Kristian Barry, Gareth Starling & Jason Godden, Merlin Cryer, Christian Mansell, Tom Sanford, Jon Cooper, James Beale, John Davies, Steve Roberts, Trudi Topham, JR Southall, Christopher Bryant, Sharon Bidwell, Prakash Bakrania, and Simon Williams.

And, of course, special thanks go to Joseph W Quintana; you will always be 'so much more'.

References

Doctor Who (BBC Television, 1963-2013)
Doctor Who Magazine (Marvel, Panini, 1979-2013)
The Encyclopaedia of the Worlds of Doctor Who by David Saunders (Knight Books, 1989)
Doctor Who Novels (Virgin Publishing, BBC Books, 1991-2013)
The DisContinuity Guide by Paul Cornell, Martin Day and Keith Topping (Virgin Publishing, 1995)
Doctor Who Audios (BBC Audio, Big Finish, 1996-2013)
A History of the Universe by Lance Parkin (Virgin Publishing, 1996)
Doctor Who: The Television Companion by David J Howe & Stephen James Walker (BBC Books, 1998)
I, Who 1, 2 & 3 by Lars Pearson (Mad Norwegian Press, 2003)
Doctor Who: The New Audio Adventures – The Inside Story by Benjamin Cook (Big Finish, 2004)
Doctor Who: The Inside Story by Gary Russell (BBC Books, 2006)
Torchwood (BBC Television, 2007-2010)
Inside the Hub by Stephen James Walker (Telos Publishing, 2007)
The Sarah Jane Adventures (Children's BBC Television, 2008-2012)
Doctor Who: The Encyclopaedia by Gary Russell (BBC Books, 2012)
The Comic Strip Companion by Paul Scoones (Telos Publishing, 2012)
TARDIS Data Core (www.tardis.wikia.com)
The Doctor Who Reference Guide (www.drwhoguide.com)

Coming Soon from Candy Jar

Just Sarah
Forty Years of a Doctor Who Companion

On 15th December 1973, Sarah Jane Smith joined the Doctor on his travels and became one of the most recognised companions throughout its initial twenty-six-year run.

In 2006 she returned to *Doctor Who* and span-off into her own series, *The Sarah Jane Adventures*, which became the most successful show on Children's BBC. This is the story of the most successful companion to ever enter the TARDIS.

Just Sarah…

For more information on the Candy Jar range of books visit:
www.candyjarbooks.co.uk